Have you ever had one of those days when nothing seemed to go right?

It all started when you smashed your head on the night table trying to shut off the alarm clock. The toast got stuck and the whole house filled with smoke. The freeway was shut down because of an accident and you were late for work. Your boss got mad at you for something you didn't even do. Then, to top it all off, the waitress at lunch spilled spaghetti sauce all over your shirt.

It has happened to all of us. Chances are, it was a test.

A test?

We are all tested. At each point in time and space, we are dealing with intersecting arcs of light and of darkness. We are also dealing with the effects of actions we set in motion long ago—or just the day before. The interplay of these forces is what results in the tests and challenges of life. And all of this can be plotted according to the laws governing cycles—a science that has been called the Cosmic Clock.

We've all had tests like this one, and most likely, we've flunked some of them. This may have been a test of control, to see if you could keep it together when all the world, seemingly, was conspiring to make you mad. Many tests are as mundane as this. Others may be more complex. And sometimes the stakes can be much higher.

But what if you could know these tests were coming *before* they arrived? What if you could prepare for them? How much better could you do?

What if you could *predict your future?*

You don't need a crystal ball. It's not magic or mystery. By knowing the science of the cosmic clock, the wisdom of the Mother, you can learn to anticipate the tests of life and be the master of your fate, of your cycles, of your destiny.

Predict Your
FUTURE

CLIMB THE HIGHEST MOUNTAIN® SERIES

The Path of the Higher Self

The Path of Self-Transformation

The Masters and the Spiritual Path

The Path of Brotherhood

The Path of the Universal Christ

The Masters and Their Retreats

Predict Your Future:
Understand the Cycles of the Cosmic Clock

Predict Your
FUTURE

UNDERSTAND THE CYCLES
OF THE COSMIC CLOCK

ELIZABETH CLARE PROPHET

Summit University ☙ Press
Corwin Springs, Montana

To the children of the Mother

PREDICT YOUR FUTURE: UNDERSTAND THE CYCLES OF THE COSMIC CLOCK
by Elizabeth Clare Prophet; compiled and edited by Annice Booth
Copyright © 2004 by Summit University Press
All rights reserved

Library of Congress Control Number: 2004105852
ISBN: 0-922729-98-0

SUMMIT UNIVERSITY 🕯 PRESS®
The Summit Lighthouse, *Pearls of Wisdom*, Science of the Spoken Word,
Keepers of the Flame, and Summit University are trademarks registered in
the U.S. Patent and Trademark Office and in other countries. All rights to
their use are reserved.

Printed in the United States of America

Note: Our understanding of life and the universe is that all things are in
polarity: plus/minus, Alpha/Omega, yin/yang, masculine/feminine. The
worlds of Spirit and Matter are in polarity as two manifestations of God's
universal presence. In this relationship, Spirit assumes the positive-yang-
masculine polarity, and Matter assumes the negative-yin-feminine
polarity. Thus, we have used masculine pronouns to refer to God and
feminine pronouns to refer to the soul, the part of ourselves that is
evolving in the planes of Matter. Also, in order to avoid the sometimes
cumbersome or confusing expressions of gender-neutral language, we
have occasionally used masculine pronouns to refer to the individual.
These usages are not intended to exclude women.

08 07 06 05 04   5 4 3 2 1

CONTENTS

EDITOR'S PREFACE

I have always loved the changing of the seasons. It is my great joy to observe every year how the warm colors of autumn fade into the winter-white landscape, eventually giving way to the green growth of spring and the lazy days of summer. I also like to observe the cycles of the earth, for even as the seasons change, so do the cycles within and the cycles in the heavens shape events in the world and in the microcosm of our own lives.

It is my fervent hope that this book will bring you to a new understanding of the cycles of the world and the cycles of your own life. I also hope that through applying these precepts, you will gain a new confidence and a sense of mastery in meeting life's challenges.

The teachings you hold in your hand were given to Elizabeth Clare Prophet beginning about thirty-five years ago. I can vividly recall seeing Mrs. Prophet in her prayer tower, kneeling in gratitude before a life-size golden statue of Mother Mary, praising and thanking the blessed Mother for releasing the precious gift of this teaching. She was so humble and joyous to be chosen by Mother Mary as the one who would bring this transcendent new understanding in its entirety to the world.

I well remember the conference in 1970 when Mrs. Prophet first began to share these new revelations with the students of the ascended masters. For the next thirty years, she taught on the science of the cosmic clock, adding further pieces to the puzzle as

Mother Mary revealed them to her. I know that this subject was dear to her heart, for she knew from personal experience what a difference these teachings made in her own life, and she wanted to share them with everyone.

The material on the cosmic clock was intended to be included in two of the original thirty-three chapters of *Climb the Highest Mountain,* the landmark series by Mark L. Prophet and Elizabeth Clare Prophet that sheds so much light on the science of the Spirit. The very basic teachings on the clock we had received in the early 1970s were to be part of chapter 21, "The Law of Cycles," and chapter 30, "Integrity." However, as Mother Mary continued to reveal new understandings of this science in the years since *Climb the Highest Mountain* was outlined, the material soon became much more extensive. Thus, what was originally to be a brief explanation has evolved into a complete introduction to the teachings on the cosmic clock and many of its applications, now worthy of an entire book in the series.

The information in this book has been compiled from the many lectures Mrs. Prophet has given on the cosmic clock, taking the best and most complete explanations of each point. We have also included many figures and diagrams to graphically illustrate this profound science. Many of them are based on the ones Mrs. Prophet used in delivering her own lectures on this subject. Some of the originals were hand-drawn by her as she saw them on the inner planes in her meditations.

The teachings of the Divine Mother on charting the cycles of the cosmic clock are among the most liberating you may ever read. As you learn to understand your past and anticipate your future, I sincerely pray that you will take these teachings and use them for your own freedom and your ascension in the light.

Annice Booth
Royal Teton Ranch
Paradise Valley, Montana

INTRODUCTION

The first impulse of the cosmic clock that I was given came to me very early in life. As a tiny child, as I lived the year, I saw myself walking on a circle; and around the year I would walk, day by day. And I would remember dates and experiences according to where I had stood on this giant circle where my soul was walking.

After I became a messenger for the Brotherhood, Mother Mary came to me and showed me the science of the cosmic clock for the charting of the cycles of our own self-discipline. This is not traditional astrology. It is an inner astrology of the white-fire core whereby we can chart the cycles of our karma—cause-and-effect sequences of energy in motion.

Karma cannot simply be defined: "as a man soweth, that shall he also reap." It is more than this. It is the entire flow of energy throughout cosmos over the figure-eight pattern. Karma is the indomitable law of God that is outworking, outpicturing itself. It is set in motion, and it continues to be in motion.

All that we are is karma. Everything that we are is the result of everything that we have ever been. To contemplate this fact is almost to suddenly feel oneself a prisoner of unseen causes. And so there is the tendency to rebel against one's karma. But one's karma is oneself.

Some say that we cannot change the past, that we can only

change the future. But Saint Germain, the master of the Aquarian age, has shown us that we *can* change the past. There is a way to be free from past causes and present effects. There is a Science of the Spoken Word whereby we can ride the crest of the wave of karma and not be overcome.

To ride the crest even of a difficult karma to victory is an exhilarating sense of life becoming life. You can feel the mounting pressures of past conflict cycling into your life, but you need not be inundated by them.

You can be the master of your fate, your cycles, your destiny. To do this, you need the wisdom of the Mother as the science of the cosmic clock.

As well as our karma, this science allows us to chart the cycles of our *dharma*. Our dharma is our duty to be ourselves, our Real Self. It is the duty to fulfill one's reason for being. One's reason for being is a nucleus of fire, an inner blueprint, and it is itself a cosmic clock that ticks off our divine destiny, our fiery destiny.

To paraphrase Brutus in *Julius Caesar,* "There is a tide in the affairs of men, which, taken at its crest, leads on to victory."[1] We've all had that feeling in life where we feel that we're right on. We've taken the wave exactly at the moment. We are in command.

And we've all had that feeling of missing that wave. We haven't quite made the wave of our inner cosmic clock, and it goes on ahead of us. Riding the cycles of a cosmos is the challenge of the path of initiation, it is a challenge of self-mastery, and it leads to soul freedom.

The amazing thing about karma, about cosmic law and about energy is that the more we attain, the more we find that we are subject to a mathematical formula that is so vast as to govern every area of our life, waking and sleeping.

At first glimpse, this mathematical formula seems confining. At the second glimpse, we realize that it is the opportunity for the soul to take flight out of time and space and to become the

Infinite One.

Meshing our consciousness with the mathematics of a cosmos is this challenge of initiation, this riding of the crest. It demands the listening grace, listening with the inner ear to the commands of conscience—a conscience not programmed by society, but a conscience that comes from within the soul, from its divine origins.

Listening for the command, responding with alacrity, responding with the swiftness of the wings of an eagle, obeying the inner clock, we find that we are at the right point in time and space at all times.

The exactness of the flow of energy-spirals in the cosmos is a wonder. But the wonder of wonders is to perceive how this cosmic clock works in conjunction with the scientific and systematic use of the energy of the Holy Spirit to transmute the misqualified energies of your subconscious, to balance karma, and to hasten the day of your victory.

We are all walking a path of initiation, and we all have a choice. We can either keep going on a treadmill of failing our tests—perhaps getting irritated or angry at the circumstances of life—or we can determine to pass these tests and move on with our spiritual development. We can get off that treadmill and begin hiking up the mountain.

These exams in earth's schoolroom have been going on for thousands of years. In the Bible we read that Job asked the Lord, "What is man, that thou shouldest magnify him? and that thou shouldest set thine heart upon him? And that thou shouldest visit him every morning, and try him every moment?"[2] What kinds of tests could we have every moment? They are those of everyday life.

Each test that we pass gives us the right to carry a greater concentration of the sacred fire in our heart chakra and in all of our chakras. Thus, initiation is cumulative. What we earn on one line has to be carried to the next line, and it becomes the foundation for mastery in that line. Likewise, what we do not pass on one line cannot be built upon in the next. So we must prepare.

As the wheel of the cosmic clock turns day by day and you experience the cycles of your tests and initiations in life, do not sigh with the burden of the lines of your destiny, but greet them with the joy of the flame. And remember that God, desiring to see mankind pass these tests, has given us the science of the Divine Mother known as the Cosmic Clock.

Elizabeth Clare Prophet

This is the teaching of the
stars for the golden age.
And it has to be an inner teaching
of the ascended masters.

It cannot be a teaching
that is based on what we see
only with our eyes
in the heavens—
because the universe is on a curve,
and we do not see clearly,
nor are all the manifestations
of the hierarchy in physical
manifestation.

The whole Cosmic Egg
in which we live
is nothing more than a series
of spirals within spirals within spirals.
These are the wheels
that Ezekiel saw—
wheels within wheels within wheels.

Start thinking about the atoms
within your being,
composing molecules, composing cells,
composing organs
and systems within systems.

And then look
at the matter around you,
and the trees,
and the entire organization of cosmos—
it is all a collection
of billions upon billions,
infinite numbers of these spirals.

But they will all have
the same basic pattern of light
descending from Spirit
to Matter.

CHAPTER 1

The Law
of Cycles

While the earth remaineth,
seedtime and harvest,
and cold and heat, and summer and winter,
and day and night shall not cease.

—Genesis

CHAPTER 1

The Law of Cycles

One of the great sources of comfort that has come to me in this life has been an understanding of the mathematical formula of the law of cycles whereby Spirit cycles through Matter and Matter cycles through Spirit.

We approach the law of cycles with reverence for the Creator whose Self-expression it contains. All evidences of its outworking in man, the earth, the elements and the stars are but the tracings of his Being, footprints in the sands, tracks in the upper snows. Wherever we behold his markings as cyclings of infinity tumbling through the finite coils of time and space, there he has been, there his awful, wonderful Presence is—just beyond the veiled spirals of his creation.

Attempting to penetrate the law of cycles, we find secrets sublime and all-encompassing—the being of man the microcosm, in man the Macrocosm. These secrets have remained closely guarded by the adepts of the mystery schools for thousands of years, for an understanding of these laws provides a predictable platform of evolution—and the power to initiate cycles of our own.

Where shall we start our excursion through the vast ocean of

God's creation? The wonder of it all is that no matter where we start, by following any cycle of life to its origin, there we stand face to face with God. For he is the originator of all cycles. He is the driving force spinning at the pivot point of all form.

The Cycle Defined

A cycle is an interval of time during which a sequence of a recurring succession of events or phenomena is completed. It is also defined as a "recurrent sequence of events which occur in such order that the last event of one sequence immediately precedes the recurrence of the first event in a new series."

Place your hand on your heart and feel the cycles of your heart's pulsation, the beat of your physical life sustaining the vehicles of your soul's evolution in Matter. Look up at a light bulb and know that it shines because electricity is pulsating at a cycle of sixty times per second through its filament. Listen to a piece of music and hear the cyclic vibration of the violin strings resonating through the eardrum as sound.

All of cosmos can be comprehended in terms of cycles. The warp and woof of creation is manifest in currents of spiritual sound vibrating according to cyclic law. The very atoms and electrons of this world of form bow to the cyclic interchange of Spirit into Matter, Matter into Spirit—all encompassed in the one element from which all of life issues forth.

The Cosmic Magnet

To understand one of the basic tenets of the law of cycles, we must delve into the deepest mysteries of our Spirit-Matter universe. Here we contact the simplest and grandest of all cycles: the dual pulsation that is the heartbeat of cosmos. Here we find the one element, forever in equilibrium, forever pulsating in the rhythmic cycles that reverberate down to the inner core of every atom.

The entire religious philosophy of the yin/yang of Taoism is built upon the existence and importance of the cyclic interchange between an infinite hierarchy of opposing, or complementary, forces. It is the grand cycle of Alpha to Omega.

We hear it singing the song of the atom within our very own cosmos. It is the inhalation and exhalation of the Godhead. This primary cycle is the simplest relationship of two forces—and the most all-encompassing action. If we clearly embrace the cyclic flow and unity between the Spirit/Matter, or Father/Mother, principles of motion, it is as if we are given a library card to God's storehouse of universal knowledge. This divine polarity exists throughout cosmos—from the balanced pulsation of the Great Central Sun to the systemic equilibrium of the hydrogen atom.

We learn from the science of sound and from the archives of the Brotherhood that all manifested cosmos is the interplay of vibrations—a vast web of electromagnetic waves oscillating at different numbers of cycles per second. And what is a vibration if not a cyclic motion related to a framework of time and space orientation? The range of cycles is infinite—from one cycle in billions of years to billions of cycles each second.

The Law of Transcendence

As we ponder the immense odyssey of God's Being through eternal rounds of beginnings and endings, we can ask the fateful question: Why? What is the purpose of it all if the universe is just an endless cycle of rounds with man floating on a speck of dust in space cast loose on a shoreless ocean? What is the nature of the Godhead as he exists through endless cycles in infinite space?

The answer, we are told, is that the law of cycles implements the law of transcendence. God is a transcendent being, and with each new outbreath, he evolves to a greater state of cosmic perfection and beauty.

The cycles are not really circles or sine waves but they are spirals—spirals of infinite expansion according to the geometry of the golden ratio (1:1.618...). Each cycle of evolution takes in more of God. Each round sends us into wider spheres of the body of God's cosmos.

As the cycles of cosmos spiral upward into greater and greater dimensions, so man can forever transcend the veils of Matter that form the schoolrooms for his soul's evolution.

The Circle of Life

The riddle of eternity and evolution is contained within the symbol of the circle. The circle is the two-dimensional representation of the spiral that begins in the square base of the pyramid and rises to the apex of realization in the capstone of life. And there in the center of the capstone, the law of transcendence functions through the eye of God. For when the spiral passes through the All-Seeing Eye, it transcends the dimensions of form and passes from Matter to Spirit.

This is the fulfillment of the law of cycles that begins in the heart of God and culminates in every perfect creation. The eternal Logos is the dot in the center of the circle, the beginning and ending of cycles that are composed of circles, layer upon layer. Energy that begins as a spiral in Spirit descends into Matter, there to coalesce around the flame and then—in the twinkling of an eye—to return to Spirit over the descending and ascending spirals of God's consciousness.

The heavenly bodies are undergoing cyclic evolution within the larger infinite spiral of God's Being in Spirit—passing through material manifestation and returning to Spirit. In the Macrocosm as well as in the microcosm, circling spirals trigger the flow of energy into and out of form.

Throughout the universe, the pattern of cyclic return is reproduced again and again with infinite precision, traversing realms of eternity, expanding according to the golden ratio.

Man as Co-Creator

The circle represents a cross section of a spiral that has neither beginning nor ending but appears to be finite as it passes through the physical universe in the form of planets, stars, galaxies—and man himself. Although the circle itself is without beginning or ending, at any point on the circumference of the circle the hand of God may draw an intersecting line, thereby creating a beginning and an ending. Thus cycles are initiated and worlds are born.

Drop a stone into a still pond and watch the cyclic wave patterns continue to flow and flow in smooth rhythm. Drop a stone into an agitated pond, and there results a complex of wave-pattern interchange, but the cycle initiated by the stone continues to affect the water. Thus it is by the hand of God and by his emissaries. The entire universe is the interplay of cyclic vibrations, initiated somewhere, somehow, by someone.

That someone could be you. As we ascend the scales of evolution, we are entrusted with the divine power and authority to initiate cycles that may last forever. Who is to say that the candle glow of your love in this very moment will not exist forevermore in the continuum of God's Being?

Within the form of the circle the mystery of the beginning and the ending of God is solved. God himself is the circle that has neither beginning nor ending of cycles. Until man becomes one with God, he is but a dot on the circumference, caught up in the flow of the Infinite and fulfilling cycles of life, cycles perhaps that he is unaware of. But once man has passed through the cycles of the initiatic process—the spirals of destiny that unlock the total pattern of his identity—he earns the right to be congruent with the dot in the center of the great circle of life.

The Return to God

The cycle of the heartbeat of cosmos exudes life's energies to all creatures great and small. Through it, we can contact a sense of everlasting comfort during the trials and tribulations of our lives. The law of cycles is thus the instrumentation of the Comforter's own flame. It is a swaddling garment wound round about the earth. The very currents of the earth's surface, the very emanations from its sun center, the law of cycles, the comfort flame, the hum just below the level of our own hearing transfer to us this comfort of the cyclic law of the sounding of God's Word.

Life is ongoing, and the law of cycles promises us that life will go on. God's heart will beat on. The wheel of cyclic return will rotate on the spokes of our karmic creations.

By the law of cycles, then, we are set upon our courses spiraling through once again the nexus of being, the nexus being the Word itself, the law of cycles being the emanation of the Word—the eternal Logos. "In the beginning was the Word, and the Word was with God, and the Word was God." And without this Word "was not any thing made that was made."[1]

As we become congruent with the dot in the center of God's circle, the power is bestowed upon us to imprint the cyclic energies of God with the pattern of our God-oriented idea or desire. This is the way to return to God as a permanent atom in his Being—through this Word that has incarnated in the avatars with the cyclic law of manifestation. The great manus, the law-givers of the ages and of their races, upheld the cycle of the Word whereby all seed going forth from the great Tree of Life might return through the Word as the law of cycles.

There is joy in this law of cycles. And the joy of this marriage of science and religion is you at the nexus of infinity, you converging with that living Word.

God has neither beginning nor ending because his Being takes in the universe of cycles and all that precedes and follows them in the formed and unformed dimensions of Spirit. Man, on the other hand, seems for a brief interim to have a beginning and an ending because he identifies with a slice of the spiral that initiates in Spirit, evolves through Matter, and returns to Spirit. When man's beginnings and his endings are seen as part of the never-ending cycles of God's Self-awareness, he will realize that although the spirals of his own life travel in a linear pattern through the limited spheres of outer manifestation, there is, in reality, no end to the involution and evolution of his consciousness.

When man returns to God, aligning the energies he has gathered in spirals with the Great Spiral that is God's Being, both God and man transcend their former state, and the law of cycles implements the law of transcendence. God transcends himself as man transcends himself, for God is in man and man is in God. Through the merging of cycles, man becomes more of God and God becomes more in man; hence new creations are continually being born into spirals that expand the circle of the Infinite One.

Aquarius

CHAPTER 2

The Psychology of Being

Man, Know Thyself!

— Temple of Apollo, Delphi

CHAPTER 2

The Psychology of Being

As we contemplate the love of hierarchy and of the master for the chela, for the disciple, and we feel that love whereby the master says, "I cannot leave thee, I will not leave thee," we see how that love comes forth from the Father-Mother God. When Jesus took his leave of his disciples, he said: "I will not leave you comfortless. Behold, the Comforter will come who will teach you all things."[1] The Comforter as the Holy Spirit gives us that teaching whereby we are not left alone to drift in our own sea of impurities, our own subconscious, our own karma. We are not left alone, because the teacher has left us the teaching.

One of the greatest examples of the love of hierarchy that I have found is the teaching on the cosmic clock. The cosmic clock is the Comforter. It is that agency of the Holy Spirit that remains with us after the master ascends, while the angels ascend and descend on the ladder of life.

The cycles that unfold in this clock are cycles of love—the love whereby we ascend, the love whereby the consuming fire of all who have gone before us transmutes those elements that are not desirable, that are not permissible in the hallowed circle of the AUM.

There is a poem by Robert Frost that has always been dear to me, which conveys the cycles and the fiery core and the burden of karma that is upon us.

"Stopping by Woods on a Snowy Evening"

> Whose woods these are I think I know.
> His house is in the village, though;
> He will not see me stopping here
> To watch his woods fill up with snow.
>
> My little horse must think it queer
> To stop without a farmhouse near
> Between the woods and frozen lake
> The darkest evening of the year.
>
> He gives his harness bells a shake
> To ask if there is some mistake.
> The only other sound's the sweep
> Of easy wind and downy flake.
>
> The woods are lovely, dark, and deep.
> But I have promises to keep,
> And miles to go before I sleep,
> And miles to go before I sleep.

The snowy evening represents the fiery core of Being, the God-source out of which the soul descends—cycling through the cosmic clock, its cosmic destiny. And here we find ourselves at a certain point in that destiny. We stand on a point of the clock; and we cannot tarry in our cups, for we have miles to go, promises to keep. We have cycles to turn, commitments to meet to Lords of Flame, to hierarchies, to humanity. And before we lay this mortal form to rest and shuffle off this mortal coil, we must fulfill those promises; and we have many miles to go.

The Law of Karma

The law of karma, of perfect retribution, is intimately related to the law of cycles. We can know with absolute surety that if we send out hatred or negative vibrations, sooner or later they will cycle back to ourselves—and we will have to expend energy to requalify our murky creation.

We can also know that the self-generated impulse toward God, toward good, toward service of our fellowman will, with infinite precision, cycle back also and add to our momentum of light and our return to wholeness. This is the law of karma. It is the mathematically predictable law of cycles. It is the most simple yet profound manifestation of justice.

By willingly coming into congruence with the cycle of involution, evolution and ascension, we know that at the end of this round, we shall indeed see the face of God.

Can we imagine what it would be like if the law of cycles didn't exist, if we had no way of knowing where to direct our striving to return to a state of wholeness?

Be Your Own Psychologist

After you study the cosmic clock in its entirety, you will be able to be your own psychologist and analyze yourself and see where your weaknesses are, where you are constantly stumbling, constantly having problems. The chart of your cycles will analyze this for you and help you to know how to recognize a specific weakness, how to be objective about it, how to overcome it, how to put it in the flame.

You must always remember that you are the Christ standing in the center of this circle. And the circle of this clock is the circle of your awareness. Either you are manifesting the divinity of God's consciousness on the lines of this clock, or you are going to be manifesting a perversion of those lines in the human consciousness. It will become very clear to you which is the case. And when you see a negative manifestation, you simply stand in the center of this circle and say: "Well, I don't want to be that manifestation. I demand that it be consumed, and I demand that the correct concept replace it."

The Path of Personal Christhood

Since all of cosmos is built upon the same plan, you have the same authority that God does. God stands in the Central Sun and commands the solar hierarchies, and they expand his awareness of his qualities. You are a co-creator with God standing in the center of your own circle, and it is up to you to decide each hour and each day what you will manifest on the periphery of being. When that periphery becomes perfected, you begin passing the initiations of Christhood, and then of the Buddha, and then your ascension. And soon you find that you are manifesting your own cosmos with hierarchies that emanate from your central sun. This is the vast opportunity for evolution that you have if you will diligently practice the science of the cosmic clock.

In order to attain your individual mastery and the realization of personal Christhood, it is necessary for you to take dominion over the earth and over the heavens. The heavens are the etheric octave, and the earth and the heavens combined form the etheric, mental, astral and physical planes in which we abide. Taking dominion means to gain mastery over what is called our astrology.

Because the forces of astrology are in one sense so powerful, so dominating, and because so many people on this planet are actually creatures hour by hour and day by day of their personal astrology, we need to establish a point of co-measurement. We need to define the relationship of our self to our God-source, our I AM Presence, and of our self to the great center of God, the Great Central Sun in the heart of cosmos.

The Chart of Your Divine Self

The Chart of Your Divine Self (page 24) is a portrait of you and of the God within you. It is a diagram of you and your potential to become who you really are. It is an outline of your spiritual anatomy.

The upper figure is your "I AM Presence," the Presence of

God that is individualized in each one of us. It is your personalized "I AM THAT I AM." Your I AM Presence is surrounded by seven concentric spheres of spiritual energy that make up what is called your "causal body." The spheres of pulsating energy contain the record of the good works you have performed since your very first incarnation on earth. They are like your cosmic bank account.

The middle figure in the chart represents the "Holy Christ Self," who is also called the Higher Self. You can think of your Holy Christ Self as your chief guardian angel and dearest friend, your inner teacher and voice of conscience. Just as the I AM Presence is the presence of God that is individualized for each of us, so the Holy Christ Self is the presence of the Universal Christ that is individualized for each of us. "The Christ" is actually a title given to those who have attained oneness with their Higher Self, or Christ Self. That is why Jesus was called "Jesus, the Christ."

What the Chart shows is that each of us has a Higher Self, or "Inner Christ," and that each of us is destined to become one with that Higher Self—whether we call it the Christ, the Buddha, the Tao or the Atman. This "Inner Christ" is what the Christian mystics sometimes refer to as the "inner man of the heart," and what the Upanishads mysteriously describe as a being the "size of a thumb" who "dwells deep within the heart."

We all have moments when we feel that connection with our Higher Self—when we are creative, loving, joyful. But there are other moments when we feel out of sync with our Higher Self—moments when we become angry, depressed, lost. What the spiritual path is all about is learning to sustain the connection to the higher part of ourselves so that we can make our greatest contribution to humanity.

The shaft of white light descending from the I AM Presence through the Holy Christ Self to the lower figure in the Chart is the crystal cord (sometimes called the silver cord). It is the "umbilical cord," the lifeline, that ties you to Spirit.

The Chart of Your Divine Self

Your crystal cord also nourishes that special, radiant flame of God that is ensconced in the secret chamber of your heart. It is called the threefold flame, or divine spark, because it is literally a spark of sacred fire that God has transmitted from his heart to yours. This flame is called "threefold" because it engenders the primary attributes of Spirit—power, wisdom and love.

The mystics of the world's religions have contacted the divine spark, describing it as the seed of divinity within. Buddhists, for instance, speak of the "germ of Buddhahood" that exists in every living being. In the

The threefold flame manifests the primary attributes of Spirit: power, the blue plume; wisdom, the yellow plume; and love, the pink plume.

Hindu tradition, the Katha Upanishad speaks of the "light of the Spirit" that is concealed in the "secret high place of the heart" of all beings. Likewise, the fourteenth-century Christian theologian and mystic Meister Eckhart teaches of the divine spark when he says, "God's seed is within us."[2]

When we give prayers or mantras, we meditate on the flame in the secret chamber of our heart. This secret chamber is your own private meditation room, your interior castle, as Teresa of Avila called it. In Hindu tradition, the devotee visualizes a jeweled island in his heart. There he sees himself before a beautiful altar, where he worships his teacher in deep meditation.

Jesus spoke of entering the secret chamber of the heart when he said: "When thou prayest, enter into thy closet, and when thou hast shut thy door, pray to thy Father which is in secret; and thy Father which seeth in secret shall reward thee openly."[3]

The lower figure in the Chart of Your Divine Self represents you on the spiritual path, surrounded by the violet flame and the protective white light of God. The soul is the living potential of

God—the part of you that is mortal but that can become immortal.

The purpose of your soul's evolution on earth is to grow in self-mastery, balance your karma and fulfill your mission on earth so that you can return to the spiritual dimensions that are your real home. When your soul at last takes flight and ascends back to God and the heaven-world, you will become an ascended master, free from the rounds of karma and rebirth. The high-frequency energy of the violet flame can help you reach that goal more quickly.

We will discuss the Chart of Your Divine Self in greater detail in chapter 9, "Cosmic Accountability."

CHAPTER 3

Pisces

Your Personal Cosmic Clock

To every thing there is a season,
and a time to every purpose under the heaven:
a time to be born, and a time to die;
a time to plant,
and a time to pluck up that which is planted.
—Ecclesiastes

CHAPTER 3

Your Personal Cosmic Clock

It is on the face of a clock that we diagram galaxies, the Great Central Sun and our own universe within ourselves. We find the lines on this clock are positions of consciousness. They are points of consciousness of great cosmic beings.

Every circle or ovoid or ellipse in the universe follows the same cycle. Beginning at the twelve o'clock line and going around all the way back to the twelve o'clock line, we find that we can put our days, our months, our years on the same clock, and by determining the hierarchies of the sun that govern these planes of consciousness, we can gain mastery on these spheres.

The Circle of Infinity

Let us examine the cosmic clock beginning from the white-fire core of our own I AM Presence and see how the cycles of energy flow from the I AM THAT I AM into time and space.

We begin with the circle of infinity, which is *you*. It is the wholeness of your cosmic consciousness; it is the wholeness of God. And this wholeness, not being expressed as wholeness in time and space, is fragmented so that we can partake of the grace of wholeness.

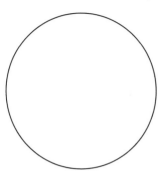

Figure 1 The Circle of Infinity
The All, the One
the Undifferentiated Whole
the White-Fire Core of Being
the Hallowed Circle of the AUM

The beginning of the fragmentation is the creation of cloven tongues of fire of the Father-Mother God, of Alpha and Omega. The one undivided whole becomes the duality of the T'ai Chi. In this symbol you will notice the thrust of the fire of Spirit as the white flame.

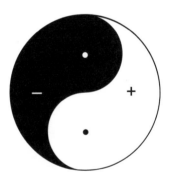

Figure 2 The T'ai Chi
The Polarity of Wholeness Showing the Flow of Energy from
Spirit to Matter, Matter to Spirit

The impetus of Spirit flowing from what would be the twelve o'clock line becomes, at the six o'clock line, the fire of Matter, the blue. And we see that these two flames in rotation, forming the circle of infinity, moving beyond the speed of light, whirling, create the negative and positive polarity of a cosmos.

All of life hangs upon the frequencies of Father-Mother, of the plus and the minus. The Spirit is the thrust of the positive, and the Matter is the return of the negative. You have the positive fling and the negative fling of life. These, then, are the action of the Father-Mother God.

If you will visualize on this circle energy moving from twelve o'clock to three, to six, to nine and back again to twelve—that is a clockwise movement. That is the way creation comes forth. It comes forth as the thrust of Alpha's energy and the return of Omega. On this hangs all of life.

When you get the feel for this motion of the Father-Mother God, you sense the balance scales of Libra, of cosmic justice, of your own inner karma, of night and day, of the movement of the planets, the cycles of the solar systems, the galaxies moving around the Central Sun. The flow of energy to your heart chakra from your I AM Presence is in spirals—always clockwise spirals—moving energy from the Source unto their fulfillment.

That movement of energy itself is karma. We have to broaden our sense of karma to encompass the yin and yang of the flow of a cosmos. And we have to become a part of this movement of the T'ai Chi. Your personal cosmic clock comes forth out of this movement.

The Dividing of the Circle

The circle is the circle of your wholeness with your twin flame, and then it becomes the T'ai Chi, the two in one. Each time there is the descent of the light of God into the earth, there is the breaking down from the one to the two, then it becomes the four, and then it becomes the twelve; and all of these represent cycles.

Life is a series of unfolding cycles. When we understand the law of these cycles and what governs them, when we understand that we can be the governor in the point of the Christ Self, we can determine the unfoldment of cycles, and we can always be at the right point in time and space—and always there fulfilling the balance of karma and the dharma that is the inner blueprint.

The Birth of Twin Flames

The fiery ovoid, the wholeness of God, produces that focal point of Alpha and Omega (fig. 3), Father-Mother God carrying the torch of life, going forth to carve a cosmic destiny.

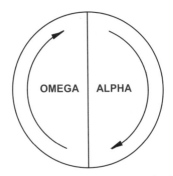

Figure 3 The Father-Mother God
The Going Out and the Coming In
of the Cycles of Alpha and Omega

Therefore, out of the whole single circle that represents infinity, there emerge two Monads each having the polarity of Alpha and Omega, the plus and minus of Being, each having the same electronic blueprint of life—twin flames with a cosmic destiny.

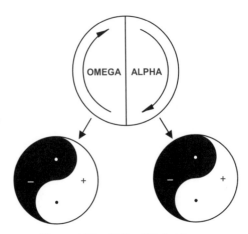

Figure 4 The Birth of Twin Flames

Out of each of these halves, which in turn has become a whole, there descends a soul—counterpart of the Spirit of the living God. The soul then descends into Matter and is clothed upon with coats of skins, an allegorical term used in Genesis meaning the four lower bodies—four frequencies for the realization of the four dimensions of being, the four quadrants of the whole (fig. 5).

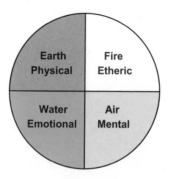

Figure 5 The Four Elements Corresponding to
the Four Lower Bodies and the Four Planes of Matter

The Four Lower Bodies

The four lower bodies that surround the soul enable us to experiment with the alchemy of fire in the first quarter of the circle, the plane of the memory, with the frequency of white; with the alchemy of air in the second quarter of the circle, the plane of the mind, with the frequency of yellow; with the alchemy of water in the third quarter of the circle, the plane of the feelings, with the frequency of pink; and finally with the alchemy of earth, the plane of the physical body, with the frequency of blue. And so we come, trailing clouds of glory.

Those who descended into form in the early root races[1] did not put on the density we now wear, because their consciousness never entered into the area of relativity—of the energy *veil* that is called *evil*, which is created by man by his free will through the misuse of the sacred fire. And so, twin souls descending from the twin flames of the I AM Presence in the early root races ascended back to that fiery core without ever having created what we are going to diagram later, which is known as the electronic belt—the accumulation of the misqualification of God's energy as it collects in the subconscious.

Fire, Air, Water, Earth

These four frequencies of being are known by the terms of the ancient alchemists: fire, air, water and earth. The modern-day chemist or physicist would find these terms obsolete. That is because they are thinking of them in terms of their understanding of the alchemist's division of Matter into four parts. But this is not what the alchemist had reference to. The alchemist was defining frequencies, planes of consciousness—dividing north, south, east and west, the four sides of the City Foursquare, the four sides of the pyramid of life, and the four lower bodies of man. Alchemists were initiates of the Great White Brotherhood,* but they did not allow their initiations to be known.

The four quadrants of Matter give us keys to self-mastery and keys to the flow of energy. Our seven chakras relate to these four quadrants. Each of the chakras is for the release of a certain energy of God's consciousness at a certain plane. We need to get used to dealing with these terms as a way of experiencing God and as a way of perceiving God. We need to use them to relate to outer coordinates of the actual substance of fire, air, water and earth; and we need to use our experience with these outer manifestations to relate to inner experience in the inner manifestation.

Therefore, we can take physical fire and let it relate in our subconscious to spiritual fire, to the spiritual matrix of fire, to sacred fire. We need to feel the physical fire being translated, and

---

* The Great White Brotherhood is a spiritual order of saints and adepts of every race, culture and religion. These masters have transcended the cycles of karma and rebirth and reunited with the Spirit of the living God. The word "white" refers to the aura or halo of white light that surrounds them.

when this translation occurs, we move from the sphere of Matter to the sphere of Spirit.

In the same way we speak of air—air relating to the mind, the airy quality of thought that moves as the wind. We speak of the Holy Spirit as the wind that "bloweth where it listeth." And so we go from our experience in air and in the wind and make the translation to God as a moving Spirit. And then, with our inner senses of the soul, we begin to experience a new dimension, a new vibration of God corresponding to that air element.

We have experience with water. We touch water. It is substance that flows. It needs a matrix to have form. And so we begin to talk about the flow of the Mother, because the Mother has dominion over the sea and is symbolized in the sea and the great power of the movement of waters. From our experience of the joy and the movement of water, we come to know God as his feelings flow in the realm of Spirit. This is how we can use nature as a point of meditation, as a take-off point whereby our soul slips, as it were, into the dimensions of Spirit.

And finally, the earth element itself gives us a sense of the bedrock of Reality, of the highest focus of God in the Great Central Sun, of an earth that is not an earth that we hold in our hands but an earth that is the solidness of the consciousness of God.

Four Aspects of God: Father, Son, Mother, Holy Spirit

Coming to experience the patterns of these four, we relate them to the four aspects of God, which we define as Father, as Son, as Mother and as Holy Spirit.

We understand the meaning of God, Father, as fire, as the fiery dispensations of the Law and the fiery discipline of the Law and the cracking of the whip of cosmic consciousness.

We understand the meaning of Son, the Word being the communication of the Father, the Logos, the understanding, the wisdom. We remember the mind of Christ, whose parables taught us the meaning of the inner Logos. And so the flaming Son (Sun) consciousness of our own Christ Self we now relate to mind, and mind to the element of air. With the fingers of the mind, we begin to touch and to move and to feel and then to become, because we have felt.

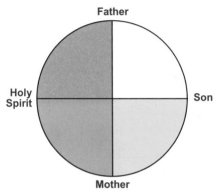

Figure 6 Four Aspects of God

Mother, then, is the great love, the love of water and the movement of water. Out of water is all life, and out of the womb of the Mother is all life. This is what we know we must ensoul in our emotional body. We experience God as Mother in every feeling that is pure.

And finally, God as Holy Spirit is the fusion of Father and Mother and Son, the fusion of the light of cosmic consciousness for action, the infilling of the temple with the breath of life. If you have ever watched a child being born and you have seen how this form that is white begins to turn pink from the heart out as it is infused with the breath of life and the threefold flame is ignited by the Holy Spirit, you have experienced the wonder of this Holy Spirit, and you see how the Holy Spirit infuses all of Matter with life.

And so you have the understanding of the meaning of Matter, of the physical plane, and of God as Holy Spirit—all the while remembering that energy is movement. Energy is cycling in this clockwise direction, moving and continuing to move so that

Figure 7 The Flow of Energy in the Expansion
of Cosmic Consciousness

nothing is remaining static. The turning of the wheel of the Law is Father becoming Son, Son becoming Mother, Mother becoming Holy Spirit, Holy Spirit becoming Father. And this movement, faster than the speed of light, is the whirling of cosmic consciousness.

We think of God the same yesterday, today and forever. That which is the same is the coordinates of Reality, but the God whom we know, the God that is a consuming fire,[2] is a God that is continually transcending himself, as the cosmos is continually expanding. This God, who is experiencing himself as you in this moment, is expanding his own Self-awareness; and you are increasing your awareness of selfhood through Father, Mother, Son and Holy Spirit. These quadrants form the cosmic cross of white fire that you are, upon which all of your karma hangs, in which your dharma is fulfilled. It is energy in motion, continually in motion. Fire becomes air. Air becomes water. Water becomes earth.

If you contemplate the thought, it defies human reason. Can you imagine fire suddenly becoming air? Air suddenly becoming water? Water suddenly becoming earth? Yet in God's consciousness, the perpetual motion of the elements is this life becoming Life—Life with the motivating principle of expansion.

Why creation? So that God can expand the awareness of Self *in* the creation. And then God draws the creation back to himself, assimilates the creation, and begins another round, another manvantara.

Four Personalities of God

Saint Germain speaks of these four aspects of God in *Studies in Alchemy*. He speaks of God the Father as an Impersonal Impersonality, of God the Son as an Impersonal Personality, of God the Mother as a Personal Personality, and Holy Spirit as a Personal Impersonality.[3] When we can experience and be these aspects of God, we know him in a wholeness that we have not known before (fig. 8, page 40).

What is an Impersonal Impersonality? It is a Law. It is a

principle. It is a Spirit. That is why it is written, "God is a Spirit: and they that worship him must worship him in spirit and in truth."[4] But we need not leave God as a Spirit, as an Impersonal Impersonality, for he did not leave himself as such. The Word became flesh and dwelt among us, and we beheld his glory.[5] The only way you can behold an impersonal God is if he will personify an aspect of himself.

And so in the Christed ones and sons and daughters of God, we find revealed a personality that is yet impersonal. The Christ is a personality, a figure, someone we can know, yet who is impersonal to the extent that he dispenses the laws of a cosmos equally among the multitudes, among his followers. He teaches the Law. He does not enter into human relationships or family ties. He remains the teacher—impersonal, yet personal.

Then God enters the heart of the Mother in Matter, and we experience God as Mother, the most personal person we will ever know, the most intimate relationship we will ever have—the Mother and the child. We get to know God in the nearest, dearest sense of that ever-present Mother, that flame of love omnipresent, very personal. The face we can always see is the face of our mother.

At the line of the Holy Spirit, God becomes a Personal Impersonality, just the reverse of the Impersonal Personality. And the reverse comes as a matter of frequency, as a matter of vibration. The Holy Spirit is a very present yet unseen help. It is the Comforter who comes when the avatar ascends, who teaches us all things. We can almost touch the Holy Spirit, yet not quite. We converse with the Holy Spirit. We feel that presence in each breath we take, and yet it is the unseen one. It is the Personal Impersonality.

When we meditate upon these words, we have a closer contact with God and a greater ability to define our own inner clock. And so the corresponding four planes in our four lower bodies—or the four lower bodies of the Earth or Mars or Venus or Jupiter—reveal the same principle of life becoming Life according to the four quadrants of being.

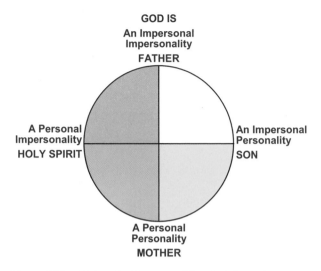

Figure 8 The Alchemical Nature of the God Consciousness

Out of the two, then, of the yin and the yang, come forth the four; and we find that Spirit and Matter become the four quadrants of consciousness. The four planes of existence are found in the sphere of Spirit and in the sphere of Matter. If we put these spheres alongside of one another, we have a figure-eight pattern (fig. 9).

The Trinity in the Four Quadrants

Having experienced four frequencies of being as the four quadrants of the clock, we now see the trinity of manifestation within each quadrant. Frequencies are becoming more articulate; they are becoming defined. We see, then, that our cosmic clock divided into four quadrants becomes the twelve; and each of the four quadrants becomes a threefold flame. From the whole to the half to the four to the twelve is simply a further breaking-down of the individualization of the God flame (fig. 10).

The threefold flame of life burns within each of the four lower bodies, in every side of the pyramid of life. In each aspect of God the Trinity is fulfilled: the blue ray of the Father, the yellow of the Son and the pink of the Holy Spirit.

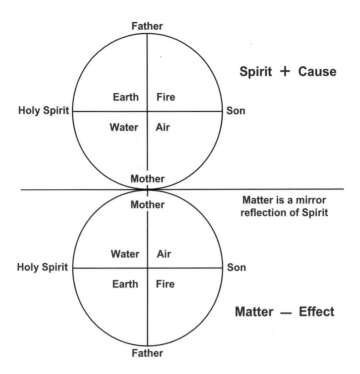

Figure 9 Four Frequencies of Being in Spirit and Matter
The Figure-Eight Flow
"As Above, So Below"

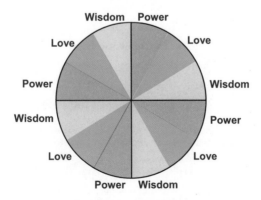

Figure 10 The Balance of the Threefold Flame
in the Four Quadrants of Being

These are the masculine aspects of God, and they are made real in the flame of the Mother. And the flame of the Mother is always the white-fire core of being, the white chakra, the white light of purity, which ignites and gives meaning to Father, Son and Holy Spirit. It is the Mother who teaches us who the Father is. It is the Mother who gives birth to the Son. It is the Mother who is the bride of the Holy Spirit. By the addition of the feminine principle, the masculine is quickened in Matter, and we see God face to face.

This diagram shows us that on each side of the pyramid—in each of the four lower bodies—we must balance the threefold flame. We must balance the expression of the threefold flame because the threefold flame develops according to our expression of these qualities. Because of the energy veil, or what we call effluvia, lodged in each of the four lower bodies, the threefold flame does not always shine with the same balance in the memory, the mind, the feelings and the physical body.

We all have our strong points. Some of us are strong mentally. Some have a very strong etheric body—the fiery body, the fiery blueprint. Others are strong in the heart and the feelings, and others have the maximum health and flow of energy in the physical form. All of the four lower bodies must be perfected as vehicles of the sacred fire, of the threefold flame in the heart. The impediments that block the flow of the sacred fire in these four lower bodies also block the flow of light within the chakras. Therefore, the cosmic clock is a means of diagramming the mastery of the chakras (fig. 16, page 54) as well as the trans-mutation of karma and the charting of the daily initiations.

The God-Qualities of the Twelve Lines

Each line of this clock describes a frequency, a vibration (fig. 11). That energy is sent forth from the Central Sun. It is stepped down to the hierarchies of the cosmos and then to the hierarchies of earth. It is released to the earth. It comes into the atmosphere, into the four lower bodies of the planet, and it is then assimilated.

We call the twelve principal divisions of God's consciousness and the beings who ensoul them the twelve solar hierarchies, or the twelve hierarchies of the sun. We know them by the names of the twelve signs of the zodiac (fig. 12). It is not too important whether or not in actuality these are the names of these hierarchies; this is the vibrational pattern they go by in our octave, and we are happy to use these names.

The Twelve Solar Hierarchies

You will note that the cosmic hierarchies are placed on the chart in a clockwise direction, beginning at the twelve o'clock line with the hierarchy of Capricorn. That is a hierarchy that releases the light-energies, the fohatic light, of God-power through the constellation, the configuration of stars, that we see and call Capricorn.

We use these names not because we think these hierarchies are, in fact, those constellations. As we know, stars in a constellation may not be near each other at all, but only appear to be clustered together from our vantage point on the earth. But the magnificent cosmic beings who make up these hierarchies, whose consciousness extends through worlds beyond worlds beyond worlds, focus themselves in the star formations that bear these names. The stars are not the hierarchy; the beings in the hierarchy simply use these and many other stars to release their energy.

Some have argued according to the world's astrology that these groupings of stars are changing because the axis of the earth is moving and because the stars themselves are moving. However, this has no bearing on the divine astrology, which is based not on the stars but on the *hierarchies who ensoul the stars* and who focus a certain aspect of the Creator's consciousness.

These star formations are only one tangible manifestation of the twelve solar hierarchies. There are lesser focuses of these twelve hierarchies around every sun and around every star. Your causal body has a focal point for the release of energy of the hierarchies, and your four lower bodies are capable of releasing that energy if you can transmute all impediments to that flow.

Figure 11 The God Consciousness, or God-Qualities,
of Lines of the Clock

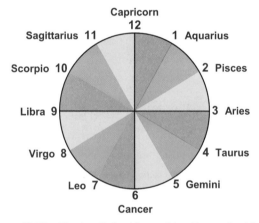

Figure 12 The Twelve Solar Hierarchies Focus the Mastery
of the Trinity in the Four Quadrants of Being

On this clock, the hierarchy of Capricorn is on the twelve o'clock line, the hierarchy of Aquarius on the one o'clock line, the hierarchy of Pisces on the two, the hierarchy of Aries on the three, the hierarchy of Taurus on the four, the hierarchy of Gemini on the five, the hierarchy of Cancer on the six, the hierarchy of Leo on the seven, the hierarchy of Virgo on the eight, the hierarchy of Libra on the nine, the hierarchy of Scorpio on the ten and the hierarchy of Sagittarius on the eleven. That is the order of their release of God's consciousness.

We are intended to become this sundial, this cosmic clock. We are intended to create the spiral within the heart, to release the spiral that forms the clock, to become that pinwheel that whirls in time and space, delivering into the planes of Matter all of these frequencies in exact measure, in the cadences of the cosmic heartbeat. This is cosmic flow! It is flowing now, this very moment, from your causal body. Yet very meagerly are we the recipients of the flow unless we have that attunement that is called cosmic consciousness.

Your Sun Sign

According to where your birthday fell when you came into incarnation, you say "I am a Taurus," or "I am a Virgo," or whatever your sign may be. What that means is that you were born at a period when the hierarchy of Taurus or Virgo or your own sign was the predominant hierarchy releasing light energy to the earth. It is under that hierarchy that you will serve in this embodiment to take the disciplines of the four aspects of God's Being—Father, Son, Mother and Holy Spirit.

The initiations under the twelve hierarchies of the sun that you need most to pass in this life come under the hierarchy of your sun sign at birth. The quality of that sign is like a tincture dropped into a glass of water; it colors the whole glass. And all the other tests must all be considered in relationship to that sign.

You may find that the points of your greatest attainment are under the sun sign, so that when you approach the gate of that hierarchy, you bring with you an ongoing attainment. You may also have attainment in other signs as indicated by the presence of planets in those signs in your astrological birth chart.

The reason we are born under a particular sign is also to attain mastery. If you were born when the sun was in Aquarius, it is your mission in life to amplify the power of God-love to the planet unto the victory of the Aquarian age. It is also your mission to transmute all that opposes that love. That is the key to your Christ consciousness. You would not have been born under that solar hierarchy if it had not been your time to go through that initiation.

Above all, you should not miss that one test. That is the key test of your entire life. That is the star that your crown requires, and you must let no man take your crown. Come what may, brook no interference to the amplification of the God-quality of your sun sign.

People who are born on the cusp, right when the sign is changing, have the equal influence of two signs. Therefore, they have the opportunity to master the circumstances of and to serve under two hierarchies.

The Rising Sign and the Moon Sign

In this life, you will also have the testings of the hierarchy of your rising sign—the astrological sign that was on the horizon at the hour of birth. In addition, you will have the testings of the hierarchy in which the position of the moon was fixed at the hour of your birth. Generally speaking, one can say that the sun sign governs your God consciousness, the rising sign governs the Christ consciousness, and the moon sign would be the soul (solar) consciousness—which is your outer personality.

The sun sign is the destiny pattern, the divine-plan pattern, the over-all ruling consciousness of the individual. If the individual is aligned with the God-self, it will be the divine aspect of the sun sign that manifests; if he is aligned with the human self, the lower nature, it will be the lower aspect of the sign that will manifest, or a combination of the two.

In people who are not striving for God consciousness, Christ consciousness and solar consciousness, you find that the outer personality follows the moon sign in its negative aspects. Once the individual transmutes the lower part of his electronic belt, he puts the moon under his feet—the moon sign under his feet—and he manifests the positive aspects of that sign.

The Cycle of the Years of Your Life

The next cycle to be aware of is the cycle of the years of your life. Draw a circle and divide it into twelve. Whatever your age is, you find that age on the clock by putting your birth on the twelve o'clock line, age one on the one o'clock line, and continuing around the clock until you come to your age.

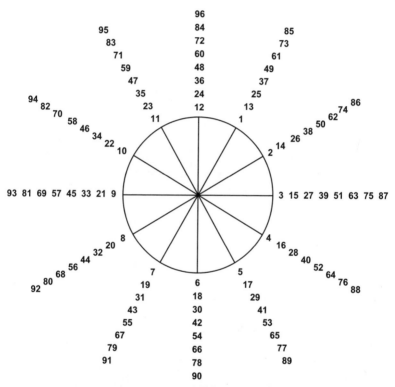

Figure 13 The Years of Life on the Cosmic Clock

Each year of your life, from one birthday to the next, the entire twelve-month cycle is governed by the hierarchy of that line, and you move forward one line each year. For example, if you are thirty-six years old, you are on the twelve o'clock line of Capricorn for the whole year. If you are twelve, twenty-four, forty-eight, sixty or seventy-two, you are also on the line of Capricorn for the year.

Within that year you will also have the opportunities that the planet has; everybody has the cycles of the planet in common. In addition, within that year you will walk through the twelve hierarchies month by month on your individual clock.

I encourage you to make a general outline of your life's history, of what you can remember of the most crucial events, positive as well as negative, and to put them on the clock. What happened to you when you were two or five or ten? Perhaps there was something very important that you remember.

If it was a great event, note it as a key cycle in your cosmic destiny. Make the most of it. Amplify its momentum by calling to the hierarchy of that sign to purify and perfect that happening in your life. And if it wasn't so good, if it was a bad record, call for it to be consumed by the violet flame under the hierarchy in which it happened and under the ascended master serving on that line.

The violet flame is God's energy of transmutation, which means change. You can change the atoms and electrons of your four lower bodies, clear the records of those tests that you have failed in the past and be ready with a clean, white page. When you do this, it makes the testing that much simpler, because you are there ready to seize that energy and welcome the initiator of your cycle. (See chapter 8 for more information about the violet flame.)

The Cycle of the Months

We have discussed how the clock unfolds year by year from birth. Now we will discuss how the clock unfolds month by month—the clock of the months of the year. We will chart one year in your life—any year.

Draw a circle, which will represent a year. Divide your circle into twelve months. The first day on the chart is your birthday. Place the day and the month of your birth on the twelve o'clock line. Your year begins on that day. New Year's Day might be the beginning of the year for the planet, but for you as your own microcosm, your year begins on that particular day. On the one o'clock line, place the same day of the next calendar month. Then simply continue around the clock in this way for all the remaining lines.

For instance, if your birthday is June 5, put June 5 on the twelve o'clock line, July 5 on the one o'clock line, August 5 on the two o'clock line, and so on. This will tell you, month by month, how your initiations fall under the twelve hierarchies of the sun.

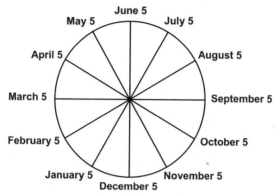

Figure 14 Chart of the Months
(This example shows the chart for someone born on June 5.)

The day of your birthday is the day when you start your initiations under the hierarchy of Capricorn—the twelve o'clock line. Three months later to the day (e.g., September 5), on the three o'clock line, you will be initiated under the hierarchy of Aries, and for one month you will have the initiations of God-control. This is the test of the Divine Ego versus the human ego, the opportunity to transmute the human ego and develop the Divine Ego, which is your own Real Self, the Christ Self as it represents the I AM Presence. This testing comes under the hierarchy of Aries.

Six months after your birthday to the day (e.g., December 5), you will have the testing of the hierarchy of Cancer, the testing of the Mother flame, the testing of your harmony; and you will have the testing of the flow of water in the emotions. Nine months after your birthday to the day (e.g., March 5), on the nine o'clock line, you will have the test of the hierarchy of Libra—the test of the Holy Spirit, the test of Reality, the opportunity to prove what is Real and to transmute all kinds of karma of unreality that comes to you to be cycled into your flame for transmutation.

Therefore, each year of your life, you are on the line of the hierarchy for that year according to your age. And within that year you will walk through the twelve hierarchies month by month. For example, if you are twenty-six, you are on the two o'clock line of Pisces for your year; but on your birthday, you start the first month of that year under the hierarchy of Capricorn. (Remember, all cycles begin in Capricorn.) It is like two dials on the meter that measures electricity—one dial is for the yearly cycle and one dial is for the monthly cycle.

When you are in your Capricorn month, you can anticipate that from your causal body will descend your attainment of God-power. You have God-power in that great sphere of light, the Sun behind the sun. It is a momentum that you stored in previous initiations under that hierarchy. You have momentums of God-love, God-mastery, God-control, and so on. When that month comes, it's like the opening of the door of the causal body. The light of your good karma comes down. At the same time, the negative karma on the same line rises out of the electronic belt. Therefore, every month of your life you can anticipate exactly what kind of energy of your personal karma will be up for transmutation.

For example, in the first month of your year, you will be facing all the records of the misuse of God-power, which we identify as criticism, condemnation and judgment. You will deal with the karma of situations where you have misused your chakras to condemn other parts of life or yourself, thus misusing God's power and therefore not having it for the good purposes of the affirmation of God-good.

In that month you will tend to experience criticism directed at you and yourself directing it toward others. If you don't know about it, you'll just carry right along, fulfilling your karmic cycles. If you do know about it, you'll put the violet flame through it and transmute that momentum of negative energy into the positive manifestation of God-power.

Testings of the Trines and Polarities

This is your personal cosmic clock. There are other phases to it; there are other ways to break it down. There are other things that you can learn about it, such as the trines and the polarity of the signs.

For example, when you are having a test in Aries, you have to remember that there will be secondary tests of Libra, because it is the polar opposite, the polarity of Aries on the clock; and you can be aware of this testing. Simultaneously, there is the testing in the fire trine, because Aries is a fire sign. The triangle, the grand trine, of testing in the month or year of Aries comes on the three, the seven and the eleven o'clock lines, which are respectively the fire signs of Aries, Leo and Sagittarius (fig. 15). They form a threefold flame, as you can see by the colors in figure 12 (page 44). Aries is the blue fire sign, Leo the pink fire sign, and Sagittarius is the yellow fire sign, according to the unfoldment of the threefold flame.

The water signs—Pisces, Cancer and Scorpio—come together as the two-six-ten. The two is the yellow, the six is the blue and the ten is the pink. This is your threefold flame for the mastery under the hierarchies of water. If you are in a Scorpio year, you will also have some testing of Pisces and Cancer substance, because that is the grand trine of your testing—to balance that triangle and that threefold flame. The mastery we learn under these three hierarchies will see us through when it comes to balancing our own emotional body, which is the third quadrant of the clock.

The trine of air is Aquarius, Gemini and Libra. These hierarchies teach us the mastery of God-love, God-wisdom and God-reality. The hierarchies of Capricorn, Taurus and Virgo teach us the mastery of the earth element in the physical quadrant. They teach us this mastery through the energies of God-power, God-obedience and God-justice.

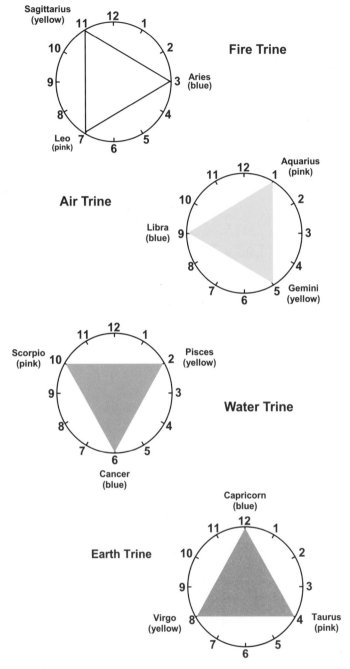

Figure 15 Triangles of Initiations in the Four Elements

We face the tests of these signs not only according to our personal cycles of the clock and the cycles of the sun and the moon, but also when planets happen to be in these signs. Energies are released by these configurations because, just as we individually have an accumulation of negative energy, each one of those planets also has an accumulation of negative energy that is the subconscious of the entire lifewave of evolutions who have evolved on that planet. (Even if there is no evidence of physical life on a planet now, there may have been life there in the past, or life may be evolving in other dimensions. In either case, the record of consciousness creates a forcefield and a magnetism interpreted in astrology.)

Therefore, each planet has a frequency of its own untransmuted substance, of its collective evolutions, as well as the frequency of its causal body of the good that has been outpictured collectively—the good works of all of its evolutions. The combination of the two—influences that are benign and not benign—makes up the identity of the planet. When we say the name of a planet, we have a sense of a personality, a vibration, a consciousness, just as we do when we speak of friends and individuals.

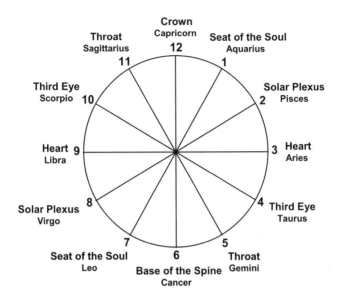

Figure 16 The Chakras and the Lines of the Clock

The twelve lines of the clock are related to the seven major chakras in the body of man. The initiations of the lines may also be understood and plotted as initiations of the corresponding chakras. The victory of the heart is won through the mastery of the three and the nine o'clock lines. The crown chakra is on the twelve o'clock line and the base chakra is on the six. These are the four cardinal points. The third-eye chakra is mastered on the ten-four axis of God-vision and God-obedience; the solar plexus is on the two-eight; the seat of the soul is on the one-seven; and the throat chakra is on the five-eleven.

CHAPTER 4

Aries

Hierarchy

Order is heaven's first law.
—El Morya

CHAPTER 4

Hierarchy

Order is heaven's first law, and that order manifests in the release of light from the Great Central Sun all the way down from the coordinates of hierarchy to our point in time and space.

We can say that God is everywhere, but what is it that is everywhere? It is God's *energy* that is everywhere—God's energy, which is the Holy Spirit. But that Holy Spirit, that energy, is man's to use as he will. Therefore, we can see that where man has chosen to amplify God-good, there will be a greater concentration of Spirit and of light.

As we consider the vastness of the universe, we realize that there must be a place where there is a far greater concentration of God than we have ever known or seen upon this earth. That place we call the Great Central Sun. Don't let the term disturb you. We call it the Great Central Sun because it is a pulsating center, the highest concentration of energy of God, the power of Spirit, in cosmos. It is not a physical sun but a spiritual sun.

Now, if you suddenly were dropped into this center of Being of God, what would happen to you? You would be consumed. Why? Because you would be totally unlike it. You are imperfect; that center is perfection.

This is why it is written in the Old Testament, "No man can see God and live."[1] You cannot see God and any longer live as man. You must become God. If you have not yet become God, when you enter into his flaming Presence, you are dissolved. This is why there is a separation between heaven and earth. Earth is not allowed to contaminate heaven, and people evolving on earth are not allowed to enter the higher reaches of cosmos.

God wants you to have the energy that is in the Central Sun. How is he going to get that energy to you if you are going to be consumed when you contact it? Now we see the reason for hierarchy.

Beginning in the heart of the Great Central Sun, hierarchy manifests as the stepping-down of the energies of Alpha and Omega, of the sacred AUM, of the I AM THAT I AM that is the fiery focal point for the whole of creation, the whole of the cosmos.

Alpha and Omega are ascended beings who represent and focus the Father-Mother God in the Great Central Sun. They are the highest expression of twin flames of which we know, and we refer to them as our Father-Mother God. John the Beloved called them "the beginning and the ending." In fact, it was Alpha who spoke, "I AM Alpha and Omega, the beginning and the ending."[2]

Energy Is Personified

The twelve points on the clock represent twelve aspects of God's consciousness. These frequencies, or vibrations, are the necessary spiralings of energy from the world of Spirit to Matter. Whenever anything is precipitated, it must start at twelve and go around and finish at twelve. As it goes from one line to the next, it is actually going through different vibrational patterns of God's consciousness.

Wherever you have a vibration, you are going to have an individuality ensouling that vibration. This is the point of the creation of man. You have God manifest through man, and every aspect of God's consciousness must be outpictured through a different manifestation of Himself or a collective manifestation, which would mean a hierarchy of beings.

If you understand that principle, then you will know that for every idea, for every color, for every vibration, there is a being or a consciousness that must ensoul it in order to sustain it, because there is nothing that can sustain itself. In the cosmic hierarchy there are beings who have evolved under those frequencies and who have reached cosmic attainment, who have been assigned by God to hold the pattern of that frequency for the entire cosmos.

Cosmic Beings and the Twelve Solar Hierarchies

Proceeding out from the Great Central Sun, beings who have earned the right through concentration of energy, of consciousness, of awareness of God, step down this release of sacred fire for lesser evolutions who have not passed the initiations required for them to contain such a concentrated manifestation of light. In each hierarchy, there are millions of cosmic beings. The Elohim and cosmic beings carry the greatest concentration, the highest vibration of light that we can comprehend in our state of evolution.

The term *cosmic being* is a title, not only a description. A cosmic being is one who is aware of Self as cosmos, who can ensoul a cosmos and be aware of energy fields and the control of energy fields that are vast, beyond our ability to even comprehend. The term simply means that their awareness of the God flame is able to approximate measures of cosmic consciousness, the highest that can be contained.

Surrounding Alpha and Omega, then, are cosmic beings and the twelve solar hierarchies. All cycles have their origin in Capricorn, and they begin in the etheric body under the hierarchies of Capricorn, Aquarius and Pisces. Mankind are not aware of the emanations of the etheric plane because these energies are at the level of the sacred fire. The first moment they become aware of God's frequencies cycling for manifestation is under the hierarchy of Aries, and this is why worldly astrologers place Aries as the first sign of the zodiac, even though it figures as the fourth in the cycling from the center of God consciousness.

Aries, Taurus and Gemini release the attributes of God in the plane of the mind. Cancer, Leo and Virgo release the attributes of God in the plane of the feelings, in the water quadrant. The hierarchies of Libra, Scorpio and Sagittarius release the consciousness of God for precipitation of the Holy Spirit in the earth plane.

Serving under these hierarchies are hierarchies of the Great White Brotherhood whom we know who are serving earth's evolutions. They take the energies of the twelve hierarchies of the sun and act as step-down transformers. They translate this energy to the level whereby mankind in the evolutions of this solar system can absorb, assimilate and become these cosmic energies.

These beings work ceaselessly throughout the cycles of the twenty-four hours to translate these energies to our four lower bodies. We are being nourished unconsciously by the living flow of this cosmic energy of the Word, and it keeps on moving, it keeps on flowing; it is anchored in the I AM Presence of each one, it is anchored in the Christ Self, and it keeps on turning as the wheel of life.

We are sensitive to these energies in a very subtle way. We receive them in certain of the chakras, we release them, and sometimes we are more sensitive than at other times to their influences. Those who have learned worldly astrology interpret the influences in a different light than they are actually in their original release.

For example, the hierarchy of Capricorn could contain as its nucleus 144,000 cosmic beings acting as step-down transformers for the flame that is released from the heart of Alpha and Omega in the Great Central Sun on this line of the clock. This is the energy that initiates cycles. We identify it as God-power, but we haven't even touched the power of God. We have seen earthquake. We have seen fire and flood. We know what land masses in motion can do, but these are a speck of dust next to the power of God.

A Vast Hierarchy of Light

Each of these twelve solar hierarchies has an appointment by God to release a certain aspect of the creative light. We find that the stepping-down of energies is invided over and over again. As the twelve hierarchies take the twelve parts, other hierarchies break these down. As frequency is stepped down, so other virtues are borne by separate lifestreams, by separate ascended masters, angels, archangels, and so forth. In the hierarchy of heaven, all have their place, all have their function.

Scientists consider that there are billions of galaxies. Billions of galaxies! When we think of the vastness of our galaxy and then try to comprehend billions of these galaxies revolving around a Great Central Sun, it almost defies our ability to equate with the cosmos in which we live. All of this is controlled by hierarchy, cosmic consciousness, beings aware of Self as God, as cosmos.

And yet all of this which scientists have observed is still only the physical spectrum of the cosmos—a very thin line, a frequency. What is above and below this frequency is yet another vastness of cosmos, of infinity, and also of planes that still are part of time and space. We see that in examining hierarchy, we do need to expand consciousness even to contain a concept of what El Morya calls *co-measurement*—the ability of the individual soul to measure itself against the Infinite, which is quite a task in itself.

The key hierarchies, then, are the twelve hierarchies that form the cosmic clock around the Central Sun. Then come the cosmic beings. Within this vast hierarchy, we see a trinity, an order of manifestation where there are three kingdoms, each serving as one of the aspects of the threefold flame.

Elohim and Elementals: The Power Ray

The Elohim, the most powerful aspect of the consciousness of God, include in their hierarchy elemental builders of form. Elementals are the salamanders that control the fire element, the sylphs that control the air, the undines that control the water and the gnomes that control the earth. These four aspects also govern man's four lower bodies. Serving directly under the Elohim are the beings of the four elements who are the twin flames who have dominion over all of the evolutions of the gnomes, salamanders, sylphs and undines.

Oromasis and Diana are the twin flames of the fiery element. Their salamanders may stand before you nine to twenty feet tall. When you see them, they are a moving rainbow fire with an identity in the fire. They are a white light—a white flame merging into the colors of the rainbow. They are a spectacular sight! They concentrate the energies of sacred fire. They are servants of man, servants of the ascended masters. They serve to keep the physical, mental and emotional bodies clean by the action of fire.

Then there are Aries and Thor, twin flames of the air element, who also govern mental action. Under them serve the mighty sylphs who control the air currents, air pressure and the purification of the air. They are fighting the pollution of the air and bearing the burden of mankind's pollution. We have the ascended beings Neptune and Luara who control the beings of the water— the undines—and the flow of energy in the feeling body of mankind. Virgo and Pelleur control the earth element and the gnomes. All of these, then, serve under the Elohim.

The seven mighty Elohim and their divine complements, their feminine counterparts, are the builders of creation. It was they who responded to the fiat of the LORD God "Let there be light: and there was light"[3] and the fiat of creation to create the worlds. The term "Elohim" is a sacred sound. It is an intonation. Even the repetition of the name releases a tremendous power, and so we give it as a chant: *Elohim!*

We find that throughout the Bible there are hundreds of references to God as Elohim, which is a plural noun, showing that man's awareness of God was as a plural being, as a dual being of the polarity of the masculine and feminine—the Divine Us. In the translation of the Old Testament, this word appears as LORD God.

The Elohim are the Spirits of God, the morning stars that sang together in the beginning.[4] They represent the power of creation—the blue ray, the blue flame in your heart. They represent the Father aspect of the Trinity. In the Hindu trinity of Brahma, Vishnu and Shiva, they represent Brahma—the thrust of creation that comes forth from the masculine aspect of the Godhead.

Christed Ones, Sons and Daughters of God: The Wisdom Ray

The second kingdom in hierarchy, corresponding to the Second Person of the Trinity, is the kingdom of the Christed ones—the sons and daughters of God. These are the ascended masters, and this is *you* in the state of becoming an ascended master. Because you are evolving in time and space, your evolution will culminate in the kingdom that falls on the second ray, the yellow aspect of the threefold flame.

It is the mission of the beings who serve in this order to anchor the mind of God, the intelligence of God, the directives of the Creator's consciousness. As we focus that intelligence, the beings of the elements become the servants to implement that intelligence, that intelling of the mind of God.

Therefore, serving in this kingdom of hierarchy, we are given tests and initiations in the correct use of mental faculties, in the correct use of free will, in the reason of the Logos. And this is the action of the Word that is made flesh.[5] It is the Word incarnate that is that Second Person of the Trinity. Ascended masters and their chelas moving upward in the spiral of God consciousness comprise the order that God has created to be the directors of creation.

Archangels and Angelic Hosts: The Love Ray

Finally, the third kingdom, functioning in the pink flame of divine love, is the angelic hosts: the seven mighty archangels and their divine complements and all of the different types of angels that serve mankind.

The angels are beings who have not left the purity of God's consciousness, except in some cases where they volunteered to incarnate in bodies like ours to help mankind. Angels that are called the seraphim and the cherubim have never touched human creation, have never incarnated and been subject to the Fall and the density of imperfection. They maintain the highest purity of the consciousness of God. There are also ministering seraphim and cherubim who make their way twenty-four hours a day standing before the altar of God and singing "Holy, holy, holy, LORD God Almighty!" They hold the frequency of purity, which they radiate to the lifewaves and evolutions in the vastness of cosmos.

The angels serve us at the level of the feeling body. They bring to us hope and joy and laughter, constancy and a quickening. They sustain the mental concepts that we receive that are ours to hold in our kingdom, the second aspect. Without the angelic hosts, the concepts that we give forth would not put on the feeling body, the desire body that draws the tremendous momentum of the Creator for precipitation in the physical plane. There is very little that we can bring forth as alchemists unless we have the feeling of the creation, the intense love of the creation, the love of that which we are bringing forth.

The angelic hosts stand by the children of the light and the sons and daughters of God. They stand guard as sentinels, as pillars of fire, guarding our creation, guarding our consciousness, giving us that quickening in moments of doubt and despair when the mission must go on, when we must conquer. They infuse us with the energy that is the feeling of God.

Balance of the Three Kingdoms

These three kingdoms working in balance, in harmony, are assigned to outpicture the trinity of the threefold flame of life on a cosmic scale. The very flame that burns within our hearts—the blue, the yellow and the pink—has all of this as ramification in the cosmic hierarchy.

Studying these kingdoms of hierarchy, we also learn something about how we apply the flame that is in our hearts. We learn, then, that it is the energy of the blue ray, the thrust of power, that gives impetus to the idea that is contained within the mind of God. Without that thrust of energy, the idea has no momentum. It is like the arrow that is shot from the bow. It is the energy of the pulling back that gives the momentum to the arrow that is the idea of God going into manifestation.

It is the action of the pink flame of love that sustains the creation. This is the action of the Holy Spirit. The angelic hosts are instruments of the Holy Spirit. When we have received the thrust of power, the Law, the blueprint of what has to be created, when we have set the mental matrix of the idea, when we have brought forth the creation through love, there is then the necessity to sustain and nourish the creation. That sustaining energy, that staying power, is always supplied by the angelic hosts. And it is supplied in ourselves by the development of love and the virtues, the qualities and the feelings that are necessary.

We speak of the balanced threefold flame as being the mark of the Christed One, the mark of attainment in the New Age. We also see that on a cosmic scale in the Macrocosm, it is necessary for these three kingdoms to function in harmony so that in a planet, in a solar system, the threefold flame, as ensouled by hierarchies, is also in balance. If mankind evolving toward becoming masters of life do not even know that that is the path they are on, do not even understand initiation or the laws governing initiation, do not understand hierarchy as a chain of being, how can they pursue even their own way, even their own kingdom of becoming Christed ones? They know not that to become the Real Self is the goal of life. And since mankind have not set that purpose and that goal for themselves, they cannot even begin to understand the fusion with the other two kingdoms —the beings of the elements and the angelic hosts.

Denial of Hierarchy and Its Purposes

I am very well aware, as you are aware, of the fact that we are living in an age when science is king. Scientists tell us there are no beings of nature, no elementals, that all things run by themselves in this cosmos. Fantastically, things run by themselves! There are no angelic beings, there are no elementals, and really, there are no Christed ones, because the scientists declare that the kingdom of the Christed ones is merely an advanced form of the animal kingdom—*Homo sapiens*, a species.

We find, then, that through a perversion of the science that is truly the flame of the Mother, there is a total denial of hierarchy and its purposes; we find that mankind are not easily taught the nature of individuality, the special nature of the flame. I often feel surprise going through an audience when I talk about the uniqueness and importance of the individual. Today, people don't think they count; they don't think they matter. They are just part of the sea of the mass consciousness, the lowest common denominator—mediocrity. And it doesn't really matter, people think, if I'm alive or I'm not alive. So there is that denial of the flame, that denial of the Real Self, that denial of purpose.

To talk to the world today about a hierarchy of ascended beings and about the order of hierarchy is to introduce something that perhaps has not been talked about since early Christian times when Origen of Alexandria described these orders of celestial beings. It is simply something too great to imagine. I think that the burden of responsibility when one accepts hierarchy is so great that it is one of the aspects that turns people aside.

The Antahkarana of Life

When we understand hierarchy, we see the importance of the flame that we carry as a link in a tremendous chain—not just a single chain, but, as it were, a golden chain mail—interconnecting links that span a whole cosmos in what is called the *antahkarana* of life. It is the web of life. It is like a vast knitting of the Cosmic

Virgin, and each stitch is a point of the individualization of the God flame.

Each point is necessary. At each point there is the converging of the spirals of Alpha and Omega that form the fiery cross of life. And where this cross, this focal point, is manifest, identity springs forth as cosmic beings, as Elohim, elementals, angels, archangels and Christed man and woman.

The awareness of God is what infuses the material cosmos with the flame, the Spirit of life. Without the awareness of the flame, the entire cosmos becomes a mechanical, physical, chemical manifestation devoid of meaning. When we realize that all of hierarchy that has gone before us in this chain, holding the frequencies above us that are greater than we are able to bear, and that all of hierarchy beneath us, all beings who hold lesser frequencies than our own, for whom we hold a key and a frequency—that all of these above and below pivot on our individualization of the God flame, then we are seized with the enormity of the responsibility we bear.

To fail to take the torch that is passed from the hierarchies above means that all kinds of lifewaves below will not receive the torch. The neglect of our responsibility is a dropped stitch in the knitting of the Cosmic Virgin—like a black hole in space. We see, then, that our striving to be free, to carry the flame of freedom at all costs, is done not for ourselves alone; it is done because of the millions of cosmic beings who stand above us and who are counting on us to carry the torch for the millions of lifewaves who have yet to evolve to the place where we stand.

You Are Hierarchy

The message of the Great White Brotherhood is simply this: *You are hierarchy.* You count. You count as the supreme manifestation of God. Your counting as this manifestation means that you must count yourself—your self-worth—not as a human being, but as a flame. It is the flame in you that doeth the work. It is the flame in you that is essential. It is the individualization of that flame through your soul that makes you unique, that makes you the mandala. So when I say to count your worth "not as a human being," I mean "human" in the sense of being limited, being mortal or having misqualified energy. Rather, count yourself as the Real Self.

The purpose of creation, the purpose of the creative fiat that brought forth your soul, was to adorn a spiritual-material cosmos with a unique aspect of the Godhead focused in the Great Central Sun. If you fail to be that flame, cosmos will be without the focalization of that facet of the diamond-shining mind of God. Now this should not make us give vent to pride, to an egocentrism; but it should lead us to the thinking of the wonder of that flame and the glory that God has placed as a portion of himself within. It should make us vastly humble—and yet not subservient, not self-deprecating, not full of self-condemnation.

Self-Condemnation

We find, then, that the condemnation of self is the first tool of the fallen ones whereby the entire hierarchy is denied. We find that chelas coming into an awareness of the ascended masters' teachings must pass the hurdle of overcoming self-condemnation. Self-condemnation is the denial that you are the potential, the living flame, of God. It is the denial of yourself as the Christed One. It is the denial of your soul's opportunity to be. This condemnation does not even originate in yourself. It is a weight of the mass consciousness that exists at subconscious as well as conscious levels. When you condemn yourself, you are condemning God. When you condemn God, this is black magic. And so, you practice this against yourself, denying yourself out of existence.

Correct Assessment of Selfhood

To seize the torch that is passed and to run with it, we must have a correct assessment of selfhood. And that always begins with "I of mine own self can do nothing. It is the Father in me that

doeth the work. My Father worketh hitherto, and I work."[6] It is
the sense of knowing that when you say "I," it is God who is the
"I." But it is not making the ego that God. It is not making the
carnal mind and all of its misuses of the sacred fire that God. It is
taking the line that is drawn by the Mediator, your Real Self, and
understanding that on one side of the line falls the Reality of your
Self-awareness as God and on the other side is the synthetic image—
the product of a synthetic civilization, of a mechanization concept.

In the *Climb the Highest Mountain* series, the structure of
which was outlined by beloved El Morya, the chapters on "Your
Synthetic Image" and "Your Real Image" show that it is not
altogether a simple process to separate in consciousness the tares
from the wheat, to define the Reality of the I AM THAT I AM
and to understand all that opposes that Reality.[7] This is why we
have hierarchy. Those who have gone beyond us on the Path, the
ascended masters, come very close to us; and they help us to
discern Truth—in ourselves first, and then in the world. They
help us see what is Real and what is unreal. Mankind cannot
truly progress without these cosmic teachers. Without hierarchy,
we would not have the measuring rod to define identity. So
hierarchy comes forth. El Morya says:

> Look up into the stars and know that there identity has
> realized selfhood in God. Know that the stars in the
> firmament of God's Being reflect the glory of the "elder
> days of Art"[8]—of those forgotten yesteryears when sons
> and daughters of God, members of the early root races of
> this and other systems of worlds, triumphed in the Law of
> the Logos, overcame time and space, and ascended to the
> plane of God-reality where they sustain the starry body
> and the starry consciousness of concentrated fire, leaving a
> counterpart in Matter to mark the point of victory. Stars
> are markers of those who have overcome. Thus you, too,
> can say: "We shall overcome. Earth shall become a star.
> The evolutions of Terra shall be free."[9]

The Ascended Masters Who Release the Light of the Twelve Solar Hierarchies to the Earth

There are twelve ascended masters who occupy positions on the twelve points on the clock to lower into manifestation for earth's evolutions the twelve qualities of the solar hierarchies. Each one, by free will, has elected to ensoul a certain aspect of God's Being. These masters have either come from other parts of the cosmos to serve earth or have graduated from earth's evolutions and stay with us out of their love for earth and their desire to see us succeed.

The names that we have for the masters are not their inner names. They have given us these names as fohatic keys that invoke the portion of their being that they can offer to us according to the Great Law. Masters release a name for a dispensation and for a people, and we call to them by that name. When we say that name in the name of our mighty I AM Presence, we automatically access from the master the light of God that that name is a chalice for and no more. The names we have of the Elohim, for example, allow us to access only a portion of their power, for we are not yet at the level where we can receive a greater portion.

This reminds us of the old Ent, a tree shepherd, in Tolkien's *Lord of the Rings*. He cautioned the impetuous hobbits against giving their real names, and would not give them his real name, which, he said, would take a very long time to say and would be the story of his existence. They had to be content with a name that in their language was Treebeard. "Real names," he said, "tell you the story of the things they belong to, in my language.... My name is growing all the time."[10]

The Great Divine Director

The infinite number of cosmic beings who make up the hierarchy of Capricorn have elected that the Great Divine Director should concentrate the momentum of God-power to the earth during the cycle of Capricorn. This means that when our initiations come under this hierarchy, we face the Great Divine Director directly and receive our teachings and examinations under his rod. The seven archangels assist him in this discipline of the evolutions of Terra.

The Great Divine Director works ceaselessly throughout the cycles of the twenty-four hours to translate these energies to our four lower bodies. We are being nourished unconsciously by the living flow of this cosmic energy of the Word.

Figure 17 The Ascended Masters Who Initiate Earth's Evolutions in the God Consciousness of the Twelve Solar Hierarchies

The Great Divine Director is the master to whom you call to hold and intensify the blueprint of your divine plan, what you are meant to accomplish on earth. He is called the Divine Director because he has mastered and taken the cosmic thesis on inner direction for the evolutions of this earth. Passing the initiations of God-power means that you have shown your ability to use the power God gives you in accordance with his inner direction.

In his capacity on the twelve o'clock line, since he contains this formula for the direction of your life, the Great Divine

Director assists you at the point when you begin new projects and cycles. Capricorn is the etheric body, which is the memory body. The Great Divine Director contains the memory and the pattern of cycles. Whenever you are starting a project, always call to him, and he will be the one who initiates the cycle and transfers to you the dispensation of energy for it.

Winter solstice, which is the time when the greatest light of the Great Central Sun is released to the planet for her evolutions, comes under the sign of Capricorn. Thus the Great Divine Director presides over the coming of the new year and new cycles.

Saint Germain

Standing for the Aquarian age on the one o'clock line are Saint Germain and the angelic hosts of light, holding the focus of God-love. Saint Germain is the director of the two-thousand-year cycle we are now entering, which is known as the seventh dispensation or age of Aquarius. He was embodied as the prophet Samuel, as Francis Bacon, Christopher Columbus and many others. After his ascension, he returned to earth as le Comte de Saint Germain. Voltaire called him "a man who never dies, and who knows everything."[11] He lived for 200 years, advising the kings of Europe. His dream was to create a United States of Europe.[12]

Saint Germain's mastery is on the seventh ray, the violet ray (the color of cattleya orchids), which is the frequency of light at which the energy of freedom and transmutation vibrates. He holds the office of God of Freedom to this system of worlds. His retreat, the Cave of Symbols, is located in the Rocky Mountains. It is an etheric and a well-hidden physical retreat. Saint Germain has stood for centuries as the defender of individual and world freedom.

Jesus

Jesus stands on the two o'clock line for the hierarchy of Pisces, holding the flame of God-mastery. The Piscean age, through which we have just passed, began with his birth. We are now concluding the initiations of Pisces, overlapping with the commencement of Aquarius.

Jesus was the archetype of self-mastery in the Piscean age. Pisces is a water sign (even though it is in the etheric quadrant), and many of Jesus' miracles demonstrate his mastery of water: walking on water, casting out demons, healing types of sicknesses that relate to the problems of the emotions, and challenging death and hell on the astral plane, which is the emotional plane, corresponding to the water element. Jesus also used the fire of the etheric quadrant for the multiplication of the loaves and fishes and for the public demonstration of the transfiguration, the crucifixion, the resurrection and the ascension.

Assisting Jesus on this line are the great hosts of ascended masters.

Helios

The three o'clock line is presided over by Helios and the Great Central Sun messengers, focusing the quality of God-control, which they amplify by the power of the Great Central Sun magnet. This magnet is the God-control of the flow of life through us, the flow of the energy of the Logos, which is the quality we must outpicture under the hierarchy of Aries.

Helios and his twin flame, Vesta, ensoul the consciousness of the sun of our solar system. They sponsor the evolutions of this solar system from the spiritual Sun behind the sun. They receive and step down the light from that Sun, making it accessible to the various lifewaves of the planets in our solar system.

Saint Patrick wrote in his *Confessions* about this mighty being, Helios.

> On that very same night I lay a-sleeping, and power-fully Satan assailed me; which I shall remember as long as I am in this body. He fell upon me like an enormous stone, and I was stricken nerveless in all my limbs. Whence then did it come into my unscholarly spirit to call upon Helias?

At once I saw the sun rising into the dawn sky, and while I kept invoking "Helias, Helias," with all my strength, lo, the Splendour of the Sun fell over me and instantly shook all the heaviness off from me.[13]

Under the initiations of Helios, we are meant to outpicture the control of the flow of life through us, the flow of the energy of the Logos, the Word.

Godfre

On the four o'clock line under the hierarchy of Taurus is God Obedience, the ascended master Godfre, whose mastery of the flame of obedience makes him eminently qualified to deliver to us the flame of God-obedience and to give us the initiations of love under the hierarchy of Taurus.

The seven mighty Elohim serve with Godfre to train millions of lifestreams in the law of conformity to the inner blueprint.

El Morya

The hierarchy of Gemini on the five o'clock line tests the initiate in God-wisdom, a yellow sign in the mental quadrant. The initiator is El Morya, with the reinforcement of the legions of Mercury. It was El Morya who brought the message of the Great White Brotherhood to Mark Prophet in 1958 and directed him to found The Summit Lighthouse.

El Morya was embodied as Melchior, one of the three wise men; Akbar the Great, ruler of the Mogul Empire; Saint Thomas à Becket and Saint Thomas More. In his final embodiment, he was known as the Master M, who directed Helena Blavatsky in founding the Theosophical Society. El Morya ascended around 1898.

During his many embodiments on earth, El Morya outpictured a great devotion to the will of God. In his etheric retreat in Darjeeling, India, he heads the Darjeeling Council, made up of 144 ascended beings with additional unascended chelas as advisors, which assists mankind by organizing, developing, directing and implementing the will of God as the foundation for all successful organized movements.

El Morya teaches the attainment of the Gemini mind, achieving the wisdom or illumination necessary for obedience to the holy will of God, for taking dominion in the earth planes, for the rule of the self, for the resolution of all division within the personality and the alignment of the four lower bodies that have been separated by centuries of misuse. He outpictures the attributes of courage, forthrightness, self-reliance and initiative.

Serapis Bey

Serapis Bey, hierarch of the Ascension Temple at Luxor, Egypt, working diligently with the great seraphim and cherubim, initiates us in the flame of purity that we call God-harmony. He was a priest in the Ascension Temple on the lost continent of Atlantis, and just before that continent sank, he carried the flame from the temple to Egypt. His watchword is discipline.

To pass the initiations on the six o'clock line, the first hierarchy in the emotional quadrant, we must master the flow of harmony. We must be able to hold the reins of harmony in our four lower bodies. This is not an easy testing, inasmuch as it is a testing of the water element, of energy-in-*motion*. It requires that we keep harmony while in motion—in action—when for some it is difficult enough to keep harmony while standing still. The initiations of the hierarchy of Cancer always involve a decision.

Goddess of Liberty

On the seven o'clock line is the Goddess of Liberty, who is the spokesman of the Karmic Board. Together with the Lords of Karma, she holds the key under the hierarchy of Leo to the quality of God-gratitude. She once said that immigration is "*I AM gratitude in action.*" She was the inspiration for the Statue of Liberty, who holds the lamp in the port of New York welcoming immigrants.

Gratitude on the seven o'clock line is continually affirming all of the gifts and graces of the Spirit and our appreciation for life. Each time we say, "I am grateful," we increase the flow in the feeling body. This plays a tremendous part in balancing karma. The flame of gratitude is an important key in the turning of the cycles of the cosmic clock.

Lord Lanto

Lord Lanto, an ancient Oriental master, keeps the flame of God-justice with the Lords of Wisdom under the hierarchy of Virgo on the eight o'clock line. He ascended after his final embodiment as an emperor of China at the time of Confucius, around 500 B.C. He was the presiding master of the Royal Teton Retreat in Wyoming until 1958, when he passed that office to the ascended master Confucius.

Lanto now serves as the lord of the wisdom ray, the second ray, disseminating holy wisdom and divine illumination into the consciousness of mankind. One of his initiations is that of co-measurement, attaining a sense of our individual worth. We do this by internalizing the principle of God-justice to realize that all have equal God-potential.

Mighty Victory

On the nine o'clock line of the Holy Spirit, Mighty Victory from Venus and the Lords of Individuality serve the hierarchy of Libra. Victory keeps the flame of God-reality for mankind. He requires us to determine the difference between our Real Self and the unreal synthetic self that is a product of centuries of self-deception.

Mighty Victory came to serve the evolutions of earth in the 1930s in answer to Saint Germain's call for assistance. He is known as the tall master from Venus, and he has legions and armies of light in his command.

He embodies, for the evolutions of this solar system and beyond, God's quality of victory in every thing we do. Victory is a flame, a consciousness, an awareness of God, which aeons ago this master from Venus determined to manifest. His name has long been dissolved into the flame that he determined to be.

Mighty Victory and the Great Divine Director are like two ends of a spectrum. The twelve o'clock line begins a spiral of a project, the correct divine matrix, and the nine o'clock line initiates it into the physical quadrant. The minute you try to precipitate on the nine o'clock line everything that has gone before—the blueprint, the planning, the logistics—you come into the blockages of the physical plane and physical karma, which are great.

And there stands Victory, inflamed with the quality of God-reality, and he helps you push through because you are Real. Through him, you can bring every project to a victorious conclusion and fulfillment in the physical plane in your life.

Cyclopea

Cyclopea is one of the seven mighty Elohim, the "seven spirits" of Revelation who sit before the throne of God.[14] He is also known as the Elohim of Music, and it is through the music of the spheres that he governs the activities of speech, hearing and sight.

Cyclopea and the Lords of Form occupy the ten o'clock line of the hierarchy of Scorpio, which teaches the correct use of the creative energies through God-vision. One of the initiations of Scorpio is that of single-eyed vision, which was lost when mankind took on the consciousness of a dual mind by partaking of the fruit of the tree of the knowledge of good and evil.

The apostle James said, "A double minded man is unstable in all his ways."[15] And Jesus said, "The light of the body is the eye: if therefore thine eye be single, thy whole body shall be full of light."[16] If we have this single-eyed vision, this knowledge only of good, we can have the light to create.

Those born in Scorpio have a tremendous opportunity in this age, but they have to learn to discipline that water energy (Scorpio is a water sign in the earth quadrant) and pass the tests of living selflessly and pursuing the path of self-sacrifice in service to life.

The retreat of Cyclopea and his twin flame, Virginia, is located high in the Altai range where China, Siberia and Mongolia meet, near Tabun Bogdo. The entire retreat is in the etheric realm, although congruent with the mountains.

Lord Maitreya

On the eleven o'clock line, Lord Maitreya, the Coming Buddha, the Great Initiator on the hierarchy of Sagittarius, initiates us in the flame of God-victory along with the Lords of Mind. He holds, at inner levels, the office of Cosmic Christ and Planetary Buddha. He was a student of Gautama Buddha, and he succeeded his master in this office. He has a focus of illumination in the Himalayan Mountains.

A Path of Initiation

The fact that hierarchy exists provides for us a path of initiation. Initiation is the step-by-step process whereby the being who is immediately above you in attainment gives you the teaching and the understanding that enables you to rise a step and assume that place, that role of the teacher. When you are prepared, you liberate the teacher and the teacher may also advance one step. This is also a law of hierarchy: the teacher cannot advance unless he has chelas coming after him who will keep the flame at the point that he is vacating.

We see that in the teachings of East and West, there have always been chelas and gurus and this correct relationship. You may find that your teacher is an unascended being. You may find that in the mastery of science or of music or of art, you apprentice yourself to a great teacher, one who knows more than you. And when you have learned all that that teacher can impart, you go on. Perhaps you surpass the teacher. This is always the prayer of the teacher—that the students will exceed the level of attainment of the teacher.

John the Baptist demonstrated this principle when he said, "He must increase, but I must decrease."[17] In a previous incarnation, John the Baptist was the guru of Jesus. Now he comes forth to pave the way for his pupil to be the Christed One. This is Elijah and Elisha, guru and chela of the Old Testament, proving the Law. Elijah ascends into heaven, and his chela, Elisha, takes up his mantle—which is the momentum, the authority of the teacher—smites the waters of Jordan, is proclaimed a prophet, and works miracles among the people of Israel. Elisha incarnates again and again and finally comes as Jesus, the Christed One. And his teacher, honoring his disciple, is given the dispensation to incarnate, to clear the way for his coming.[18] Now you understand the mystery "He must increase, but I must decrease." This is the order of hierarchy.

"When the Pupil Is Ready, the Teacher Appears"

We find, then, that when we have exhausted all worldly teachers, when we have shown ourselves willing to submit to the teacher on earth from whom we still can profit, when we have shown ourselves humble and patient and willing to take correction, willing to conform to discipline, the ascended masters—who are waiting in the wings of life, waiting for us to be ready to receive an ascended master teacher—come forth. And you know the saying, "When the pupil is ready, the teacher appears."

Morya has a famous quote that has stayed with me all the years of my, shall we say, trials and tribulations as a chela of the ascended masters. He says, "If the messenger be an ant, heed him!" You never know who the master is going to send to see how you will receive his representative. If you pass the test of receiving his representative, the representative will go on his way and you will receive the Lord himself.

Jesus said the same thing. He gave the formula for initiation: "Inasmuch as ye have done it unto one of the least of these my brethren, ye have done it unto me."[19] So we find the path of karma yoga, balancing karma through service, is won as we recognize the service of God in man, as we recognize that when we receive a prophet in the name of a prophet, we receive a prophet's reward.[20]

There are great lessons to be learned on the path of initiation. Morya is a very stern guru, and he has a very interesting sense of humor. He keeps at the entrance to his retreat in Darjeeling a very gruff chela who has no appearance whatsoever of mastery or of even being worthy to stand at the gate of the master's retreat. He speaks gruffly. Perhaps he is not dressed in the best of attire. And those who come to knock at the door, if they come in their finery and have disdain for the gatekeeper, then the master determines that they are not worthy to be received. It's a very interesting thing.

Our Position in Hierarchy

We learned of the gatekeeper of the Royal Teton Retreat. His name is Alphas. Mention was made of him in a dictation because to him the greatest mission, the greatest calling in life and the highest honor, was to be the gatekeeper of the Royal Teton Retreat.

We see, then, that service to the masters, in whatever office, whatever humble position, is keeping that point in hierarchy, keeping that stitch in the golden chain mail until we are ready to occupy the next position and assume the responsibilities attendant upon that position.

We should be content to be in the position that we hold. We ought to see that we do well and master that focal point, whether it be a job in the world or in the household or as father or as mother or as teacher. Whatever your calling, whatever your work, that is where the masters give the tests; that is where the tests take place.

Life is the guru until we show that nothing in this world is able to deter us from the humility of the flame, from the service of the Real Self of all. We find that having passed certain tests, we come directly into contact with the ascended masters. Their lessons—the Keepers of the Flame Lessons, the books they have written through their various messengers, the *Pearls of Wisdom*[21] —all of these represent an intensification of contact with hierarchy, until you are face to face with a guru as you kneel at the altar of your own heart, the chamber of your heart where the guru appears in your meditation. The masters are guides along the way until we develop the discrimination to understand who and what are the real hierarchies.

The Y in the Path

We must understand that inasmuch as there is a path of initiation and choices to be made and the gift of free will, some have entered the Path, misused the gift and chosen incorrectly. There is the point of choice that is known as the Y in the Path; there is the point at which you must elect to take the right-handed path or the left-handed path.

The right-handed path is taking the knowledge of the Brotherhood, the initiations and the energies of the I AM Presence and using these solely to the glory of the Flame and to the service of humanity. The left-handed path is taking all of this and using it to the glory of the ego. This path has been out-pictured in the way of Satanism, in the way of the inverted five-pointed star whereby the Christ is inverted, the carnal mind is elevated, and all of the energies God gives are used for the gratification of the senses and the gratification of the ego.

A False Hierarchy

Unfortunately, the right- and the left-handed paths are not so clearly defined when the choices come. But come they will; and if we meet them with determination and humility, relying upon the flame within, we will pass the tests of life. Many have failed, however. Those who have failed through their pride, their ambition and their ego have not been content to remain in the shadows, obscured, unrecognized. And therefore, they have set themselves up as a counterfeit hierarchy, a false hierarchy. Point counterpoint, they misrepresent the ascended masters and their hierarchies. This is why John warned that Antichrist should come.[22]

Antichrist is the personification of the opposition to all who would personify the Christ. Since Jesus became the Christ, he warned of that which would come to oppose that light. We find, then, that there are false teachers and true teachers. Jesus gave us the formula for dividing the way. He said, "Can sweet water and bitter come forth from the same fountain?"[23] He said, "wherefore by their fruits ye shall know them."[24] All of the false teachers quote the same spiritual truths as the ascended masters. They quote similar teachings, though there may be variations and perversions. Therefore, it is not to the teaching that we look, but to the fruits in the life of the teacher. We examine the vibration of the teacher. We test the frequencies.

"Try the Spirits"

John said, "Try the spirits to see whether they are of God."[25] When you aren't able to sense vibration, to sense frequency, how can you test the vibration of the teacher? You pray. You pray to the Real Self. You pray to the I AM Presence. You ask for guidance. You ask to be given a sign, and you do not precipitate that sign and force some kind of a manifestation that does not come from God. It is best not to commit yourself until you are sure.

When you are going through the period of anchoring your soul's consciousness in God, you take each precept, each law that is given, and you prove it. When you can have confidence in the teacher, as we can have confidence in the ascended masters, you, as the chela, know then that it is safe to trust the guru. Therefore, we take the word of the guru that is given to us and we act upon

it in faith—not always understanding, not always knowing. We
follow the teachings of Jesus and Gautama, the true teachers of
the ages, in faith, not always knowing where they will lead us.

The reward for faith and faithfulness on the Path is understanding, and this is the order of the trinity. The blue ray must be
provided by the chela—the thrust of faith in the teacher—so that
the teacher can deliver the teaching, which is the yellow ray of
understanding. And when that yellow ray is delivered unto the
chela, then the chela bursts forth in the flame of love. The love
spiral kindles the arc that forms the chain of hierarchy whereby
your heart is indissolubly linked to the heart of the teacher.

We see, then, that the Path requires faith and that it also
requires testing. It requires the testing of the Law that is given,
the testing of the flames. The ascended masters want you to
challenge every aspect of being and consciousness and of the
teaching. When you challenge in humility, in the name of your
Real Self and in the name of the I AM Presence, God will not fail
to give you proof of the way.

We must remember that those who impersonate the ascended
masters will set themselves up as the mediator in place of your
Real Self. They will make you rely on them as the source of
information, as the source of some great thing that is coming
forth. They will keep you in a pattern of running back and forth
till you come to the place where you have to ask this individual
permission to do almost anything. You find yourself, then,
becoming subservient to the will, perhaps the human will, of a
teacher who is displacing your own contact, your own Mediator,
the Real Self that God has provided for you.

The One Path

There is really only one Path that leads to the summit of life,
your own I AM Presence. There are many lesser paths, but when
you come into the one Path, you come under the one Law of your
own I AM Presence. It is the ladder—like Jacob's ladder with the
angels ascending and descending.[26]

There are steps of initiation, thirty-three in number, which every devotee of the flame must pass if he is to make his ascension. There are no alternatives to these initiations. There is no roundabout way of getting around these initiations. Jesus said, "The kingdom of heaven suffereth violence, and the violent take it by force."[27] The violent are those on the left-handed path who want to seize the power of God without the necessary surrender of the human consciousness. They would circumvent hierarchy, circumvent the masters, circumvent initiation, and proclaim themselves as Christed Ones.

When you come into the teachings of the ascended masters, they provide the way, very sure, very clearly marked. Morya has spoken of the solitary climbers who insist on going it alone. He says that the heights of the Himalayas are strewn with the remains of those who have rejected hierarchy, who have said: "I don't need hierarchy. I don't need those teachers of mankind to pave the way. I will find it on my own."

You know, this really doesn't make sense in any area of human endeavor. When we determine to study mathematics, music or whatever else, we find the best teacher. We learn all the teacher can impart, and then we forge ahead on our own when we find no other teacher. Why should we spend an entire embodiment discovering for ourselves all of the laws of chemistry or physics that have been discovered over hundreds of years with many lives investing their time and their effort? We take that which comes to us from the hierarchy of science; it is our foundation. We may check, we may challenge, we may disagree. We may attempt to see and prove whether or not all that has been said is true. But we go forward.

The Passing of the Torch

This is the passing of the torch! This is how civilization moves forward! And when you cross the threshold from this life to the next, it will be the carrying of the torch of all that has been gleaned by the souls of humanity and the offering of that fruit upon the altar of God. The torch has indeed been passed—the torch of the teaching of the ages, the teachings of the ascended masters, and the torch of a higher frequency into which this world must merge.

The light has been sent forth from the Central Sun. The planet Earth is expected to rise in initiation of planetary dimension. The entire planet is expected to go up a notch. It has to, because the solar system is going up, the galaxy is going up, this sector of the cosmos is going up.

This torch, this light, is passed from the Great White Brotherhood, from the ascended hierarchy, to those who will take it, to those who will seize it. We have a sacred opportunity. We have a sacred commitment. Let us consider, then, the meaning of hierarchy and our role in hierarchy.

SUMMIT UNIVERSITY PRESS®

Non-Profit Publisher since 1975

Tell us how you liked this book!

Book title: _____

Comments: _____

_____

_____

What did you like the most? _____

How did you find this book? _____

☐ **YES! Send me FREE BOOK CATALOG**   ☐ **I'm interested in more information**

Name _____

Address _____

City _____ State _____ Zip Code_____

E-mail: _____ Phone no. _____

Your tax-deductible contributions make these publications available to the world.

Please make your checks payable to: Summit University Press, PO Box 5000, Gardiner, MT 59030.
Call us toll free at 1-800-245-5445. Outside the U.S.A., call 406-848-9500.
E-mail: tslinfo@tsl.org   www.summituniversitypress.com

491-PYF#7035 7/04

BUSINESS REPLY MAIL
FIRST-CLASS MAIL   PERMIT NO. 20   GARDINER MT

POSTAGE WILL BE PAID BY ADDRESSEE

SUMMIT UNIVERSITY PRESS

PO Box 5000
Gardiner, MT 59030-9900

Taurus

Charting
the Cycles
of You
and Your
Family

Life, and all that lives,
is conceived in the mist
and not in the crystal.
And who knows but a crystal
is mist in decay?
—Kahlil Gibran

CHAPTER 5

Charting the Cycles of You and Your Family on the Cosmic Clock

We have seen that God's consciousness expands and is stepped down successively in twelve measures so that it can be realized by us in manifestation in the physical plane. Energy is stepped down from the etheric level of God's being to the mental level, to the emotional, and finally to the physical through these twelve hierarchies of the sun that surround the Great Central Sun. Millions of cosmic beings ensoul each one of these positions on the clock and each one of these virtues. And this release of light occurs in cycles.

Within the cycle of your life, there are many other cycles. And these cycles interpenetrate each other. We can all understand that seconds contain microseconds, and that seconds are contained within minutes, minutes within hours, hours within days, days within weeks, and weeks within months and years and millennia. Each cycle that is contained in another cycle is like a wheel within a wheel. The entire universe is built upon cycles within cycles, and these cycles can be charted.

The First Twelve-Year Cycle of Life

To chart the years of your life on the clock, take the twelve o'clock line and place there the day, the month and the year of your birth, or your child's birth. If your birthday is June 5, place June 5 and the year of your birth on the twelve o'clock line.

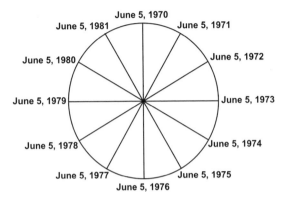

Figure 18 The First Twelve-Year Cycle
(This chart is for someone born June 5, 1970.)

At the hour that you were born, you began your first initiation, the initiation of the hierarchy of Capricorn, of God-power. The initial thrust of God-power was your first breath and your first cry, and the initiation you passed was to seize the flame of life and take it and claim it as your own. As you know, some unfortunately do not pass this test.

All through the first year of life, you were serving under the Great Divine Director and the hierarchies of Capricorn, testing the power as that power manifested in the stretching of the limbs, in the flow of the energy of the heart, in the exact working of the physical body.

On your **first** birthday came the first initiation in this life under the hierarchy of Aquarius, and God-love infused your soul with a new wonder. Your identification with love and with loved ones increased.

On your **second** birthday come the initiations of Pisces in the water element. It is a testing in the etheric body of the flow of water—the emotions. It is the flame of God-mastery. In this year you master many things. Scientists tell us we learn more in this year than at any other time in our life—in fact, in the first several years of our life. So the flame of God-mastery comes with a great thrust to the two-year-old, who is eager to master everything in sight.

Then at **three** comes the awareness of the Christ Child. The child gains a tremendous sense of identity, of "I AM WHO I AM," the awareness of the name, and "I want to do it all by myself!" This is the development of the ego; it is the Divine Ego aborning in the child. The greatest mistake the parent can make is to do for that child what the child diligently desires to do for himself; and when the child cries that you have done something for him, quickly undo it and let him do it himself. It is terribly important that the flame of individuality develop in this third year under the hierarchy of Aries. It is focusing the balance for a lifetime. All the while, the records are being recorded in the subconscious; and all that occurs on these lines—all of the impressions, all of the sounds we hear, the interaction with life— all of this is going into the record of the four lower bodies.

In the **fourth** year comes the test of the hierarchy of Taurus. More and more we are precipitating into the physical, gaining mastery of the physical. There is now that certain stubbornness that carries through the flame of individuality—the stubbornness that is not a bad stubbornness. It is a will to be, to have a separate identity, to forge out that mind that is beginning to work. Children are developing reading skills, and they are working with numbers. They are mastering the physical element, the earth plane of Taurus. The entire year is marked by this energy.

As we see in the aspect of the circle that shows the threefold flames, Taurus is a sign of love (fig. 12, page 44). It is by love that we precipitate determination, and it is actually a determination within the soul of the child to conform to the law of the inner being. The problem here is that not all children have the sense of the inner law, and they have laws imposed upon them from without that society and parents and schools deem more important than the inner law of the child. So the child is taking into himself, line upon line, whatever he contacts and composing the law of his life at subconscious and conscious levels.

At this period of time and earlier, the Montessori system[1] is able to give the child the contact with the inner law; but many other educational experiences that children have at this age are to the detriment of the child. These experiences tear from the child his contact with the inner law of life. This, then, will be a pattern that is set for life, for good or for ill. The cycles come; the cosmic clock is unfolding.

On the **fifth** birthday, the child comes under the hierarchy of Gemini, which tests the wisdom of the Christ mind. It is a sign of air. The mental development increases. The child is precocious. The child wants to learn. Most of our educational systems hold the child back in games and playing, saying, "This is what children do!" But Maria Montessori found out that children are brilliant, have a tremendous desire to learn and have the keys whereby they *can* learn. Though she did not describe it in this way, she shows in her system how children can draw forth from the causal body and the I AM Presence the inner genius of the soul.

On the six o'clock line, on the **sixth** birthday, the child learns under the hierarchy of Cancer the flow of energies-in-motion, the flow of harmony. This is a time when parents must take care to see that the child is not allowed to have tantrums and to throw energy in order to control others. For the next three years the child will be testing the emotional body and the flow of energy: What can the child get away with? What can the child do with energy?

The child discovers that if he throws energy through the solar plexus or through screaming, he can command a whole group of adults. So the child becomes very powerful and at that very moment begins to control the mother. This is the time when the mother and the father must define their positions, and it is the time when the child must be taught how to govern energy-in-motion. Many of the tools in the Montessori system teach this governing, this control, which extends to the physical body and the mental body and sets the correct patterns at the etheric plane.

At age **seven** the child is dealing again with an action of love under Leo and the mastery of God-gratitude—learning manners, learning politeness, learning to say "Thank you," developing an awareness of social action and interaction.

On the eight o'clock line, at age **eight,** the hierarchy of Virgo anchors into this earth sign the flame of God-justice, the equality of the flow of energy in the four lower bodies.

At the age of **nine,** the child comes again into a new increment of awareness—awareness of life as the Holy Spirit and the flame of God-reality. A greater measure of independence is coming here, and parents must take care to see that the child is taught what is Real and what is not real.

There is a confusion that results from the media today whereby children are given all kinds of cartoons and stories and fantasies with which they identify; they float in and out of the astral plane, in and out of illusion. Here we define Reality. And we find that in our educational institutions there is also a desire to define Reality. Yet in their ignorance, some educators tell our children that that which is unreal is real and that that which is real is not real. My children came home telling me that their teacher said, "There are no angels. There isn't any God. No one believes in God anymore." This shows the importance of the role of the parent, who must reaffirm Reality and the standards of the Holy Spirit, the cosmic honor flame that *must* be inculcated in this early cycle.

The **tenth** birthday marks God-vision, dealing with the energies of Scorpio, the test of the ten, selflessness, a lesson of giving, a lesson also in the water element.

In the **eleventh** year comes the flame of God-victory—a flame of light, a flame of illumination—dealing with the energies of Sagittarius, the fire of Sagittarius anchoring in the earth quadrant the sign of victory, the development of the physical body.

Each twelve years marks the turning of a cycle of the cosmic clock. On the **twelfth** birthday the child returns to the place of origin and now has a set of records to be dealt with from the first turn of the clock. The child faces the initiations of puberty on the twelve o'clock line in a new cycle of God-power surging through the four lower bodies, and he will also deal with all of the records of impressions of the first year of his life.

Twelve o'clock also marks the year when the first increment of karma from previous lifetimes descends. Unless the child is an advanced soul, an initiate, or has requested that the karma be given earlier, it is the plan of the Lords of Karma to allow children to have twelve years and to allow parents and teachers to have twelve years to correlate in the child's consciousness the blueprint of life, the mastery of the mind, the standards of culture, the standards of religion—all the right things that children should be taught as the legacy of the thousands of years of culture on this planet.

Unfortunately, parents are sometimes ignorant of this culture and of this teaching. Our educational institutions do not ensoul it, and we find many times that in the first twelve years of the life of a child, more harm is done than good. Nevertheless, these twelve years are the supreme opportunity to pass on to children the torch of all of the values we hold dear, spiritual knowledge and an understanding of the cosmos. Maria Montessori found out that little children are enthralled with astronomy and the study of the stars, because they have the co-measurement with the infinite. Mathematics and physics and chemistry also intrigue the child.

The Second Twelve-Year Cycle

During the first twelve years, the pattern of what the child will bring forth is set. Ideally, the child will have developed a strong sense of cosmic law, which parents call right and wrong. But right and wrong, of course, move on the scale of relativity as the decades roll by; and so we prefer to speak of cosmic law itself as the measuring rod of right and wrong. After the child is given that supreme contact with the soul in the first twelve years, when he has that grounding, then he faces the tests of karma and the tests of puberty. With a firm foundation in the Law, he is equipped to face that energy that is oncoming and that presents a great testing in the next twelve-year cycle—the years between twelve and twenty-four.

Let us study these years as we take up an examination of the perversions of the twelve hierarchies of the sun. On the **twelfth** birthday, the child receives the impetus—actually a sphere of light that descends from the causal body—of God-power. It is a blue sphere of energy. It is delivered to the Christ Self, to the Christ flame, just as cosmic hierarchies deliver a sphere of light at winter solstice for the turning of the cycle of the year.

So, this gift of energy now is within the heart of the child. How will he use this energy? The child will use the energy as he has been taught. If he has been taught obedience, he will use it in obedience. If he has been taught God-control, the energy will flow with God-control. If he has been taught the proper behavior patterns, the proper discipline and learning techniques, all of this God-power will be used as an adornment to amplify all of the other twelve aspects of the clock. However, the child is also going to deal with the first increment of karma in this year. And this frequency of energy that is the misuse of God-power we define as *criticism, condemnation and judgment* (fig. 19). It is the misuse of the etheric body and the alchemy of fire.

This condemnation manifests in many subtle ways, including self-condemnation and self-belittlement. It may be a period when the child withdraws, feels uncomfortable with his peers, doesn't know quite how to interact. The self-belittlement and sense of worthlessness at this age, which may continue all the way through the next twelve years of attempting to integrate with peers, can be the result of past karma delivered on that twelfth birthday. As the I AM Presence delivers the sphere of fire, of God-power, so the Lords of Karma, through the Christ Self, also deliver the package of karma that contains the soul's misuses of

God-power in previous lifetimes.

These misuses do not fall strictly into the category of these three words, yet they can be sensed as such. When initiations of Capricorn are prevalent in the life of the individual, there is that feeling of being weighed down, of being condemned, the feeling you can't do anything right no matter how hard you try, the feeling that people are speaking ill of you—and perhaps they actually are, but it can become a burden to the point of a psychological complex of paranoia. All of this is often the result of the misuse of God-power in past incarnations.

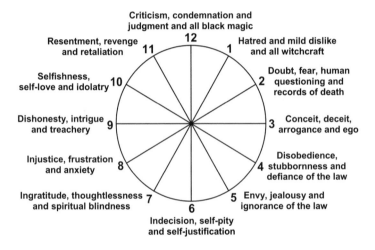

Figure 19 Human Perversions of the God Consciousness
of the Twelve Solar Hierarchies

The wise parent who has the teachings of the cosmic clock will take the child in hand. The twelve-year-old has the complete capacity to understand the clock. He will understand that he has choices to make. He can choose to increase his momentum of power by invocations to the blue flame and to the masters who serve on that ray, especially to the Great Divine Director; or he can choose to indulge that condemnation as it cycles back to him for transmutation.

Instead of letting it go into the flame, he may take that condemnation and begin to condemn his parents or his brothers and sisters or children at school. He may become hypercritical of everything and everyone, including himself. When parents observe this trend, they should warn the child, "It is time to give an invocation to put into the flame all that is less than the perfection of God-power and your divine plan that ought to be fulfilled this year." Children will see the difference, and they will also run to greet the opportunity of balancing this karma.

Where there is ignorance of all that is taking place, you find that people can go through an entire year of taking all of that momentum of karma and re-creating it. *People re-create karma.* For an entire year they can be misqualifying the flame of God-power. And when the cycle turns and that flame and that torch that should have been carried is to be exchanged for the flame of God-love on the line of Aquarius on the next birthday, the flame that has not been carried cannot be exchanged for a new flame. Thus we see that *initiation is cumulative.* What we earn on one line must be carried to the next line, and it becomes the foundation for mastery in that line.

Therefore, on the **thirteenth** birthday, the child who has correctly used the flame of God-power lays it upon the altar; and the momentum of God-power gives him the mastery to claim the love of Aquarius and to anchor that love as purity, as divinity. The age of thirteen is for the adolescent the testing of love in many ways. It is a time when love must be garnered in the heart, when the wise parent will show the child how to raise the energies coursing through the body, how to release that energy in the heart, how to expand the heart chakra, to begin to understand life as a path of service, and to continually be giving in love in order to use these new energies that are arousing new feelings within his form. These energies can be used for the service of life, and the child can gain a great sense of mastery of that flow in this year.

However, with the release of that flame of love, the karma of hatred and mild dislike, which are the misuses of love, also comes up for transmutation. We find that young people at this age like to get together in groups and cliques and clubs, and there is the stratification into social levels. Some are left out and some are included, and intense likes and dislikes build up. They move in groups, and there is the feeling that some are on the inside, some are on the outside. There is that substance of intensity in relationships. All of this, of course, can be dissolved by the alchemy of divine love when parents and teachers are there to show the child how to use these energies.

As we go around the clock, then, to the **fourteenth** birthday on the two o'clock line, we find that there is mastery to be gained, especially over the increments of karma coming at this age—a very important age, especially for the devotee who is born to attain God-mastery in this life. The training in the walk of Jesus and of the Christ will be a tremendous bulwark in the life of the adolescent, the teenager—understanding the teachings of Jesus, his words, his counsel; understanding Jesus as the guru, the master of the age; understanding that there is a very intimate communion that we can have with Jesus giving us the strength to overcome temptation, to walk in the way of mastery. The entire Piscean dispensation is the gift of Jesus to the fourteen-year-old. As wise parents, we will see that our children understand and develop a very personal relationship with this beloved master.[2]

With that increment of God-mastery and the walk with Jesus, there comes the increment of karma that is a momentum of fear and doubt, including all past records of the experience and the initiation of death. At fourteen there is a great deal of torment that the adolescent faces in coming to grips with past records of death. In this year we find young people across the world even considering suicide and the forms of violence that come from these records of death.[3]

Coming to the **fifteenth** birthday on the three o'clock line, the child enters into his own sonship—his awareness of himself as the Christ. He truly comes into the awareness that "I AM a son of God!" He is not simply affirming this, but he is realizing what it means to be a son of God. The Christ Self releases an increment, a momentum, of the Great Central Sun; and the Christ flame actually blazes forth through the child. With proper guidance, even miracles can happen in the lives of children this age, for they are pure and of the virgin consciousness. They have a very special contact with the angelic hosts and with Mary and Jesus that they have not lost since their incarnation, since they were little children and had that attunement in the fiery core of life.

When children at age fifteen face that awareness and potential of the Christ, they also are faced with that increment of karma that is the ego, or the carnal mind. We find that it is an age when young people become aware of themselves as personalities and they move and push the personality and the ego first—with all of its demands and flirtations and movement and inter-action—to the neglect of the soul, to the neglect of the development of the Christ flame.

At age **sixteen,** there is a supreme opportunity for building, for anchoring the talents of the child in the earth plane. This year falls in the mental quadrant. It is the year when application in school is very important; preparation and decisions for the sacred labor are being made. "What will I do with my life? What is my divine plan? How will I forge a future for myself, for my family? How will I bring forth the talents of my causal body?" All of this the hierarchy of Taurus shows the young adult of sixteen. And this application of the flame of love, in study, will bring the reward of the foundation that is necessary for life.

Unfortunately, there are many distractions at this age. Besides the increment of the flame of love and God-obedience that is given on this birthday, there is also that package of karma—the record of all that the Lords of Karma require the sixteen-year-old to transmute of past records of rebellion, disobedience, stubborn-ness and defiance of the Law—the inner law of being.

The age of sixteen (and even younger) is the age when experimentation with all forms of abuses of the body often takes place—the taking-in of drugs, the taking-in of impure substance, impure foods—all of this misusing the flame of the Law and the action of love in Taurus. We find that because of the way the foundations of civilization are made, young people of this age, going with their peers, do not have the guidance needed to pass the tests on this line; and usually they make more karma than they balance.

With the **seventeenth** birthday on the five o'clock line comes an intensification of God-wisdom by the hierarchy of Gemini. The age of seventeen is an age when a great deal of knowledge can be gleaned from the causal body, when all of the hierarchies of heaven stand waiting to impart to the soul its inheritance of the yellow sphere of the causal body.

The increment of karma that comes up for transmutation in this year is the increment of envy, jealousy and ignorance of the Law. We find that when the individual is personality-oriented and doesn't get out of that socket from age fifteen on, there are envies and jealousies and vying for relationships. Sometimes this all-consuming energy takes all of the young person's time in relationships with the opposite sex—in determining whether or not this is going to work out or that is going to work out—which is a part of the testing of the hierarchy of Gemini, the twin flames of Gemini.

If this energy can be transmuted and placed in its proper perspective, the right relationships can bring about the fusion of energies for the drawing forth of a vast amount of wisdom. The mind of the seventeen-year-old, when freed from these other concerns of personality, has the capacity for amazing input, study and accomplishment, especially accomplishment in the sacred labor.

At the age of **eighteen** on the six o'clock line comes the testing in the flame of God-harmony and the Divine Mother. Eighteen marks the beginning of a three-year cycle—eighteen, nineteen and twenty. In these years the feeling body is at its prominence and there is the testing of that feeling body by the substance of karma up for transmutation that must be consumed if we would gain the mastery under the hierarchies of Cancer, Leo and Virgo.

The karma that comes to the fore under Cancer is indecision, self-pity and self-justification—feeling sorry for oneself for not being accepted in college, not going on to higher opportunity as others are going, feeling sorry for oneself because of one's own failures, that idling of energy, the inability to make a decision. "What will I do with my life? I'm out of school. Now where will I go?"

The mastery of this flow is necessary to forge ahead into the higher learning of advanced educational institutions, which were destined by the masters to be the focal point for the release of the culture of the Divine Mother. The high-school years are intended to be for the release of the energies of the Christ Self, the Christ mind. Entering college, vocational school, business school or some training after high school is a time to glean from the hand of the Mother the knowledge of our sacred labor and to complete this training in the four years that culminate on the line of the Holy Spirit.

When we come to the line of the Holy Spirit after that training, it is time to go forth into the world of form to make our mark, to get a job whereby we precipitate with our hands, with the correct use of our energies, that which we are intended to manifest in this life. The years twenty-one, twenty-two and twenty-three are periods when we can take advanced training, mastering further phases of postgraduate work in the increments of the Holy Spirit; or we can go forth, our training completed, to take our place in the world community.

Now, there are misuses of these lines to watch for in those years: at **nineteen,** under the hierarchy of Leo, ingratitude and disturbance in the emotional body. There is a certain nervous tension. Then, at **twenty,** comes the mastery of Virgo: anxiety, the sense of injustice—the sense of *human* injustice—the outrage of particular experiences or particular individuals with whom you are interacting who you feel have been unfair. It's a time to take up social causes, social justice and injustice. It's a time to be careful that we don't squander the increment of light that is given from Virgo for God-justice by getting completely caught up in a sense of injustice whereby we re-create and amplify injustices in our personal life and on a planetary level.

At **twenty-one** the testing of Libra, of God-reality, comes again. On this line we find the perversion of Libra, of Reality, as unreality. It is that deceit—the deception, the intrigue and the treachery—that the ego uses to justify its position. We must be careful to correct the tendency to lie, to fib, to expand on the facts so that they are slightly distorted so as to suit one's needs. And we must see that we do not allow our imagination to make us believe that we have an attainment we do not have or to make us rationalize the deliberate betrayal of the laws of society to the detriment of the interaction of lifestreams.

Twenty-two, the year of Scorpio, is the year of the testing of the sacred fire, the testing of the uses of the sex energy. Of course, this testing comes all through adolescence, but in this year it comes as the release of the karma of many misuses of the sacred fire in the past. This is also a year when people start families. It is a year for the mastery of the flow of the sacred fire and the using of that energy to bring forth children. It is the year of vision, of seeing the plan of life, carving out that vision, selecting one's life partner.

The momentum of selfishness of the past is very strong in this year. We must see to it that we do not base our lives, our plans, our marriages on selfishness, on possessive love. Partnerships based on residual karma that is not transmuted will not be lasting. We must call forth the sacred fire from the hierarchy of Scorpio and the Elohim Cyclopea for clear seeing, for the transmutation of these misuses of energy so that we can make our decisions based on clear seeing.

Finally, completing this second twelve-year cycle with the **twenty-third** year, we have the hierarchy of Sagittarius giving us an impetus for the victory of life. Opposing this victory is the entire dragon of the carnal mind—our own human creation symbolized in the form of the dragon in the Book of Revelation.

And this energy comes with a momentum of resentment, revenge and retaliation. When we are eleven years old and playing, it is the year when we have the hostilities and the cruelties that children are noted for—the fights, and so forth, the resentment, the revenge, the getting even with So-and-so because he did this to me. Well, it comes again at age twenty-three. And we must see to it that we do not allow resentment in its subtle form of silent seething to take from us the crown of victory, which is a release of victorious, golden illumination.

The Third Twelve-Year Cycle

Coming back again to the twelve o'clock line, we are at the **twenty-fourth** birthday. The next cycle of twelve years is for the mastery of the Christic light and the Buddhic light. In these twelve years we have the opportunity to become the Christ and the Buddha. At age **thirty-three,** Jesus manifested the victory of the Christ consciousness and earned his ascension. We have the opportunity to do likewise. Thirty-three is the number of the initiation of life that begins at birth and culminates in the thirty-third year.

On the **thirty-sixth** birthday is the initiation of Buddha; at age thirty-six, Siddhartha attained enlightenment. From there on in life, if we have passed the tests of Christic initiation, we are given intimate contact with Gautama Buddha and other Buddhas who have gone before him in the testing of our souls according to the Buddhic light.

Now if all follows like clockwork and all we outpicture throughout our lives is the God-qualities of the twelve hierarchies, of course we ascend. And that is the spiral of the ascension that you weave with the threefold flame in each of the four quadrants. The threefold flame becomes the fire in the center of the base of the pyramid that begins to turn as a spiral when you are nigh your ascension. It envelops your form, your four lower bodies, and you are completely consumed and return to the heart of the Father-Mother God.

Predict Your Future

The Cycles of Jesus' Clock

Jesus came into embodiment with 93 percent of his karma balanced. As he went through the cycles of his clock during the years from his birth to the age of twelve, he received from his causal body only increments of the flames of God-power, God-love, God-mastery, God-control, God-obedience, God-wisdom, God-harmony, God-gratitude, God-justice, God-reality, God-vision and God-victory. He, the avatar of the age, was, however, required to balance planetary karma even while increasing the sphere of the Christ consciousness during these first twelve years.

At the age of twelve, he was given the opportunity to balance personal as well as planetary karma and to begin the initiations for Christhood. His acceptance of this responsibility even when it conflicted with family obligations is evident in his statement to his parents when they found him discoursing with the doctors in the temple, "Wist ye not that I must be about my father's business?"[4]

During the next eighteen years—one and a half cycles on the cosmic clock—Jesus prepared for his three-year mission, both in and out of the retreats of the Great White Brotherhood in the Near and Far East.[5] Each line was a major initiation under Lord Maitreya, who was his guru and who put him in contact with the Cosmic Christ. With each increment, he was fortifying himself with the God flames of the solar hierarchies for the three-year ministry that culminated in his crucifixion, his resurrection and his ascension.

If we come into embodiment with karma and yet qualify God's energy and the returning energy of our karma with the flames of God, we have the opportunity to consume that karma by invocation to the sacred fire, by the momentum of light in our causal body, and to manifest considerable attainment in the Christ consciousness by our thirty-third birthday. This is the year when we enter our divine mission. We go forth with our ministry, able to deliver the teachings of the ascended masters to the world, to serve the souls involved in the karma of our mandala.

The ascended masters are concerned that the youth coming into the teachings at this time come in at an early age—in their teens, in their early twenties—so that they will have a decade to prepare for that cycle of life when the tremendous culmination of victory in the thirty-third year can anchor within them the full complement of the mastery of Jesus the Christ, Lord Maitreya and other ascended masters, such as the guru of the chela or the chohan of the ray on which the chela serves. The three-year mission following this year then culminates in the fulfillment of the power of the three-times-twelve. Three times going forth in the cycles of the cosmic clock brings us to the age of thirty-six and the Buddhic initiation.

Applying This Teaching

When we train children in our schools from the age of two and a half in this teaching, when they grow up with the training of Maria Montessori all the way through high school and then enter our institutions of learning such as Summit University,[6] when they have this training combined with a liberal arts or a specialized education and all that must be mastered in the fields of human endeavor, they will be truly equipped to face the initiations of the ascended masters, to take dominion over the earth and focus the energy within their chakras to bring about the manifestations of alchemy that will be the mark of the sons and daughters of God in the Aquarian age.

Gemini

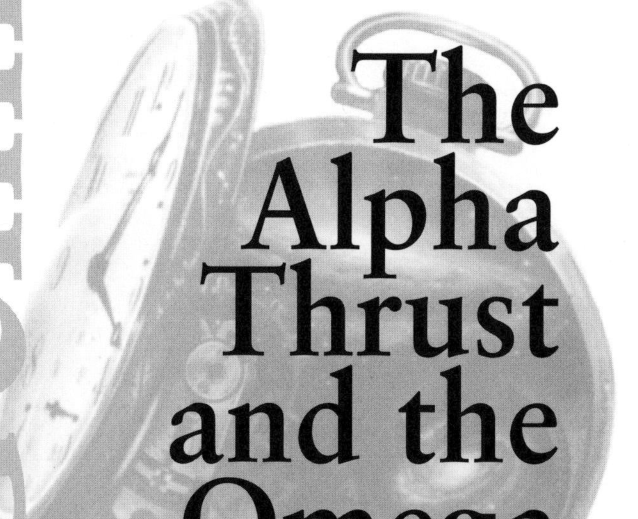

The
Alpha
Thrust
and the
Omega
Return

I am Alpha and Omega,
the beginning and the ending.
—Revelation

CHAPTER 6

The Alpha Thrust and the Omega Return

The circle of the clock is the great T'ai Chi of the Father-Mother God, and the name of that divine force is Alpha and Omega. The first side of the clock is the Alpha thrust, and the thrust is the descent of fire as it comes out from the heart of the Father-Mother God.

We begin our evolution in the center and we go right to the twelve o'clock line, which becomes our first station, our first stop. We go through the first half of the clock. And when the Alpha thrust reaches the bottom of the clock, the six o'clock line, it changes direction. And from that point on, it is called the Omega return.

That cycle is an increment of energy. It could be a microsecond long or it could be a million years. It is one cycle, depending on how you're counting cycles—"One day is with the LORD as a thousand years, and a thousand years as one day."[1]

You can see your entire evolution of incarnations as one turn of that clock. The going out from the heart of God, the sowing of the seed of karma and energy, would be the Alpha thrust. On the six o'clock line, you make the decision to return Home to the center of the "OM." When you make that decision to return, you are on the Omega return.

The scriptures say that "the LORD shall preserve thy soul. The LORD shall preserve thy going out and thy coming in from this time forth, and even forevermore."[2] We go out from the Great Central Sun, from the white-fire core of being, from our point of origin, and it is always with the impetus of Alpha and the return of Omega. This is the pattern of our soul's journeyings round and round the cosmic clock.

The return is always more difficult. Even pictorially, it's an uphill climb—we are having to go up. And the only momentum we have to go up is the momentum by which we came down. The thrust is like the downward ride in the roller coaster. If we have a tremendous thrust of light going down, that thrust will take us all the way back up.

But if in coming down we start misqualifying the energy of God on the various points of the clock and we've dissipated our Alpha thrust, by the time we get to the six o'clock line, we have no momentum to carry us back to the twelve. Then we are stuck in our karma, and it is an uphill climb all the way home. We have to start invoking the light of God to replace the energy that we should have—but don't because we've squandered it, like the prodigal son.

Every day, every hour, every moment, the energy of our lifestream is somewhere on a sine wave. The Alpha thrust is the downward motion, and during that time our energy should be increasing, because we are descending into Matter and we should be increasing in velocity. Our energy should be intensifying because we are going to get to the point of the base chakra—the point of the Divine Mother, the point of the ascension flame—and with that tremendous thrust, if we don't misqualify energy, we will go right back Home and be home free in that cycle.

Every day we have the momentum that comes from the light of our I AM Presence, the light of Alpha, and it is the charge of the day. And if we qualify it positively, if we don't let ourselves get stopped by every little thing that happens, if we have a plan for the day that we set the night before and we go into our day with that charge, that momentum will carry us all the way back through all the things that we have to accomplish.

Essentially the Omega return is a duplicate of the Alpha thrust except in polarity. Alpha is the plus sign, Omega is the minus. We are going to experience on the negative polarity of being (in other words, in Matter and in our karma) what we experienced coming out.

If we had followed the example of the twin flames in the first three golden ages, we would have the full-gathered momentum of our thrust at the six o'clock line. Because all energy we had used was to the glory of God, we would have the same momentum and greater momentum than that with which we left. It would be merely a matter of riding that momentum on the upswing and returning to the heart of God in the ritual of the ascension. That is exactly what happened to the first three root races: they came forth, fulfilled the divine plan and ascended.

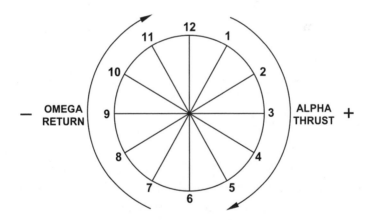

Figure 20 The Alpha Thrust and the Omega Return

But if, from the moment we leave the heart of God, we are misusing the energy from the twelve down to the five o'clock line, we are going to have to transmute that energy in order to build a new momentum to carry us Home; and that momentum is the cycles of white light, the coil of energy in the pyramid. It is the

ascension flame. It is the seamless garment. We have to weave the seamless
garment if we have lost it or if we have
abused the delicate membrane of the
aura.

This Alpha thrust and Omega
return is occurring every hour, every
day, every week, every month, every
year. Ezekiel saw the cycles of God in
the chakras as wheels within wheels.[3]

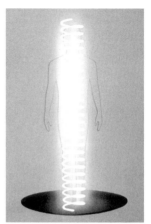

The Seven Rays

Fig. 21 The Ascension Coil

The Alpha thrust contains the first seven rays. On the twelve
o'clock line we put the first ray, and helping you in your Alpha
thrust is El Morya, the chohan of the first ray.* Lord Lanto is the
chohan of the second ray, the one o'clock line. The third ray is
the two o'clock line, and Paul the Venetian is the chohan.

The three o'clock line is the fourth ray, whose chohan is
Serapis Bey. The fourth ray, the white ray, is always the pivotal
ray. It follows the first three rays, which represent the Trinity, the
threefold flame in your heart. That Trinity represents the octaves
of Spirit, and so we see that those three lines are found in the
etheric quadrant. In this quadrant you balance the threefold
flame under the hierarchies of Capricorn, Aquarius and Pisces,
with the chohans of those three rays.

Three o'clock is the transition point, where you affirm
through the threefold flame I AM WHO I AM. From this point,
the fourth, fifth and sixth rays are bringing the threefold flame
into the first major shift from the etheric body, the memory body,
to the mental body.

Hilarion is the chohan of the fifth ray on the four o'clock

---

* As we plot the seven rays on the clock, we understand that the chohan of
each ray may assist us in developing mastery on that ray and that line. Some of
the chohans of the rays also hold offices under the twelve solar hierarchies.
These offices are on different lines of the clock from their positions as chohans.

line. Nada, chohan of the sixth ray, is on the five. Saint Germain is the chohan of the seventh ray on the six o'clock line. The fifth, sixth and seventh rays are all for precipitation of the first cardinal qualities of God—the first, second and third rays.

The fifth ray is the emerald ray of precipitation by the All-Seeing Eye of God. It is science. It is music. It is industry. It is technology. It is healing. It is everything that makes things physical.

However, you can't make things physical through the green ray alone. What really makes things physical is the ray of ministration and service, the ray of Nada—and also the ray of Jesus—which corresponds to the love ray. Ministration and service is love in action. And that love in action in service is what anchors and precipitates through the fifth ray, the green ray, and the seventh ray, the violet ray of alchemy.

The seventh ray is the ray of ritual, of religion, of mysticism, of alchemy, and also a ray of science. The two forms of science, of the fifth and the seventh rays, would not be manifest and could not become concrete without ministration and service.

The Secret Rays

When you have your mastery on those seven rays and you are looking for your Omega return, you come into the initiations of the rays known as the secret rays. There is precipitation on the fifth, sixth and seventh rays, but the five secret rays are the mastery of the astral plane, or the desire body, and the physical body. So without those five secret rays, which are on the next five lines of the clock, we are not able to bring into manifestation and make permanent our creations.

The making permanent of your creation in the Matter cosmos is through your God-mastery of the five secret rays. You see how little mastery there is of the five secret rays by the fact that we live in a band of mortality and everything that we are and everything we do is in a process of disintegration. But through the resurrection flame and the violet flame (the sixth and seventh rays), which are the open doors to the secret rays, we make permanent what we are. And that is the flame of immortality. We are in a very low spectrum of vibration, but we are learning to accelerate into dimensions where what we create can be made permanent.

Because these are secret rays, we are not told their colors; they are shielded in a shaft of white light. Because we are in a level of mortality and these are the components of the creative force that would make us immortal, this gift is not given to mortals. The very fact that we can name the five secret rays and that we can name the beings that are on those lines means that we can make calls and God can allow us to receive the portion that we are able to receive without making karma.

The Ritual of the Atom

The clock answers many questions. We all came forth from the source of Oneness, and to it we shall all one day return, with or without our individuality. But at this point in time, we see neither the beginning nor the end of our existence. Both are remote in the distant past and future.

Having lost the perspective of both shores, we try to fashion meaning out of relativity. Actors on a stage playing many roles, we are no longer able to distinguish the Real Me. We make merry and join clubs, playing the games people play. And if we dare to think, we attempt to find a rationale for our *weltanschauung*—our world view—which at best is incomplete. Then, when we think we have found the logic of the way, we close our minds to all other interpretations, dismissing them as heresy. I think the scientific mind can be the most religious mind, when it is imbued with the Holy Spirit.

We all came forth from the center of Oneness. That is the beginning of this quest for Reality. The center of Oneness is the dot in the center of the circle. No matter what chart we study, we are always aware of the fact that the Real Self is the dot in the center. That is the nucleus, the center of Being.

We come forth and we have an opportunity to expand God's Being, God's awareness of himself. And so we can say as a mantra:

> I AM God's awareness of himself.
> I AM God's awareness of himself.
> I AM God's awareness of himself.

I am God's identity. Without me, God will lose a certain pattern of his awareness of his own identity. It's a beautiful thought.

God is a sphere. A circle is a spiral of God's consciousness. And in order, then, to expand awareness, there is a going-forth from the point of the center.

Let us not even talk about Matter. Let us dwell purely in planes of consciousness in Spirit. In Spirit there is both the formed and the unformed—the form and the formless. In other words, when you get out of Matter, all does not become a filmy mist of spiritual substance. The masters are ascended. They have form. They have identity. They have substance. They have density. And yet, they are pure Spirit.

Spirit is another realm from which Matter derives its pattern. Nature is the hem of the garment of God. All of the material universe, all of the patterns that we perceive in material substance are simply a way God has of showing us, "If you can find all of this in Matter, imagine what Reality there is in the plane of Spirit." God is enticing us to explore Spirit, the kingdom of God, by creating this whole material universe.

God's awareness of himself, which is the dot in the center, must expand to become the entire circumference of being. This dot must learn control. It has control in the center. It is a fiery core or a fiery ovoid. It must suddenly make that leap and extend itself in all directions at once and be in control of that much more of what we would call time and space, or that much more area of God's consciousness. It doesn't just make the leap suddenly. It makes it in a spiral, which always moves up and toward the twelve, which is the opening.

Now at this time, it isn't even twelve—it is a flame. It is a facet of God's consciousness. It is a point where another identity has said, "I AM God's awareness of himself." And this is another law of hierarchy.

Before this point came into being and had the need to expand the awareness of God, other points had already gone forth and already manifested the flame. "Before you have called, I have answered."[1] In the center of Being, identity makes the call for expansion because expansion is the nature of God. And the answer is already found in the pattern and the matrix.

We can learn to feel the flow of that expansion of God's consciousness by the names of the God-qualities. We call the identity on this first point God-power. The first point of the geometrization of being outside the fiery core is the release of God-power. Instantaneously, then, what was the white sphere of simply an Alpha and Omega polarity, becomes, at this point of geometry, a flame of God-power.

When it goes back to the center after experiencing the twelve o'clock line, it brings with it the net gain of experience in the manifestation of God-power, and God's being takes on another ring of God-power around the center. It then goes out releasing the flame of God-love that comes forth from the energy of the white-fire core plus God-power. The flame of love is then precipitated, and it comes back again. Returning from God-love, an additional ring is formed, one complete circle around the white-fire core, and it goes out again into the manifestation of the flame of God-mastery.

Every flame that we name on the clock is the sum of all of the previous flames. God-power plus the fiery core equals God-love. God-power plus the fiery core, God-love plus the fiery core equals God-mastery. God-power plus the fiery core, God-love plus the fiery core, God-mastery plus the fiery core equals God-control.

That is why energy is a spiral, because each turn adds to the sum total, and the spiral is always in the proportion of the golden ratio. This is the fundamental pattern of this evolution.

If you study these flames, you will see that they are getting more complex. The flame of mastery is an illumination of the previous two. God-control is the flame that gives you the control of the first three flames. God-obedience makes you want to put the whole unit together in orderly fashion and to keep your being in conformity to it.

Obedience requires a certain amount of experience. There is nothing to be obedient to, unless you have power or energy. There is no reason to be obedient to God unless you understand his love and love him so much that you want to conform to his laws. Obedience doesn't mean saying "Yes, sir," and "No, sir." It is making ourselves congruent with the patterns of time and space, the patterns of the atom, the patterns of being.

Now, what happens when the center is on the periphery? There is another forcefield of a sphere on each line that makes up that flame. And there is an orbiting around that focal point for a certain increment of time and space before the return. Between the center and the sphere on the outer circle, a forcefield develops that causes the identity in the center to expand. And that is what you see in the whirling of the electron. As it whirls around, a forcefield, a pattern, is established that makes up grids whereby energy in space is now going to be controlled by the consciousness that inhabits space.

Each time it goes out, it is establishing coordinates or points around the circle, and each time it goes out, another flame is anchored and another sphere is built in the center. With each turn, the nucleus, or the center of awareness, is getting what we would call more dense. There is a greater weight of light focusing in the center. The dot in the center, by this sweep around, is gradually becoming the whole.

There is a point in the travels of this electron where there is a critical mass in the center. The center then explodes to the periphery. God's consciousness leaps into an expanded awareness of Self, and there is a new white-fire core that is the extension of the nucleus to the outer circle and the inclusion of its awareness of all of these qualities.

This is ritual that may be accomplished by meditation and invocation. We start in the center with the mantra "I AM God's awareness of Alpha and Omega in the white-fire core of being," and then go to each of the twelve lines in turn.

When you meditate upon this concept, you begin to be the observer watching the mind of God cogitate within you and observing how God is increasing his awareness of himself in you. You are simply a coordinate in time and space for the release of what God is doing. You are just a grid, and you are aware of this mind thinking, of this eye blinking, inside of you, and you are watching this vastness of Being functioning. And, of course, you say, "I of mine own self can do nothing," when you stand in awe of True Being within you functioning as its awareness of itself.

The Ritual
(Give each affirmation three, nine or thirty-three times.)

I AM God's awareness of Alpha and Omega
in the white-fire core of being.

I AM God's awareness of himself as God-power.

I AM God's awareness of Alpha and Omega
in the white-fire core of being.

I AM God's awareness of himself as God-love.

I AM God's awareness of Alpha and Omega
in the white-fire core of being.

I AM God's awareness of himself as God-mastery.

I AM God's awareness of Alpha and Omega
in the white-fire core of being.

I AM God's awareness of himself as God-control.

I AM God's awareness of Alpha and Omega
in the white-fire core of being.

I AM God's awareness of himself as God-obedience.

I AM God's awareness of Alpha and Omega
in the white-fire core of being.

I AM God's awareness of himself as God-wisdom.

I AM God's awareness of Alpha and Omega
in the white-fire core of being.

I AM God's awareness of himself as God-harmony.

I AM God's awareness of Alpha and Omega
in the white-fire core of being.

I AM God's awareness of himself as God-gratitude.

I AM God's awareness of Alpha and Omega
in the white-fire core of being.

I AM God's awareness of himself as God-justice.

I AM God's awareness of Alpha and Omega
in the white-fire core of being.

I AM God's awareness of himself as God-reality.

I AM God's awareness of Alpha and Omega
in the white-fire core of being.

I AM God's awareness of himself as God-vision.

I AM God's awareness of Alpha and Omega
in the white-fire core of being.

I AM God's awareness of himself as God-victory.

I AM God's awareness of Alpha and Omega
in the white-fire core of being.

There are endless invocations to be made between the center
and each point. There are more meditations, more invocations
that we can give to expand our awareness of being.

This is the Ritual of the Atom.

AUM

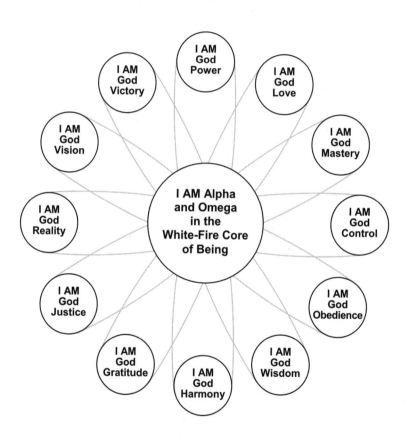

I AM God Power

I AM God Victory

I AM God Love

I AM God Vision

I AM God Mastery

I AM God Reality

I AM Alpha and Omega in the White-Fire Core of Being

I AM God Control

I AM God Justice

I AM God Obedience

I AM God Gratitude

I AM God Wisdom

I AM God Harmony

I AM THAT I AM

CHAPTER 7

Cancer

The Decades of Life

Build thee more stately mansions, O my soul,
As the swift seasons roll!
Leave thy low-vaulted past!
Let each new temple, nobler than the last,
Shut thee from heaven with a dome more vast,
Till thou at length art free,
Leaving thine outgrown shell by life's unresting sea!
— "The Chambered Nautilus"

CHAPTER 7

The Decades of Life

Saint Germain has explained that we can also chart the decades of life on the clock. If we do so, we can see that our life expectancy should be one hundred and twenty years to fulfill a decade for every line. And it may very well be that we will achieve this if we watch our diet, use the violet transmuting flame and follow other of the ascended masters' teachings.

The First Decade: The Twelve o'Clock Line

The first decade begins at birth on the twelve o'clock line. The first ten years of our lives are sponsored by the Great Divine Director, and in those years we are intended to set the foundation of the divine direction and the human direction of our lives.

Saint Germain reminds us of the words of Proverbs, "train up a child in the way he should go: and when he is old, he will not depart from it."[1] Those ten years are the shaping of the tree, and as the tree and the branches grow, so will they be for life. People are at thirty what they were at three or eight. We need to be mindful of this in our children.

Those first ten years are when we are formed. This is the blue ray of the power line. It is also the time of child abuse, child molestation, the criticism, condemnation and judgment of the child, the putting-down of the Christ in the child and the raising up of the human intellect in place of the true development of the crown chakra, which is on that line.

I think that all children receive an inheritance of condemnation at some time or another, whether from parents or from teachers or other elders who have a nonresolution in their own psychology. And I think that those bruises and those wounds and scars are among the most deadly that a child carries with him throughout his life—they make him believe that he cannot succeed.

The giving to the child of the matrix of God-power in those ten years means that that child must be reared as a devotee of the will of God. If the parents are not devotees, they will not instill this devotion in their child. If the parents are rebellious, they will instill rebellion in their children.

This decade is crucial to all else. And the violet flame is the only thing that can change what is set—or perhaps one person in a child's life whom the child looks up to, who compensates for burdens, who becomes more important than the negatives in the home.

Age 10–20: The One o'Clock Line

The one o'clock line, years ten to twenty, is sponsored by Saint Germain—the flame of God-love. The child is going to be entering puberty and reaching the age of twenty. The child may participate in the scouting movement, which is sponsored by Saint Germain. He may be in college for a number of years or in various other kinds of training.

Self-worth and interpersonal relations are very important in this decade. It is a time when the individual must understand what it means to be the friend of God, the friend of the master, to be the friend of anyone or the friend of himself.

True self-appreciation, preparation for life, comes through the seat-of-the-soul chakra. It is the coming of age of the soul. The soul will be an adult by the end of these two decades, bringing forth from the etheric body the greatest light as well as old records.

When you see how greatly love is opposed in the world today through drugs, through rock music, the turning of love into sensuality of every kind, the introduction of bad diet—all of these things happening in those years—it is the crowning of love through the initiation of Saint Germain that is opposed. Saint Germain, the great initiator of our youth, stands with Portia waiting to initiate every child when that child reaches his tenth birthday. And parents and community members must prepare children for that hour.

Age 20–30: The Two o'Clock Line

We then come to the two o'clock line of Jesus Christ. According to his upbringing, the child may be grounded in the teachings of some world religion. In this decade, he is doing what Jesus did at that age, the last ten of those "lost years" in the East—perfecting himself in his studies, in his profession, and in being a disciple of Christ, a servant of God, a minister of the Word. This is the time of the sponsorship of Jesus Christ in becoming a career son or daughter of God. The decade of twenty to thirty is the period when people decide to be married, to have families, to settle down, and to build a foundation of their calling in Christ.

The line of Pisces corresponds to the solar plexus chakra, and thus it relates also to the desire body. These first three decades are the preparation for that year of thirty-three, the year of personal Christhood. If the desires are not mastered, if the energies are not mastered, the individual will not be successful in his profession or calling. And therefore, unless he submit himself to a certain level of self-discipline, he will not be a leader in his field.

The failures come between age twenty and thirty by the inability to control the solar plexus. This chakra is in correlation with the throat chakra,* and when the solar plexus is disturbed, it is often expressed through misuse of the throat in unkind or angry speech. So it is a time to get that control over the emotions and the solar plexus chakra.

Age 30–40: The Three o'Clock Line

At age thirty, you enter the decade of Aries, the three o'clock line. Here you are ready to make concrete in the mental world your ego—your positive ego. (In this case, we think of the term "ego" as a positive sense of selfhood, the positive sense of our spirit and who we are.)

Who are you? What are your values? You have garnered them these thirty years. What is the profile of your character? How are you viewed? Are you trusted? How are you a servant of the people?

This is the decade when the solidification of your personal Christhood comes under the sponsorship of none other than the beloved Helios. Here in the central sun of this system, that sun of Helios endows you with a personal identity that is strong because it comes from the I AM Presence and Holy Christ Self.

In the decade of the thirties, you have to become who you are. If you don't know who you are and you have not resolved your psychology in the etheric quadrant, you are going to solidify and incorporate into that ego personality your psychological problems. And as you go through the mental belt, they will become solidified and much more difficult to undo.

The etheric quadrant—from zero to ten, ten to twenty and twenty to thirty—is the time for resolution. The great opportunity of being on the Path in those years is that when you get to the mental quadrant, you do not bring a fragmented personality, a split personality to that quadrant.

Helios, then, helps us to seal the divine wholeness, the Alpha-

---

* These are the chakras immediately below and above the heart. They are on the lines of the yellow cross: two/eight and five/eleven.

Omega, the sense that "I am in the Central Sun—the Central Sun is in me."

Age 40–50: The Four o'Clock Line

The four o'clock line is sponsored by God Obedience and the seven mighty Elohim. This line gives us the opportunity for absolute oneness with God by obedience to his laws.

There is a great security in the Law of God. One is protected from all returning karma when one is on the right side of divine Law and human law—loving these laws, loving the will of God more than anything else in life and not hesitating. We can say this, but when we come to a test of something we want more than anything in this world and God says no, are we going to love him still? That is a test we all must face.

Age 50–60: The Five o'Clock Line

What is the meaning, then, of fifty? It is the yellow ray of the mental quadrant. It is El Morya's line, the hierarchy of Gemini, which gives us great access to the mind of God.*

What do we learn in this decade? We learn the mastery of the mind, the sealing of the teachings of the masters, the sealing of the mental body and of all that we must learn through the mental body. People learn the teachings through their hearts and souls and through all of their chakras, but until they have a setting forth of their doctrine and their theology, they don't become the masters of the teachings.

This is the decade of completion of the first half of the cosmic clock, the Alpha thrust. The completion of this line will bring us to the point of the Omega return, which is the ascension back to the heart of God, all the way back to the twelve o'clock line.

---

* El Morya has defined the Gemini mind as "the mind that is poised at the point of the Christ, betwixt the current of Alpha in the crown chakra and the current of Omega in the base-of-the-spine chakra—parallel lines of consciousness." [*Pearls of Wisdom*, vol. 24, no. 43, October 25, 1981.]

This is a time when we are expected to intensify and increase the capacity of the mind, to clear the mind, to open the crown chakra, to raise the sacred fire in preparation for the time when we come to the six o'clock line—the line of the Divine Mother and the point of the lowest descent—and we enter the emotional quadrant of the clock and the astral plane.

Those of us who are not destined to live 120 years have to realize that in the decades on the right side of the clock we also need to accomplish the lessons of the corresponding lines on the left side of the clock, the Omega side. So when we are working on our one o'clock line, we are also working on the seven, when we are on the two o'clock line, we are also working on the eight, and so forth.

Age 60–90: The Emotional Quadrant

When you come to the decade of sixty to seventy, if you are not on the path of discipleship and have not conserved your light, there can be an acceleration of the aging process. There is the reaping of the karma in the astral plane that we have made in the first half of the clock, and that energy solidifies very quickly.

In the third quadrant, that karma is cycling into the astral body and it starts cycling into physical manifestation. This is the aging process. This is the period when people develop the diseases of old age and when they begin to start thinking that they're in the class of the elderly, they can't get around like everybody else, and depending on their outlook, they can become feeble at a very early age.

At this age, those who are the chelas of the masters are the shining ones in the community. They show us that when you have carried the light for lifetimes and you get to these levels, you embody that light, the light becomes very apparent, and you are waiting for your victory.

Age 60–70: The Six o'Clock Line

The decade of the sixties is the six o'clock line going to the seven. It is the base chakra, and we are reaping the karma of the misuse of the sacred fire in that chakra in this and previous lives.

Age 70–80: The Seven o'Clock Line

We then come to the seven o'clock line, where we deal with the karma of all misuses of the light in the seat-of-the-soul chakra.

Age 80–90: The Eight o'Clock Line

On the eight o'clock line, we deal with all misuses of the light in the solar plexus.

Age 90–120: The Physical Quadrant

The nine o'clock line is when you bring this entire clock into the physical. The decade of the nineties is the line of the Holy Spirit and the line of the heart chakra. The ten o'clock line brings you to the age of 100 and the eleven to 110, and the completion of that decade is the twelve o'clock line and 120. The great patriarchs of old and some in other societies have done this.

The purpose of this teaching is not necessarily to inspire you to desire to live to a ripe old age, per se, but rather to intensify the quality of the sacred fire in the decade where you are and to gain the maximum mastery, the maximum blessing, the maximum initiation from the masters who are sponsoring that line of the clock. If you do this, then at any hour that you may be called to other octaves for your ascension or for whatever reason, you will have garnered enough light in the decades up to that time to also count for the future decades and the completion of all the lines of the clock.

CHAPTER 8

Leo

Karmic
Dust

...for the elect's sake
those days shall be shortened.

—Matthew

CHAPTER 8

Karmic Dust

There are some people who will tell you that, by some logic or reasoning, they are not responsible for their past karma and they don't have to do anything about it. As long as they meditate on God, this will take care of everything.

Well, it doesn't happen to be so. We all are responsible for every jot and tittle of energy that we have used since the time we came forth into the world of cause and effect. There is no getting around it. You can't rationalize it, you can't shove it under the rug, and you can't pretend it doesn't exist.

We have a responsibility to balance this energy, and there is a science involved in doing this. And you can systematically, day by day, get rid of the karmic dust that settles.

You stir up the dust when you misqualify energy, and you may stir it up so much that it may travel far and wide. But there is a magnetic forcefield to that dust because it has your electronic imprint upon it; and so it comes back and it settles. It settles according to polarity, positive and negative—according to the Godly virtues and according to their perversions.

We desire to bring all of heaven down to earth, all of the causal body down into our consciousness. The karmic dust settling in the electronic belt in opposition to the twelve virtues is what prevents us from bringing the kingdom of heaven into manifestation upon earth.

Just as the light of the sun becomes distorted by the atmosphere, so the mass consciousness that surrounds our planet as an astral plane of misqualified energy distorts the pure release of God's light. Your own four lower bodies with the records of karma, records of imperfections of the human consciousness, receiving that light, impress upon that light the misqualifications that are there already. It's like pouring pure water into a dirty vessel—it takes on the coloration of the vessel.

All of this karma is not there waiting to be transmuted at a given instant. Karma only comes in cycles, and most of it is sealed. But at a certain moment in time and space, according to the position of yourself in relation to the cosmic hierarchies, you will find a certain amount of karma that is there for you to transmute.

The Electronic Belt

Within the etheric body there are two forcefields. These are sometimes called the higher etheric body and the lower etheric body. The higher etheric body is designed to record the perfection of the I AM Presence and to anchor in man the divine blueprint of his Christed individuality. The lower etheric body is the subconscious mind, the computer that stores the data of man's life—all of his experiences, his thoughts, his feelings, his words and his actions, which are expressed through the mental, emotional and physical bodies.

Every vibration that ripples across man's being, every subtle mood, every hidden motive, every idle thought or word spoken by man is impressed upon the plastic substance of the lower etheric body. The impulses of the world that pass before the mind or play upon the feelings are also recorded upon the subconscious mind.

Obviously, the bad harvest of unwise sowings cannot ascend

into the causal body, which is a magnet of perfection, drawing unto itself only the good, the pure and the beautiful. Man's misqualified energies sink to the lowest level of his subconscious being, forming a negative spiral around his four lower bodies, a forcefield of density called the electronic belt.

Figure 22 The Electronic Belt

The subconscious mind is in layers, like sedimentary rock, and the electronic belt may be described as being a kettledrum. The top of the drum is about at the navel or the solar plexus, and the base of the kettle is beneath the feet. The electronic belt is very weighty. It is actually that energy that makes our consciousness dense and that keeps us in embodiment and keeps us on earth.

When Jesus walked up Bethany's Hill, he was weightless, but weightless in the sense that he no longer had karmic weight, nor did he have the weight of world density upon him. When you have transmuted, or requalified, all that lies within your subconscious as patterns and momentums, you become karmically weightless. There is nothing left to hold you to earth. You are free from the round of rebirth, and you become one with God, because that is the only self that you know. You know yourself as God because you have surrendered all that is less than God within you.

As your causal body in heaven is separated into twelve bands, which actually represent frequencies or levels of vibration, different aspects of the Christ consciousness, so the perversions of those energies also assume different frequencies. These frequencies cause the energy to separate and become congealed at certain points.

All that is less than God is therefore diagrammed as the lines of a clock, and each line of that clock represents a twelfth of the subconscious. You could divide this kettledrum of the electronic belt like a pie into twelve parts, and you would be able to determine approximately where in the subconscious, in the layers of sedimentary rock, these momentums lie.

The planet upon which we are evolving has a collective subconscious that is subject to the same laws. Mankind are collectively responsible for the wrong they have done as a group, and the universe, the cosmos itself, is based on the law of cycles, the same law of cycles that you are subject to. You can therefore determine, by placing your soul in relation to the universe, the body of the Mother, what aspects of misqualified energy are available for you to transmute at a certain period in your life, a certain month of the year, at a certain time.

The times and the seasons and the cycles were noted by Ecclesiastes, the Old Testament writer who said, There is a time to be born and a time to die.[1] This time is measured in cycles.

Layers of the Subconscious

You may think that you know yourself or your outer consciousness quite well—not your God Self, but your human awareness of life that you have evolved since you were born. But that awareness and that consciousness is perhaps less than one percent of your being. It's like an iceberg: only the top appears above the surface. All that is beneath is unknown to you except in glimpses—and this is the mercy of God.

No one of us could bear the full weight of our sin or our karma at a certain time or in a given embodiment. And so by increments, the Christ Self and the Lords of Karma release to us the energies that we are able to successfully and victoriously deal with each day. This is why Jesus said, "Sufficient unto the day is the evil thereof."[2]

The evil, the *energy veil*, that you have created by taking the love of God and misqualifying it as hatred or as sensuality or as lust has become your own subconscious and is part of that electronic belt, that kettledrum. That energy may have been sent forth to other parts of life, but it must return to you. It is just like a ball on the end of a string that you hit with a paddle. You send it out, it comes back. And it comes back with even greater intensity than you send it out, because as it goes out into the world as energy, it attracts more of itself, more of its kind. If you send out hatred, that hatred will gather more hatred and return to you for redemption. If you send out love, it will gather more love and return to you for blessing.

Let us then consider these energies for which we are responsible. The difference between being a child of God and a son or daughter of God is a difference of responsibility. This is not easy for most people to face, because it is so simple and so sweet and so easy to accept that someone else has taken your burden for you, that someone else has died for you, and if you will only say that you believe on this person, that is all you have to do.

Violet Flame to Transmute Negative Karma

When you begin to use the violet flame, you can transmute the energies of this electronic belt. The violet flame is the light of the Holy Spirit, and using this light gives you a more than ordinary amount of energy to transmute your past. And so you begin to step up your ability to balance karma. You are no longer taking an entire embodiment to go through, perhaps, one layer of this electronic belt to settle your debts with individuals. The more you give the violet-flame decrees and mantras, the more you invoke the flame, the more quickly you go through these layers.

The violet flame is invoked through the use of the spoken Word, using the power of speech. It is a two-fold action of visualization and recitation. As you say violet-flame mantras, you can visualize this flame, the "wine of forgiveness," cleansing all of the records of past trials and testings, repolarizing the atoms and molecules of your being, like a magnetic current erasing a tape. It leaves only the perfect matrix of you as God intended you to be. The following is a simple violet-flame mantra:

I AM a being of violet fire,
I AM the purity God desires!

As you repeat this mantra over and over again, picking up speed as you go, your atoms begin to vibrate faster and faster. You can make a daily ritual of this mantra and see how it changes your outlook.* You can see the flame within your heart as a vortex of light infolding itself, as a spiral of energy so intense that it draws into itself and consumes every last jot and tittle of the law of misqualified energy in your world, every burden of karmic weight, whether it be a million years old or it happened yesterday.

Some people seek out life readings to find out about their past lives, but you can do your own life reading, because as you go through these layers, you will definitely become aware of past experiences. It may take several years before you attain this attunement, but until you do, it is pointless to have these readings. As soon as you know an embodiment of the past, you are immediately responsible for the energies of that lifetime and its karma, and therefore, these energies descend upon you. If you do not have the knowledge of the sacred fire, you may be overwhelmed and overcome by them.†

It is important, then, that you realize that you can scientifically and systematically use the energy of the Holy Spirit to transmute the misqualified energies on the twelve lines of the clock in order to balance karma and hasten the day of your victory. It is written in the Bible that the days shall be shortened for the elect.[3] To some, this is a mystery. To you who understand that the Holy Spirit gives the gift of fire for transmutation of the past, it is clear that days means cycles: the cycles of the return of

---

* Some additional violet-flame mantras are found at the end of this book. For other decrees and further explanation of the violet flame, see *Violet Flame to Heal Body, Mind and Soul,* by Elizabeth Clare Prophet, and *The Science of the Spoken Word,* by Mark L. Prophet and Elizabeth Clare Prophet.

† Another danger with life readings is that people may become burdened with guilt over past misdeeds or puffed up with pride by their greatness— and neither one really leads anywhere. This may occur even when the reading is inaccurate, as often happens.

karma will be shortened because as karma returns, you are transmuting it steadily day by day.

Overcoming the Negative Momentums with the Positive

For each of the twelve lines of the clock, there is the aspect of the Christ consciousness that overcomes the human condition. For example, on the twelve o'clock line there are momentums of criticism, condemnation and judgment—we have judged and condemned others. This includes the practice of black magic and all malicious thoughts toward individuals. These have accumulated, and they are a perversion of the power of God. Therefore, we invoke the power of God on the twelve o'clock line and consecrate that power to the redemption of this specific condition.

We may think that we have never had a critical thought in our entire lives, that we have never been critical of anyone. This does not guarantee that beneath the surface of the iceberg there are not layers and layers of the misuse of power through condemnation. You may not have observed this trait in your world simply because in this life it was not given to you to transmute. You had other karmic conditions, other energies to deal with. Nevertheless, you can assume from the trend of civilization and history over the last ten thousand years that at some point or another you may have released that energy. And so at the right time, at the proper cycle, you can use God-power to call for its transmutation.

And if perchance you could go through and transmute all of these layers of ten thousand years or more (and most people have been evolving on this planet two hundred to two hundred and fifty thousand years on the continents of Lemuria and Atlantis), you would still have a responsibility, as long as you were unascended, to make invocation for the collective subconscious energies of mankind.

What is this energy of condemnation directed against? There is only one thing that we are actually condemning—we condemn God in man, we condemn the Christ, we condemn the Divine

Mother and the Holy Spirit. And this force is known as anti-Christ, anti-God, anti-Mother (or anti-Matter*) and anti-Spirit.

Round the Clock Protection
for You and Your Twin Flame

We have been given a decree so that you and your twin flame can daily make the invocation for the energy of God to clear your cosmic clock of this anti-Christ substance. Each day, we are dealing with the configuration of our personal cycles, which are affected by all of the cycles of the universe and our relative position in relation to those cycles. There are millions of cycles that are simultaneous. All of these cycles in combination go to make up our cosmic clock, or our cosmic astrology.

It is well to assume, when we are on the homeward path, now reaping what we have sown, that each day there will probably be a little bit of substance, a little bit of dust or ash representing this misqualified energy that we have sown and that is now returning to us. The decree "Round the Clock Protection" is a general call for the clearing of each of the twelve lines. This will free our cosmic clock of misqualified energy, enabling us, then, to restore the God-qualities on those lines.

The address and the invocation in this decree is to the beloved I AM Presence, to the Christ Self, and then to the specific hierarchies serving on each of the twelve lines (listed in section A) to seize, bind and lock the conditions that represent the perversions of the God flame on those twelve lines (listed in section B).

In section C of the decree, we are asking that the negative karma be bound, taken into the circle and sword of blue flame of Astrea, and we are calling for the transmutation of all that is interfering with the manifestation within us of the God-qualities listed there.

---

* The word *matter* comes from the Latin *mater,* or mother. The term *Matter* is thus used to describe the feminine (negative) polarity of the Godhead, of which the masculine (positive) polarity is Spirit. Matter is the chalice that receives the invigorating, life-giving essence of the sacred fire.

ROUND THE CLOCK PROTECTION

In the name of the beloved mighty victorious Presence of God, I AM in me, Holy Christ Selves of all mankind, all great powers and legions of light,

A (12) Beloved Great Divine Director and the seven archangels,
  (1) Beloved Saint Germain and the angelic hosts of light,
  (2) Beloved Jesus and the great hosts of ascended masters,
  (3) Beloved Helios and the Great Central Sun Magnet,
  (4) Beloved God Obedience and the seven mighty Elohim,
  (5) Beloved El Morya and the legions of Mercury,
  (6) Beloved Serapis Bey and the great seraphim and cherubim,
  (7) Beloved Goddess of Liberty and the Lords of Karma,
  (8) Beloved Lord Lanto and the Lords of Wisdom,
  (9) Beloved Mighty Victory and the Lords of Individuality,
  (10) Beloved Mighty Cyclopea and the Lords of Form,
  (11) Beloved Lord Maitreya and the Lords of Mind,

Beloved Lanello, the entire Spirit of the Great White Brotherhood and the World Mother, elemental life—fire, air, water and earth! I decree:

Seize, bind and lock! Seize, bind and lock! Seize, bind and lock!

B (12) all criticism, condemnation and judgment and all black magic
  (1) all hatred and mild dislike and all witchcraft
  (2) all doubt, fear, human questioning and records of death
  (3) all conceit, deceit, arrogance and ego
  (4) all disobedience, stubbornness and defiance of the Law
  (5) all envy, jealousy and ignorance of the Law
  (6) all indecision, self-pity and self-justification
  (7) all ingratitude, thoughtlessness and spiritual blindness
  (8) all injustice, frustration and anxiety
  (9) all dishonesty, intrigue and treachery

(10) all selfishness, self-love and idolatry
(11) all resentment, revenge and retaliation

and all that is not of the light into mighty Astrea's cosmic circle and sword of blue flame of a thousand suns, and lock your cosmic circles and swords of blue flame of thousands of suns from the Great Central Sun and blaze megatons of cosmic light, blue-lightning rays, and violet fire in, through and around all that opposes or attempts to interfere with the fulfillment of

C (12) my God-power and my divine plan fulfilled in all cycles
   (1) my God-love and my divine plan fulfilled in all cycles
   (2) my God-mastery and my divine plan fulfilled in all cycles
   (3) my God-control and my divine plan fulfilled in all cycles
   (4) my God-obedience and my divine plan fulfilled in all cycles
   (5) my God-wisdom and my divine plan fulfilled in all cycles
   (6) my God-harmony and my divine plan fulfilled in all cycles
   (7) my God-gratitude and my divine plan fulfilled in all cycles
   (8) my God-justice and my divine plan fulfilled in all cycles
   (9) my God-reality and my divine plan fulfilled in all cycles
(10) my God-vision and my divine plan fulfilled in all cycles
(11) my God-victory and my divine plan fulfilled in all cycles

and my victory in the light this day and forever.

And in full faith I consciously accept this manifest, manifest, manifest! (3x) right here and now with full power, eternally sustained, all-powerfully active, ever expanding, and world enfolding until all are wholly ascended in the light and free! Beloved I AM! Beloved I AM! Beloved I AM!

Note: The decree may be given one of four ways: (1) Following the preamble, give sections A, B and C straight through, ending with the closing; (2) give the decree twelve times, using one insert each time from sections A, B and C, beginning with number 12; (3) give the trines on lines 12, 4, 8; 1, 5, 9; 2, 6, 10; 3, 7, 11, in sections A, B, and C; or (4) give the crosses on lines 12, 3, 6, 9; 1, 4, 7, 10; 2, 5, 8, 11, in sections A, B and C.

Transmutation Line by Line

As we are called to transmute the dust of karma line by line according to the cosmic clock, the beings and the hierarchies on each line can assist us as we call to them using this decree.

For example, under the hierarchy of Capricorn, there are thousands of cosmic beings who ensoul that particular vibration of God. That is their office in the universe; they are keeping that flame for billions of souls evolving. In this system of worlds and on earth, the particular ascended master who serves as the initiator under the hierarchy of Capricorn is the Great Divine Director, and assisting him are the seven archangels. Therefore, in Section A on the twelve o'clock line, the hierarchy of Capricorn, we are calling to the beloved Great Divine Director and the seven archangels.

When we have a problem in our world where we feel that we're being critical and we're entering into spirals of condemnation of other people, we know we have a Capricorn problem and that we have recourse to call, in the name of the mighty I AM Presence, to the Great Divine Director and the seven archangels, to all the hosts of heaven, to come and lock the cosmic circle and sword of blue flame of Astrea* around the cause and core of the condition in our subconscious that is causing us to be overly critical and in condemnation of other parts of life. We can ask that the All-Seeing Eye of God penetrate the subconscious record of all previous embodiments and that the origin of that momentum be transmuted, and we can call for the cause and core of the condition to be removed from us in the lower etheric body. We can call for the clearing of it in the mental body, in the emotions or feeling world, and finally at the physical level.

---

* Purity and Astrea are the Elohim of the fourth ray (the white ray) of purity, perfection, hope and wholeness. This is the flame of the Mother and the flame of the ascension. Purity holds the divine pattern of the perfection of the Christ for all that is in manifest form, focusing the white fire that is in the heart of every sun and atom. Astrea, the feminine complement of Purity, works twenty-four hours a day wielding the cosmic circle and sword of blue flame to free the children of the Mother from all that opposes the fulfillment of the divine plan held in the heart of Purity.

When we call for that substance to be transmuted, it is always returned to us with the positive vibration of that line of the clock. So God-power on the twelve o'clock line is the virtue of the God-quality and the flame that will be restored to us when we make that specific invocation.

This is a scientific ritual. We are systematically traveling through these twelve focuses or galaxies of light one by one, invoking the light of the twelve hierarchies, transmuting day by day the misqualified energy of the centuries that is burdening the chakras. Every day our cosmic clock looks different because it has on it that day's portion of our karma, which is there waiting to be transmuted.

The God-qualities named on each line are the original flames, pure and unadulterated, and they represent the initiations that we should pass through in order to earn these jewels of light. God-wisdom is a jewel. It resides in the throat chakra (see fig. 16, page 54). We earn it by passing initiations under the hierarch of Gemini on the five o'clock line. Each of these jewels becomes a vortex of energy that is added unto our aura, unto our chakras and ultimately unto our

Figure 23 The Seven Chakras   causal body. So everything we do each day can accelerate and accrue to our lifestream more and more of this cosmic consciousness.

Planetary Cycles—Tests of Capricorn

At the same time that we are dealing with the cycles of our personal cosmic clock, there are also planetary cycles to consider. The yearly cycle of planet Earth begins at the time of the change of signs from Sagittarius to Capricorn, which is winter solstice. Thus, winter solstice, approximately December 22, is actually the new year, even though we celebrate the new year on December 31. And that new year commences with the testing of the entire planetary body under Capricorn.

As the energy of God-power released from the hierarchy of Capricorn enters the energy field of the four lower bodies of the planet and its evolutions, it tends to be misqualified as criticism, condemnation and judgment and black magic. We find, then, that the test, the initiation of the hierarchy of Capricorn for the initiate, for the disciple, for the self-disciplined one, is to meditate on the pure energy of God-power, to assimilate that power and that energy without misusing it, without responding to the magnetism of the world that tends to press upon our consciousness this quality of criticism, condemnation and judgment.

We will find that those who are born under the sign of Capricorn will have this initiation in this life. They will have great power, and they will be faced with the opportunity of using God's energy as power. These people can be starters, organizers, executives. They will have the capacity, because of this power, to probe the mysteries of God. They will have a contact with the etheric plane, because this hierarchy is in the etheric quadrant, the fire quadrant.

They will have to guard against the momentum of the mass consciousness to misuse that power in petty analysis of people, in petty condemnation, criticisms, the hen-pecking quality of finding fault with the little splinters of the human personality. Engaging in that activity dissipates the power of God. It is gossip; it is judging people, not with righteous judgment,[4] not with the judgment of God and the compassion of God, but with the criticism and the narrowness of the human consciousness.

If you are reading the papers, if you are watching the news media and simply being observant in the world, you will see how nations and their governments and their economies and every phase of human activity will come under the testing of the hierarchy of Capricorn in that month. And if you are working for world order and for God-government and you are interested in helping society and serving in your community, you will notice that leaders, important people, are burdened by the weight of light and darkness peculiar to Capricorn and that their functioning is hindered by the mass-consciousness misuse of the sacred fire in Capricorn. So when you are giving your decrees for world action from approximately December 22 to January 20, you should take care to make invocations for the transmutation of the world karma of criticism, condemnation and judgment—misuses in the etheric body of the flame of God-power.

Planetary Cycles—Tests of Aquarius

The cycle of Aquarius begins in the year at the end of Capricorn. When we enter this cycle, we feel the intensity of the light of love. Valentine's Day falls in this cycle. It is a very creative cycle. We find our own karma cycling out of our subconscious, and all of a sudden we will feel crimson flashes of hatred that we have not felt, and we say, "What is this? I don't hate that person. Why is this energy passing through me?" If you don't know, you are likely to identify with it and to begin the process of hating, in which case you will have failed a cosmic initiation to reject hatred and to ensoul love.

The perversion of love is hatred and mild dislike in any form: irritation, uncomfortability around people, subtle criticism, subtle irritation because we're not in harmony with another part of life. The misuse of the energies of love comes in selfishness, possessiveness, attachment, desire, misuse of the sacred fire.

Mild dislike is even more diabolical than hatred. We mildly prefer not to be with a certain individual. Because we don't identify it as hatred, we are not determined to exorcise this from our consciousness. So it sinks to subconscious levels, and we carry with us these little splinters, thorns of irritation, of dislike of this and that; even dislike of inanimate things is a negative vibration that impedes the flow of love in our world. Hatred comes as race hatred, as prejudice, as hatred for members of various religious faiths or various nationalities. It comes in the most insidious ways.

If we know the test is coming and we know that Aquarius gives us the option of choosing hatred or love, then we can use the flame of Saint Germain, who serves under the hierarchy of Aquarius. We can use his flame of freedom and of transmutation. We can invoke that violet flame of the Holy Spirit and demand the transmutation of the cause and core of all of our karma involving the misuse of the energy of Aquarius. We can say:

> I claim my freedom now. I claim my freedom to be love, and I will ensoul no other quality but love. And I call forth the violet flame to pass through the cause, effect, record and memory in my four lower bodies of all misuses of the sacred fire in Aquarius. Let God's will be done.

The hierarchy of Aquarius governs the entire two-thousand-year cycle. During this age, this hierarchy overlays all of the frequencies of the twelve hierarchies with the frequency of God-love. There is an intense action of love cycling through the cosmos at this time. There is a vast opportunity now in this cycle for us to redeem all of our karma in the correct use of love.

Planetary Cycles—Tests of Pisces

The final line of the etheric quadrant is the hierarchy of Pisces—the test of the flame of God-mastery. The perversion of God-mastery is fear, doubt, anxiety, questioning and death.

Even though it sits in the etheric quadrant, Pisces is also a water sign. In Pisces we are tested in the mastery of the flow of water in the fire of the etheric plane. Pisces is also the yellow plume of the Trinity in the etheric quadrant.

In Pisces are the records of death. Many people in their personal cosmic-clock cycles are not able to overcome that last enemy of death, because they are not prepared for the initiation. The Piscean conqueror is the one who has balanced the threefold flame of the Christ consciousness and is able, then, to be the conqueror over hell and death: "O death, where is thy sting? O grave, where is thy victory?"⁵ The sting of death is swallowed up in the fires of the resurrection, in the flame of the Piscean conqueror.

In the two-thousand-year age of Pisces, all mankind have had the opportunity to become the Christ. This is why we have had incarnations for two thousand years: to follow the example of Jesus the Christ. Yet his true teachings were lost from the very beginning. They were destroyed, even the books of Origen of Alexandria that set forth these teachings. The fallen ones entered the churches and they put forth the false doctrine and the dogma that only one man could be the Christ. And so they took from mankind that opportunity.

Now we are advancing to the Aquarian initiation, the initiation whereby we are challenged to become the Mother, to raise up the flame of the Mother and to fuse it with the light of the Holy Spirit. We find that we are not ready for the next initiation because we have not passed the previous initiation. What do we do then? We pray for forgiveness, we pray for mercy, We pray for the opportunity to make up that which we have lost. The ascended masters are giving us that opportunity today in their teachings. They are giving us the opportunity with the violet flame to transmute the misuses of the sacred fire in all of the hierarchies.

We have the example of Jesus. We are intended to walk in that example every step of the way. We see, then, that his flame of the Christ as the flame of God-mastery can dissolve all fear and doubt, the sense of separation, all questioning of who we are and who God is, and every record of death of every incarnation when we have laid down the body.

Planetary Cycles—Tests of Taurus

Around April 21, the sun enters the sign of Taurus. This is the four o'clock line, and the hierarchy of Taurus is served by God Obedience, beloved Godfre, and the seven mighty Elohim.

During this month, the entire earth and all of her evolutions are undergoing initiations under the hierarchy of Taurus. This sign is on the pink cross, and its challenge is to obey the inner law of being by love and by devotion.

You will see a lot of rebellion manifesting under this sign. It was under this sign that Satan fell and rebelled against the living Christ. You will notice that it is in the quadrant of the mind or the mental body, and so he fell by that Satanic logic, the logic of the carnal mind that contrived a way to disobey God and still to purport that this was in the Law of God.

You find if you watch the newspapers, listen to the news, see what is acting, that you will feel the vibration of Taurus (which is an earth sign) of human stubbornness, resisting the flow of cosmic currents and cosmic energy. Now that you have the key as to why things are going wrong in the government, in the world, in the problems you are reading about, immediately when you are aware of those cycles, you say:

> **In the name of the Christ, in the name of the beloved I AM Presence, I call to beloved Godfre, I call to the seven mighty Elohim and the hierarchy of Taurus, to take command over this substance of human disobedience and rebellion. I call for the obedience of all of my atoms, cells and consciousness to the inner will, the inner law, the inner blueprint. I call for the transmutation of personal and planetary momentums of rebellion, and I ask for the flame of Godfre, the beloved God Obedience, to now be enshrined within my being for the mastery of the third eye. According to God's will, let it be done.**

And then you name the manifestation of rebellion in yourself, in an individual, in the government, in the world at large, or in whatever condition that is happening that you are seeing on the television or in the newspaper.

Then, you give your calls to Astrea, to Archangel Michael, to the violet flame. You give those calls maybe for one minute, three minutes or fifteen minutes, and you learn to give those calls until you have invoked enough light to counteract and balance that condition and you come to the place where you feel an inner release. Until you get that release, you have not fulfilled your responsibility.

Challenging Planetary Momentums through the Repetition of Decrees

The sustained call through the repetition of decrees is necessary where you have large islands of floating grids and forcefields in the mass consciousness. For example, there is the mass accumulation of rebellion over the city of New York, which is the combination of the negative momentums of all people living there and the amalgamation of rebellion in corporate power or in the Mafia that is reinforced through financial and legal structures. Now, if you're going to call to Astrea to encircle that accumulation of energy, it's going to take more than one single command.

The command will start the process, but we give the decree to Astrea twelve or fourteen or twenty-four or thirty-six or more times, because the Law says that the ascended masters can't enter this octave unless we make the call for them to do so. We must give them the energy that they then multiply and can turn around and use in our octave.

Archangel Michael

If you're tackling a planetary momentum, you can expect to realize you're tackling something that is very virulent. The prince of this world is Satan. And although he is no more, his vibration and his lieutenants are present, and we still see that dominance in the world.[6]

If you're going to stand in your sanctuary before your altar and tackle such a force, you need the full momentum of the protection of Archangel Michael, your violet flame, your tube of light, and you need to call on all the hierarchies of heaven. Then you begin the process of challenging planetary momentums of misuse of that hierarchy.

Tests and Opportunities on the Twelve Lines

These challenges continue through the year and the twelve lines of the clock. The season of winter corresponds to the etheric cycle—the fire element, going within to the fiery core. The season of spring and the testings of the planetary body that come with Aries correspond to the element of the mind. It is the time of the new birth, the resurrection fires that come with Aries.

With summer comes the testing of the emotions. Wars and demonstrations and sometimes rioting and all kinds of turbulence happen in the summer to the planet as a whole and to people as they find that their emotions are being tested. Even the heat we experience is a product of mankind's misqualified substance in the astral body of the planet; and in our coping with life in the summertime, we must take into account the ever-present tests of the emotional body. In the fall comes the earth cycle, the harvest, corresponding to the Holy Spirit and the recycling of energies; we see the fruits of the Spirit made manifest in the fruits of the earth.

The Moon: Reflector of the Emotions

During each month, day by day there is an accurate unfoldment of the initiations under the hierarchy of the sun that is at the fore in that month. Also to be considered in that month of initiation are the cycles of the moon. The moon is moving through the twelve hierarchies even as you are moving through your karmic cycles.

The moon presents an additional testing. It is the testing of your soul. It is the testing of the personality. Therefore, while you are in the month of initiation under Aries, for example, and the moon is going through its twenty-eight-day cycle, you will have an opportunity under the hierarchy of Aries to prove your mastery over what we call *moon substance*. Moon substance is misqualified substance, energy that has been misqualified under the influence of the moon.

The moon governs the astral body, the water body. In the perfection of cosmic astrology, the satellites of planets, the lunar bodies, are intended to be reflectors and amplifiers of the pure feelings of the lifewaves of the planet. In golden ages, when mankind's feelings were pure, when the emotional body was pure and clean, the moon was a crystal reflector of the pure feelings of the angels, of mankind, of elemental life.

However, as soon as mankind began to misqualify their feelings and to build up in the astral belt, in the subconscious of the planet, layers of hatred, layers of mild dislike and all of the distortions of the feelings of God, then the moon began to amplify that energy. And therefore, there is no longer the pure reflection from the moon of the light of the sun; instead, the light of the moon is the reflection of man's misuses of solar energy. This is what we have to contend with in our initiations each month as the moon moves through the twelve hierarchies.

For example, as the moon passes through the house of Aries, it will amplify the substance of the ego, the conceit of the ego. When we have a full moon in Aries (or any phase of the moon in Aries) you will notice that people's interactions with one another are very much at an ego level. Everyone is putting forth an aspect of the ego and relating at the level of the ego.

When the moon is in Aquarius, it will not amplify love; it will amplify lust, sensuality, hatred. When there is a Capricorn moon, you may notice a heavy weight upon the people of the substance of condemnation. And that condemnation, especially when amplified by the power of the full moon, may be a bristling energy of people criticizing and picking each other apart and looking down on each other just for nothing—just for breathing the air or walking by in a dress that maybe someone didn't like. That energy saturates the astral plane. When you are aware of it, you instantaneously make a call:

In the name of the Christ, in the name of the I AM Presence, I call to Mighty Astrea and to the lords of the violet flame to consume the cause and core of all misuses of the hierarchy of Capricorn, of God-power and of all moon substance that is a misqualification of that energy. Let it be done according to God's will.

The Challenge of the Path of Initiation

The ascended masters have given us much insight into self-mastery in all of their writings and their dictations, their books, the Keepers of the Flame Lessons and their *Pearls of Wisdom* that date back to 1958.[7]

We cannot expect to be able to explain in one book all of these many fine points of the Law. There is a reason for the words, "line upon line, precept upon precept."[8] It is because the outpicturing of cosmic law is the grand mosaic of life, and each day we are placing the pieces of this mosaic for the completion of the whole. Being a devotee of the ascended masters is studying "to show thyself approved unto God, a workman ... rightly dividing the word of truth"[9]—the admonishment of Paul to Timothy.

Studying the teachings of the masters, we extract a tremendous reservoir of disciplines, and that is what it means to be a disciple. It means that we must be disciplined, not from without, but from within. And when we are sufficiently self-disciplined from within, we magnetize the discipline of the great gurus, the ascended masters themselves.

CHAPTER 9

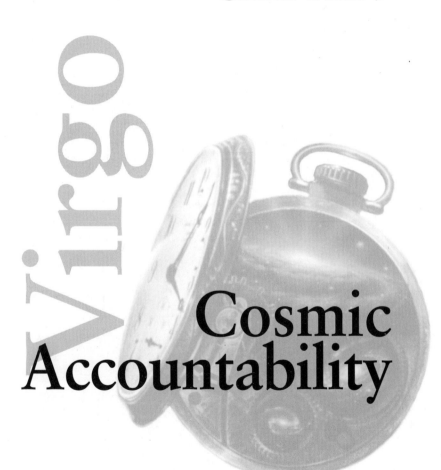

Virgo

Cosmic Accountability

We are what we think,
Having become what we thought.
— The Dhammapada

CHAPTER 9

Cosmic Accountability:
A Study of Your Subconscious
and Superconscious Mind

Buddha gave the concept that is written in *The Dhammapada:*

> We are what we think,
> Having become what we thought.
> Like the wheel that follows the cart-pulling ox,
> Sorrow follows an evil thought.

> And joy follows a pure thought,
> Like a shadow faithfully tailing a man.
> We are what we think,
> Having become what we thought.[1]

This is the basis of cosmic accountability. We look at ourselves, we look at our hands, our feet. We look in the mirror, we look at our consciousness, we look at our development, we look at our place, and we remember these words: "We are what we think, having become what we thought."

What is the thought that precedes manifestation? What is the feeling and what is the action? Cosmic accountability is the teaching of karma—"whatsoever a man soweth, that shall he also

reap."[2] Studying the subconscious and the Superconscious, we see
what we are reaping, but we don't stop there. We say, What shall
we do about it? And we find that God has given us the answers.

Responsibility for the Subconscious Mind

Many among mankind will not even take responsibility for
that of which they are consciously aware. We are going to talk
about responsibility for that of which we have no conscious
awareness, but which is lodged in the subconscious mind. We
look around us, we look at ourselves. We see that people we
know cannot even accept responsibility for their individual lives,
for their families. They rebel against authority, whether in
parents, in government or in society, not realizing that the
authority they are rebelling against is the authority of the Christ,
the Real Self within.

People are not accountable for their bodies. They take into
their bodies impurities in drugs, in alcohol, in tobacco, in all
kinds of medicines, all kinds of pills and all kinds of chemical
components that people call food. We watch TV, we take in the
media without establishing a shield for consciousness, without
taking responsibility in the knowledge that where we place our
attention, there we create an arc of energy from our mind to the
object. And over that arc, there flows to us the very substance of
the object of our attention. And so we allow the world, the mass
consciousness, to funnel in; and inevitably "We are what we
think, having become what we thought."

The Teaching—Keystone in the Arch of Being

The disciple of Christ, the devotee of Buddha, the adherent of
Reality, one who senses himself a part of the ongoing challenge of
those initiations that were demonstrated to us by Christ and
Buddha, may be separated from his own higher consciousness by
only a few days, weeks, months or years of accelerated activity on
the Path—even though he be presently enmeshed in the mass

consciousness. Whether or not we are actively engaged in the world's consciousness, we are still a part of it until we consciously withdraw from the vibrations of the "old man" and the "old woman"—the former self—that self that has accumulated human habits and a human consciousness—relatively benign or relatively off the beam—over not one but many lifetimes.

Now we must enter the new era of our own soul's liberation from the past. We must separate the soul that would strive and soar beyond the finite cage and rejoin the Infinite One.

The apostle commanded: Come apart and be a separate people[3]—a people who understand the meaning of and accept their cosmic accountability. This separation is first and foremost a step in conscientious self-acceptance, a readiness to face who and what we are—however beautiful, however ugly—and to realize that we are equipped to meet the demand for change—positive change reaching step by step toward the goal of higher consciousness.

God has provided the way through his all-consuming sacred fire. We can become who we really are—if we want to. I believe that the teaching of the ascended masters on karma and reincarnation is the keystone in the arch of being, and I think when we are willing to understand these teachings and take hold of them and then apply the Science of the Spoken Word that is given to us, that we will enter into an action of Law, an action that can enable us to evolve to a higher state of self-awareness in Christ.

We Create the Circumstances that Make Us Fail

We have entered the age of responsibility and we cannot turn back, but all around us we see a residual resistance to life and to Reality whereby whatever people can get away with, they will try to get away with. We catch ourselves trying to get away with things, trying to fool ourselves, trying to get away with not being responsible. We say we fail because circumstances prevented us from doing this or that.

The ascended master El Morya, one of the greatest devotees of Christ whom I know, says, "Poppycock!" Circumstances do not prevent us from doing what we want to do; we subconsciously create the circumstances and then say, "Something made me fail." Or we simply fail to muster the push, push, push! until we literally mow down every block, psychological or otherwise, to our victory. This drive is the key difference between the crowd and the man or woman who stands out from that crowd.

Morya says we are the controller of circumstances in our life. We make those circumstances and then we let them into manifestation to give ourselves an *excuse* for failure. We allow the mass consciousness to program us to failure, and then we make excuses for failure. We have accepted a mass programming through the media, a mass hypnosis against the Reality of the God flame within. Even sickness can be brought on from the subconscious by our own patterns of guilt—guilt that we are not living up to our highest potential.

When the apostle Paul said, "Ye did run well; who did hinder you that ye should not obey the truth?"[4] it was an indictment; and until we obey the mandate of Truth as the rock of our own inner being, we do experience guilt. And that guilt will not be drowned out by surfeiting in pleasure or the sheer noise of the current decades.

Failure and guilt go hand in hand, and they must be tackled from a sound base of the soul centered in the God flame. No one but ourselves can tackle the beast of failure and guilt. But we are never equal to the task until we stop sympathizing with the beast, align ourselves supremely with our own Christ Self, and in the sole strength of Almighty God, defeat the self-created adversary. What we have created in error, only we by free will can uncreate. This is always accomplished by the all-consuming sacred fire. Nothing else can work permanent positive change in our lives.

Yale University did a study on the aura in connection with Kirlian photography, and they found that sickness can be detected in the aura before it manifests in the physical body. This is an outstanding concept. It proves the law of cycles and of karma— "we are what we think, having become what we thought"— showing that in the subconscious is the cause and core of sickness as attitudes of hatred and fear and envy, covetousness and all aspects of incompleteness that are less than the Christ awareness. Think of that! Sickness can hardly be accounted for only by the germ theory, by bacteria, by all kinds of concepts. We attract disease to us by the negativity that is already manifesting within the subconscious. Both the positive and the negative aspects of our beings are powerful magnets.

"You Are What You Are Regardless of What You Think You Are"

Morya says, "You are what you are regardless of what you think you are." I have talked to a certain psychoanalyst who tells me that he can determine where an individual is in consciousness by the tone of the voice. A certain hollowness, a certain airy quality, a certain flightiness lets us know that the individual is not contacting the base of an inner Reality, that the individual thinks he is something that he is not, that he is acting out a part fulfilling what society expects him to be, fulfilling what he sees in the media and in his surroundings, but never finding out who he really is.

"You are totally what you are. You are totally your own manifestation," Morya says. As long as we go around thinking that this is a set of circumstances over which we have no control, we'll be sitting with the greatest gift of the cosmos—the Law itself, our own heart flame, the threefold flame of liberty held high by our beloved Christ Self—and we will not be attaining that Christ-mastery that we are ordained to have as sons and daughters of God.

Before the Lords of Karma and before the Lord of the World, *we have* cosmic accountability.

The Individualization of the God Flame

When I look into the stars and into the cosmos and I see the million points of light and more, they symbolize to me points of Christ-realization, points of the individualization of the God flame, points of children of God realizing "God created me. I AM a child of light, I live in the light, I AM the light. I will let my light shine throughout cosmos with the message of individual attainment by individual accountability."

And what we think, what we affirm in the glorious power of the Word and what we act upon forthrightly, we do become; and so we become stars of manifestation. It is written that "one star differeth from another in glory."[5] We're going to be looking at those "stars" as manifestations of the superconscious mind.

We are here, then, not by a miracle. We are here because, in exercising cosmic accountability somehow, somewhere in the past, we have earned in the present an opportunity to have a greater awareness of Selfhood in God. You are you alone by your free will, and this free will and its correct exercise has placed you on the path of Christhood.

Therefore, cosmic accountability works two ways: it is a programming of the subconscious either in Reality or in unreality. We all have many components of reality, and these components of reality bring into manifestation the joy, the beauty and the very love of life.

Another of our teachers on the Path said that it is important, when we pray to God, that we do not go through an exercise of wishing and willing before God, but that we be scientists applying the laws that Jesus Christ and Gautama Buddha taught us.[6]

Be free of superstition, be free of begging God for manifestations, but realize that "every good gift and perfect gift" is already ours in that flame, that unique flame of Christ-potential that we share through the mighty I AM Presence, whom James called the Father of Lights.[7]

Let's Put the Entire Cosmos—Cause and Effect— Inside of Ourselves

We need to remove ourselves from a primitive religion and a religion of superstition, and we can do so only by taking this accountability, by putting the entire cosmos inside of ourselves, by realizing that the atoms and molecules and cells of our bodies are a cosmos just as vast as the one we see without. When we put it all inside, then we are totally responsible for this cosmos, and we do not enter into idolatry, either blaming or worshiping others for manifestations of good or evil, but we take accountability and we are responsible for what manifests in life. Putting cause and effect within, then we begin accountability in the tests, the trials, the tribulations and the triumphs that are a part of our pathway back to God. If we take credit for our defeats, then how sweet, how sweet is the due credit for our victory.

Morya, who is very stern in his application of the will of God, has said that he will hold us responsible when things go wrong because of our supposed "ignorance" or our density. He says, "I hold you accountable for disobedience." What is disobedience? Disobedience is simply allowing ourselves to get out of alignment with the inner blueprint of life that life has stored in every cell and atom and within the heart and the soul of man and woman.

We Have Created Our Problems—We Can Uncreate Them

People who have problems created their problems. We have created our problems. We are the creator, we have the power to uncreate. The power to create is the power to destroy. If we have problems, we must have the accountability of understanding that we made them. But if we accept that responsibility, it gives us the responsibility, the opportunity, of uncreating. And so we are not at the mercy of the forces of the elements. We are no longer superstitious about life. We don't have that "woe is me" consciousness—life has dealt me a raw deal, my parents didn't give me what they should have given me, the government didn't give me what it should have given me, and so I'm miserable. And we go around with this blame and shame consciousness.

The Bible speaks of the twinkling of the eye when the last trump sounds, when death is swallowed up in victory.[8] The twinkling of the eye can be thought of as the changing of the focus of our consciousness from the two eyes, which see time and space and good and evil as relative, to the single eye of God—the All-Seeing Eye of his vision, his immaculate vision who sees us as we really are.

The change that comes is the change of alchemy where you determine that this is going to be transmuted. Transmutation—the law of change. The length of time for this transmutation, which is actually the working out of God's law of forgiveness, depends entirely upon our own conception of the energy veil.

The Energy Veil—A Mountain of Relativity

We think of the word *evil* as a code word for energy *veil*. Evil is something that we have spawned by our own thinking and feeling, by our own lack of vision. That veil settles around us almost like cotton candy wound around the pole of our being. It's this *stuff*, and it can dissolve as easily as we expect it to dissolve.

If we think that it's a tremendous mountain of concrete, of hard substance, and we imagine this tremendous struggle that is going to happen when we work against these subconscious momentums, it will be so. If we understand that that mountain is a mountain of relativity, if we understand what scientists are telling us—finally telling us what Christ already told us—that Matter really does not have substance, that it really isn't dense, that it can be molded by alchemy, that the water can be changed into wine[9] if we believe this, then our sin (which is another word for negative karma) can be forgiven and the energy we have invested in sin (in negative karma) can be transmuted in the sacred fire of the Holy Spirit. We can put it into the Flame. We can call to God, as the God of love, to pass his flame through it;

and that same energy (as energy is neither created nor destroyed) returns to us as a momentum of light instead of darkness.

Our human consciousness, as opposed to our divine consciousness, will remain as long as we entertain it, as long as we will it so, as long as the desires remain in our subconscious to be surrounded with these limitations that give us excuses for every form of behavior, every form of limiting activity that is less than the fullness of our own Christ potential—which God intended us to be, else he would not have endowed us with it.

The Subconscious Mind

Morya says, "Chelas of the masters, stop fooling yourselves. You are willfully manipulating the energies of the sacred fire of God himself by this ruse of the Fallen One. There is no such thing as accidental failure; it is entirely mechanically programmed at your own subconscious levels." We have need, then, for a brief period in our soul evolution to enter the caverns of the subconscious mind and to take with us there the light of the Christ and to let the action of that sacred fire consume the cause and core of what makes us be manifestations that are less than God expects of us.

Some say that the goal of perfection is not attainable, that only Jesus Christ could attain that goal of perfection. Yet he gave us an instruction that I think we should take literally. He said, "Be ye therefore perfect, even as your Father which is in heaven is perfect."[10]

Perfection is like the law of geometry, of mathematics. It is something that is an inner blueprint that we move toward. Striving for perfection, then, is not Antichrist; it is the fulfillment of Jesus' calling. Likewise, we need a sense of responsibility for our environment, our community, our nation and for all of the nations of the earth—finally, for the entire planet itself. But at this moment, let us consider our own little microcosm and how we can take accountability.

There is not a teacher who walks in the light of Christ who

does not admonish his disciple to take accountability for what transpires on a planetary scale. And so, what we learn about the microcosm, we can apply to the Macrocosm. It is simply easier to begin with what seems to be a smaller forcefield. Actually, it is not. Can we compare the size of the cosmos to the size of the physical body? It is relative. We cannot say one is greater and one lesser; it is only our perspective that makes it seem so.

One way of examining the subconscious mind is to begin to look at the tip of the iceberg at conscious levels of awareness and see what is taking place in our lives. I have always found that if I really wanted to know what was the dark and the ugly and the unchallenged in my world, that I could trace it because it would move through my conscious mind like a comet leaving a trail, and if I was willing to open my eyes and be honest and be humble and be willing to be corrected by God, I could see the shortcomings.

We examine, for one thing, what is around us. Is there dirt, filth, disorder, chaos, problems, argumentations, problems in the life of the family? Do we have moods? Do we pout? Do we go into moods of crying or anger, or binges of eating or smoking or drinking or partying? Do we go from one failure to another, feel worthless or inferior to everyone else? Why is it? Why are we going through these ups and downs without really being the masters of life, but kind of willy-nilly and at the whimsy of forces around us?

Could it be that in the subconscious there is a working out of desire patterns that we have not surrendered to Christ? Until we surrender these desire patterns, they remain, and so we look at the surface to key in to what is taking place at the sublevels of awareness.

Subliminal Seduction

Wilson Bryan Key wrote a book called *Subliminal Seduction* to expose the media and their use of hidden symbols in advertising to manipulate the subconscious: symbols of sex, of death, of darkness, witchcraft and black magic. He showed examples of the implanting of figures of orgies and all types of unseemly and ungodly manifestations—for example, pornographic figures in the ice cubes advertising liquor. In writing this book, he explained that a hundred or two hundred years ago, not having been programmed, we should have readily seen all of these forms, but today we do not. Our conscious minds screen out all that is unwholesome, all that is unacceptable in society.

He says that "theorists maintain that the conscious mind merely adapts itself to the basic program established in the unconscious."[11] He quotes studies that show that if you receive simultaneously a command at the conscious level—for example, that you hear or read—and a command at the subconscious level that is subliminally directed at you through pictures or through the insertion of phrases in advertising, that you will always obey the subconscious command first.

This makes us think of the words of Saint Paul, when he said: "For the good that I would I do not: but the evil which I would not, that I do."[12] And why is this? Is it because of the attempt of the fallen ones to program us to those actions that keep our souls in bondage? Or is it our own rejection of the Christ at subconscious levels that allows the mass conglomerate of emotions and motives called the "carnal mind" to dominate not only the soul but the conscious mental reflexes?

One definition of the subconscious is "the great submerged nine-tenths of the iceberg in which most of our memories and associations and drives ... reside."[13] Everything that we have ever been exposed to, even if we haven't been consciously aware of it, is contained in the subconscious. If we would reunite with God and with the flame of love, we must realize that most of this programming is unacceptable to our own inner Reality, our own higher consciousness. It doesn't fit; it can't become one with God because it is not congruent with his mind.

"Let this mind be in you, which was also in Christ Jesus"[14] is a perpetual command of our own beloved Christ Self. If we ignore it, we suffer failure and guilt, because only that Christ mind can win. None other can meet the challenge of the hour, be it small or great. It is our responsibility, then, to stand at the door of consciousness, to be the keeper of the gate and to cry out in the night "Who goes there!" We must investigate all ideas and identities seeking admittance and forbid the intruder who would encroach upon our communion with the law of love.

Let us see, now, what all of this looks like from "inner levels" of our self-awareness and what we can do about it.

Our Origin in the White-Fire Core of Being

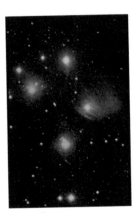

Looking at the stars, we see the representation of what I call the white-fire core of consciousness. This mass of stars and starry clusters is each one an energy field that is an effect. What is its cause? The cause is First Cause; it is God. But the effect may also be God in manifestation in his sons and daughters— a star may be not only a symbol but an actual focus of someone's self-mastery in Christ.

The white-fire core of being is the beginning of our diagram of consciousness. It is the core of the cause that is God. It is all of God; it is a sphere of light. We can think of this sphere as "the beginning and the ending," as "Alpha and Omega,"[15] the center of the fiery whirlwind of the creation of worlds whose cause-effect relationship is self-declared in the Book of Revelation:

"I AM Alpha and Omega, the beginning and the ending [of all cycles of the Spirit-Matter creation] saith the Lord [the I AM THAT I AM], which is, and which was, and which is to come [past, present and future], the Almighty.... I AM Alpha and Omega, the first [cause] and the last [effect]."[16] Alpha to Omega —the whirling energies of our own cosmos, the white-fire core out of which the soul came forth in the beginning of her cycles and to which she will return in the ending of her cycles.

The Monad

This pulsing sphere of God we call the Divine Monad. It is the original blueprint of a fiery destiny. Out of this Monad comes forth what could be considered the programming of a cosmic computer that directs every cell, the chemistry of our bodies, all that takes place at physical and metaphysical levels of consciousness—the mental body, the emotional body, the memory body. It is really beyond our imagination what is contained in this point of infinity that is our soul's origin. This point of origin is the body of First Cause, referred to as the "causal body."

When God spoke to Moses out of the bush that burned but was not consumed,[17] Moses made contact with this core of identity, this being that was the God of Moses, the very Presence of God *in* Moses—his own God Self. Moses was not satisfied to hear the voice of God, but he asked God what his name was, because he had to go and speak to the children of Israel.

Moses had an impediment in his speech and he feared that the people would not listen to him, and so he said: "Behold, when I come unto the children of Israel, and shall say unto them, The God of your fathers hath sent me unto you; and they shall say to me, What is his name? what shall I say unto them?

"And God said unto Moses, I AM THAT I AM: and he said, Thus shalt thou say unto the children of Israel, I AM hath sent me unto you. And God said moreover unto Moses, Thus shalt thou say unto the children of Israel, The LORD God [the I AM Presence] of your fathers, the God of Abraham, the God of Isaac, and the God of Jacob, hath sent me unto you: this is my name for ever, and this is my memorial unto all generations."[18]

The name of God is the confirmation of being twice: *I AM THAT I AM.* Why does God say "I AM" twice? This affirms being in the planes of heaven and the planes of earth, the planes of Spirit and the planes of Matter—"I AM" for Father, "I AM" for Mother; "I AM" for Alpha, "I AM" for Omega. The first "I AM" represents the plane of First Cause, the second "I AM" represents the plane of effect.

I believe what Moses saw represents that which we can all see—the sacred fire out of which we have come forth. And out of that fiery core of being, we experience God as Father and Mother, God as Christ and God as Holy Spirit. This is the foundation of the Path for the soul's self-realization in Reality.

The Causal Body

God gives us this potential, this potential of the Flaming One; but then he has also given us free will. And by the use of that free will, we take that energy and we create here below. And some of us become teachers and some engineers and some are in the armed forces and some are doctors and nurses. And so that means we've taken God's energy from the fiery core and we've used it to make the I AM in manifestation reflect the I AM that is in Spirit. The cosmic record continues, and we find that this is a conception of our superconscious Being—superconscious, that which is above the conscious; subconscious, that which is below the conscious.

The concentric spheres of energy that surround the Monad— the I AM THAT I AM—make up the causal body wherein there are recorded the positive causes we have set in motion that are acceptable in the eyes of God—acceptable in motive and intent, in purity of desire and vibration—and therefore, they have become an energy field of causation around that fiery core. They are spheres of consciousness that we have spun, working the works of God both on earth and in heaven.[19]

Jesus told us to lay up for ourselves treasures in heaven, "For where your treasure is, there will your heart be also."[20] This causal body is the source of the "celestial body" Paul referred to,[21] and as such it is our own individual heaven-world, our own microcosmic heaven where all of our good deeds are recorded and where these deeds register as an energy field that makes up our own sphere of higher consciousness.

There are seven distinct color spheres that make up the outer causal body, which are the seven rays for the mastery of the Christ consciousness without, and there are five inner spheres that are the five secret rays for the mastery of the Christ consciousness within (fig. 24, page 175). These five colorless bands are next to the center, the white-fire core, the white sphere, which is counted as one of the seven outer spheres.

The white-fire core and the six spheres beyond the five secret rays are the planes that relate to the evolution of God's consciousness as humanity in their present evolution are able to experience and express it. The rings of the five secret rays are positioned between the white-fire core and the yellow band of the causal body. These planes relate to man's latent divinity, which remains unrealized in most of earth's evolutions.

The twelve bands of the causal body and their virtues can be diagrammed according to color and to ray. Each of these bands is a sphere, and each sphere corresponds to one of the twelve lines of the clock.

This configuration of energy fields is a simplification of the star of our causal body. Considering the fact that we have free will, we can understand why it is written in Corinthians that "one star differeth from another star in glory."[22] It means that each one of us has that certain core of energy that is the same for all—the white-fire core of the Father-Mother God. Then the depth, intensity and the acceleration of the spheres surrounding it show our individual creativity, our individual expressions of the Christ.

If Christ is infinite—infinite in God—then there ought to be infinite manifestations of Christhood. And so we have children of God each expressing a facet of that Christ consciousness. We can look at the diagram of the causal body and consider that in each one of the spheres, in each one of the colors representing certain virtues, there is a balance of the four aspects of our awareness of God as Father, Son, Mother and Holy Spirit.

When we talk about the programming of the cosmos—including man—by the mind of God and we contemplate the fantastic organization of our superconscious Being and our God consciousness in this causal body, we must also see that the programming that is not real, which we call evil, or the energy veil, must be separate and apart from this "great wonder in heaven" that we contact in prayer and meditation.

Thus, all negative causation we have set in motion must fall by its own weight, by the gravity of the earth, to the lower frequencies of the subconscious levels of the mind. It must settle in a forcefield that is beneath the level of the heart chakra, because the heart is the focus of the energies of the Christ and the seat of the Christ consciousness—in Christian, Jew and Moslem alike.

That which we have set in motion that is pure and lovely in the sight of God and the sacred labor of our life—this energy, then, rises to the causal body of the Superconscious. All else descends to the sublevels of consciousness. It works like a separator of cream and milk.

When Jesus rose from Bethany's hill,[23] it was the acceleration of his own individual higher consciousness by which he manifested that attainment. That "going up" is really the "going in." It is the ascension into the origin, into the white-fire core of our own First Cause. We are not yet ascending because we are rooted in secondary causes of programming, and so we are bound by the gravity of our own incorrect desire and incorrect programming imposed both from within and from without.

All that we have seen as these spheres within spheres goes back to a sphere of consciousness, a white light, a presence that many of the saints and sages have seen and identified. It is painted as the halo of the saints. Often it is shown tinged with a golden yellow signifying the very next band in the causal body, the yellow band, which corresponds to the crown chakra—the wisdom flame of Alpha manifest in Christ and Buddha.

The white light contains the allness of our awareness of God because it is the sum total of the entire color spectrum accelerated into the one central sun. It also corresponds to the base chakra— the pure life force of Omega manifest in the Sons of God as the Mother flame. Thus the white and gold halo or auric light signifies God's Presence—as Immanuel—with us. It is the energy of Alpha and Omega, the Father-Mother God flowing through and emanating from the body temples of the saints.

The causal body as it is depicted in the Chart of Your Divine Self (page 24) is a cross-section of what is really a sphere. The secret rays that are in the center are at a different angle to the other spheres, because these initiations require a different plane of consciousness.

Figure 24 The Spheres of the Causal Body
The spheres of the seven rays can be seen as the color bands.
The spheres of the secret rays are in a different dimension and are
seen between the white-fire core and the yellow sphere.

Our Relationship to the Superconscious

Now we look at our relationship to that Superconscious as we are now in time and space as it is illustrated in the Chart of Your Divine Self. The lower figure in the Chart is you and me as we are evolving here on earth in a state of invocation to the

Presence of God—the upper figure in the Chart, the Divine Monad. The center figure in the Chart is Christ, the Mediator between our imperfect consciousness and the perfect consciousness of God.

Habakkuk established the concept of God as the knower of absolute Good (in contrast to relative good) when he said of Him: "Thou art of purer eyes than to behold evil, and canst not look on iniquity...."[24] Habakkuk held a concept of the perfection of God. It was an immaculate concept. As he beheld God steadfastly in light, God beheld him in the same light.

The Perfect cannot acknowledge the imperfect. The imperfect cannot see the Perfect. And therefore Christ, the Mediator, is the means of salvation, the Saviour of all mankind. Habakkuk was in the Christ consciousness, and thus he stood at the level of the Mediator, the prophet, between God and the people Israel when he made that scientific statement of God's consciousness.

When we understand that we have this direct relationship to the living Presence of God and to Christ, we do not believe the lie of procrastination in time and space that the fallen ones have told us: that God is far away, Christ is far away, they don't care what happens to us—and because they don't care, we'll have to do everything for ourselves instead of letting God work his works through us.

This Chart shows the nearness of God and, at the same time, the nearness of our realization of the Self in God. It is a chart that sets forth the goal of the Path in three steps:

1) purify the lower vehicles and the soul through the all-consuming sacred fire of God and thus prepare yourself to

2) meet the Lord Christ "in the air" (of higher consciousness) in the rapturous union of the soul with Christ (this is called the alchemical marriage—when the soul is received as the "wife" of the Lamb of God) and

3) ascend to the throne of glory as you arise with Christ your Lord to sit on the right hand of God, your mighty I AM Presence.

As Above, So Below

As we take up the step-by-step realization of the Path, let us consider that there is an action of energy flow, the concept of "as Above, so below."

When we experience joy and bliss and creativity and a sudden awareness or a sudden inspiration or we are motivated to do good, where does it come from? To me it is the cycling over a figure-eight pattern; it is the flow of consciousness. Following the figure eight, man's thoughts rise to God. They do not rise directly, but they must pass first through the nexus of the Christ consciousness, who is the sifter, sifting the hearts of mankind, giving unto the Father-Mother God only that which is pure and holy, and allowing to go beneath the heart of the individual all that is not.

We are in incarnation to master the flow of the energy that is God and the energy of God that we have misqualified in previous incarnations. It is a continual movement. That which is above in the causal body cycles here below, giving us life and energy and the talents with which we are born. The genius that some people experience simply comes forth from the superconscious mind and the programming of that mind from previous experiences. The movement of energy from the causal body is in a clockwise direction. It comes down and it anchors in form if we allow it, if we invoke it, if we call forth its manifestation and if we are not possessive of it.

Possessiveness is when we get this inspiration from God, or this energy, and we claim it as our own. And when we put out our hand and we grab the energy, we stop the flow—everything will back up and nothing will flow anymore. This is why Lord Buddha taught the law of nonattachment and desirelessness as the only way to freedom. He said if we have continual desires to possess God, we will stagnate, we will never get out of this mortal existence.

We find that God's gifts and graces that flow freely to us, flow to us in order that we may give as we receive. We give a portion back to God, and we give a portion to mankind. The

Figure 25 The Figure-Eight Flow

important thing is to realize that the flow does not stop, and so there is no need to hoard the abundance of God.

The integration of Spirit and Matter—of the Above and the below, of consciousness that is beyond our present awareness as the Superconsciousness of God and the conscious level of Christhood—comes to us over the path of initiation. This path was publicly demonstrated to us by Jesus the Christ, Gautama the Buddha and many other saints. These world teachers have given us a great example—and they have taught us that this is an example that we must follow.

They have said: "Verily, verily, I say unto you, He that believeth on me [on the I AM Presence within me as the same I AM Presence that is within himself], the works that I do shall he do also [the works that the Christ does in me, He shall also do in him]; and greater works than these shall he do; because I go unto my Father [because I AM ascended unto the Father, unto my God Presence and your God Presence, I AM become the multiplier of the works of Christ in you]."[25]

"To My God and Your God"

When Jesus ascended and the cloud received him out of their sight, he ascended into that point of the Divine Monad, having become one with the fiery core of all of us.

After his resurrection, Jesus said to Mary Magdalene: "Touch me not; for I am not yet ascended to my Father: but go to my brethren, and say unto them, I ascend unto my Father, and your

Father; and to my God, and your God."[26] And so the ascension, or if you prefer, the acceleration of Jesus' Christ consciousness, is the reinforcement of God within us all. And because we have that reinforcement, because he puts the multiplication factor of his Christhood with our own, he expects greater works, because two is a greater momentum than one. It is a multiplication factor. It follows the law of the expanding cosmos, the law of self-transcendence whereby, in each succeeding generation and each succeeding thousand years, people have greater and greater potential for self-mastery not only of the physical but also of the spiritual universe.

And so we go in the Chart of Your Divine Self from the superconscious causal body, the rainbow of God enveloping the I AM THAT I AM, to the fully conscious awareness of the Christ Self, to the soul potential that is now manifesting as the lower self that is not fully conscious of either God or his Christ as the Reality of Being. Yet seeing "through a glass darkly," to use a phrase of Paul, as it peers through the human consciousness accrued through many lifetimes of ego-centered qualification of energy, the lower self will ultimately see the Christ "face-to-face" after it shall have undergone the fiery trial of initiation and transmutation by the violet fire. This lower figure represents each one of us exactly where we are—our present consciousness in the application of devotion to the fire of the Holy Spirit. The fire of the Holy Spirit, the violet fire, is the wine of forgiveness made tangible in the "flaming flame that will not be quenched," as Ezekiel said.[27]

Figure 26

The Flow of the Figure Eight and Free Will

In figure 26 we are looking at a devotee. Let us say that this is man before the Fall, before the descent from the plane of

Christhood, before the descent into the knowledge of good and evil.

However, man is the creator of the spirals of darkness within the subconscious mind. The subconscious mind is a body, or a vehicle of consciousness, that is intended to reflect all of the vastness of the God-potential we've been talking about as the First Cause and the origin and the white sphere. It is intended to be a reflector of the Superconscious.

But here we have the exercise of free will. Will man, given the opportunity to be obedient to the laws of God, allow himself to be a reflector of God, or will he say, "I will not; I will do my own thing"? He has an opportunity to sustain the patterns of the figure eight and the flow of consciousness, or he has an opportunity to stop the flow. The subconscious is a spiral of energy just as the Superconscious is a spiral of energy.

I find it very interesting in studying the great religious teachers of the world to find confirmation of the teachings of Jesus Christ or the Holy Spirit who has enlightened me as to the deeper meaning of the Scriptures. Lao Tzu taught in the sixth century B.C., and in his *Tao Te Ching* we find a very poetic concept of the flow of energy of which we are intended to be the masters.

> Something mysteriously formed,
> Born before heaven and earth [the white-fire core].
> In the silence and the void,
> Standing alone and unchanging,
> Ever present and in motion.
> Perhaps it is the mother of ten thousand things.
> I do not know its name.
> Call it Tao.
> For lack of a better word, I call it great.
>
> Being great, it flows.
> It flows far away.
> Having gone far, it returns.

To Lao Tzu, the definition of greatness was flow, was movement. His definition of God was flow, was movement. Is not life flow and movement? Life coursing through our veins, our minds, is movement.

> Tao is great;
> Heaven is great;
> Earth is great;

This is his perception of planes of consciousness within us.

> The king is also great.
> These are the four great powers of the universe,
> And the king is one of them.

Who is the king but the Christ in all of us? Jesus said, "Before Abraham was, I AM,"[28] and so one who was before Christ perceived Christ.

> Man follows the earth.
> Earth follows heaven.
> Heaven follows the Tao.
> Tao follows what is natural.[29]

—the flow of the figure eight.

The Decision to Do Your Thing or God's Thing

In figure 27 we see an individual who is making a decision, and for the purposes of our study, he makes the decision to do his own thing. It is an action of rebellion.

Morya says that every single civilization that has fallen has done so willfully, because at subconscious levels the souls knew of their disobedience to Alpha and Omega. Is it any wonder that mankind sit in the valley of ignorance and have not the teachings, the true teachings of Christ, even of Christ Jesus? They have willfully misused the teachings, rejected the teachings and expected life to continue to serve them.

But unto the chosen few, then and now, Christ comes to re-ignite the threefold flame of the heart that they might experience the opening of the scriptures through the opening of their own

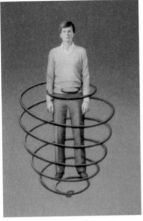

faculty of understanding. "And they said one to another, Did not our heart burn within us, while he talked with us by the way, and while he opened to us the scriptures?"[30] This is the initiation of the heart chakra of the disciples through the sacred heart of the Master.

We should pray for the same touch—heart to heart with our Lord that we may rightly divide the word of truth and of prophecy. Unless and until Christ accomplish this in his own, the people have only the husks of a dead letter and doctrine and remain fooled

Figure 27 A Negative
Spiral in the Subconscious

by serpents in the pulpit who preach the philosophy of Anti-christ—"Ye shall not surely die!"[31] We know them and their followers by the fruit of hatred, bigotry and intolerance expressed toward all others who do not interpret the letter of the Law as they do. Yet Christ's religion is first and foremost the communion of his own, loving one another "as I have loved you."

Samuel, the great prophet, said to Saul that "rebellion is as the sin of witchcraft, and stubbornness is as iniquity and idolatry."[32] Witchcraft is an aberration of the inner blueprint. You have heard of hexes that are like a hypnotic spell. Rebellion means "out of alignment with the blueprint," hence rebellion and witchcraft are one and the same.

When we feel ourselves being stubborn and in rebellion, would we say that we are practicing witchcraft? If we believe Samuel, we would have to admit it. He said to Saul: "Because thou hast rejected the word of the LORD he hath also rejected thee from being king,"[33]—from serving in the office of the disciple who understands his calling to be the representative of the

Christ Self.

Rebellion is the opening of our world to forces of Antichrist. Rebellion itself is insanity, because it is going against that which is life in the ultimate sense, that which is the law of our inmost being, and it can only result in the decay of our bodies, the disintegration and the death.

The Cosmic Clock of the Subconscious—
A Counterclockwise Vortex of the Energy Veil

The same clock that we put as a spiral, as a sphere on the causal body, we also put on the subconscious mind. Energy, then, coalesces according to cycles and spirals; and because God is the orderer of the universe, he is also the organizer of the creation, both human and divine, according to the mathematics of frequency and vibration. We discover that there are compartments of the subconscious where various momentums of being are lodged in this energy field.

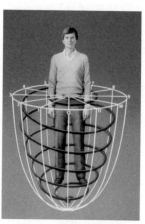

Figure 28 The Clock
of the Subconscious

Jesus spoke of those who have made the decision to be rebellious and those who have not as "the quick and the dead."[34] The quick are those who are quickened by the flow of energy over the figure-eight pattern; the dead are those who, in their folly, have attempted to possess that flow.

We come, then, to the creation of a negative spiral—not a clockwise flow that comes forth from God, but a counterclockwise flow, an energy spiral that draws us down, pulls us down into the lesser self, or into the carnal mind.

With the first decision to eat of the fruit of the tree of the knowledge of good and evil,[35] which means to partake of relativity, we lost our sense of the absolute Presence of God, the absolute awareness of the Self as Christ. So we began filling this grid, this forcefield known as the electronic belt, with negatively qualified energies. The individual in the former state enjoyed freedom. Now he is fallen man. Doing his own thing instead of God's thing, he is surrounded by that conglomerate of the programming of the mass consciousness. This programming may be entering our world consciously or subconsciously.

Figure 29 (page 186) is an attempt to show what the media does and how it plays upon the subconscious. Certain art forms and music forms, current books, cycles of education, movies such as *Crime and Passion, Mark of the Devil, The Devil Within Her, The Exorcist, Jaws, Grizzly*—all of these movies that charge people with emotions, with fear, with darkness—all of this energy coalesces in forms, in creatures, in sublevels of awareness.

Wilson Bryan Key says that "tens of millions of humans are daily massaged and manipulated without their conscious awareness."[36] This is the consequence of rebellion as the sin of witchcraft. Practicing rebellion against the inner Law of the cells and atoms of our being, we become practitioners of witchcraft against ourselves. We have programmed ourselves, allowed ourselves to be programmed to the success cult, the sex cult and the death cult.

Our electronic belt is really the sundial marking the hours of the cycles of time and space in which we have misused God's energy. All that we see here does not represent the Christ consciousness—it shows instead the perversions of the four aspects of God's consciousness—Father, Mother, Christ and Holy Spirit. Each time we pervert one of those aspects of God, it has a corresponding manifestation in the subconscious.

You see the witch form, which is the perversion of the power of God, the misuse of God's energy as self-condemnation on the twelve o'clock line. We have it written in scripture in East and West, "judge not, lest ye be judged."[37] When we look at other parts of life and we say, "That man is a sinner, that man is going to hell, that man is wicked," we are judging. Since all life is one, that judgment is meted out upon the Self—the one Great Self of all. Therefore, it registers upon our own subconscious, and we program ourselves to the very miscreations that we are judging in others. Witchcraft is the practice of inflicting upon any part of life a mental matrix of the human will or wit that is in direct contradiction of the inner Law of Being.

Now we look at the one o'clock line. It is the seat of God-love, the hierarchy of Aquarius. The perversions of love are hate and hate creation and mild dislike. We see a polar bear and a shark. They are known as man-eating beasts of prey. This is the force of hatred, man's inhumanity to man coming back upon him through the beasts of his own electronic belt. The other side of hatred is indifference. And that indifference is the other side of the viciousness of these types of animal forms.

So what we are saying here as we show the electronic belt is that hatred, anger, mild dislike and condemnation do not just go out as a mass of energy that has no shape—they take the form of animal creations. Thoughts and feelings coalesce into lower forms, dissonant forms. These may be animal forms or they may be very dark forms of perverted symbols, distortions of the human body and so forth.

On the two o'clock line, we see the skull and the skeleton, showing the record of death and dying and every manifestation of fear and doubt that leads to death. Fear and doubt are the components of death.

People say, "I have no fear," but there are records of fear in the subconscious. Perhaps you haven't contacted them. They may appear as anxiety on the eight o'clock line opposite the two. You may not normally have anxieties but you may get in a certain situation in life where all of a sudden you sense a foreboding fear. Separation from God breeds doubt and fear.

Jesus showed us that death is not real, that death is swallowed up in victory. All that is real is our belief in death, our fear not only of death but of every other manifestation of darkness. And so piling up layer upon layer, year in, year out, life after life, the consciousness of fear and doubt, we focus our own

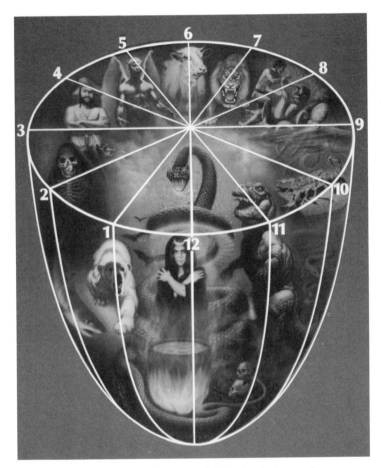

Figure 29 The Clock of Negativity in the Subconscious

self-destruction, our own death. And whether or not this results in the death of the soul is determined in the Last Judgment—the final analysis of whether we have put more energy in God or more energy in the energy veil.

The Christ is the true ego of all, the Divine Ego. On the line of Aries and Taurus we see the pirate form as the typical perversion of rebellion and the ego that is going to do its own thing—arrogance, taking the gain of others, not being willing to submit to the law of karma, the law of initiation. This is the human ego, uncontrolled, unbridled, in place of the Christ consciousness.

The five o'clock line is the green demon, the focal point of envy, jealousy, covetousness and ignorance. Demons have deified *evil* instead of deifying God. So they do not have the mind of God in Christ. They have the fallen consciousness, and this is the typical carnal mind that prevents you from realizing the Christ mind.

Now we go to the miscreations of the emotional quadrant, the perversions of the water element on the lines of Cancer, Leo and Virgo.

The six o'clock line shows the head of a cow on the line where we should be realizing God as Mother. That cow consciousness is the earthly mother with its earthly attachments and earthly densities: the overprotective, sympathetic, saccharine consciousness, the mother that smothers, chewing the cud—endless chatter, gossip, unseemly conversation, tying up the energies of the base chakra, the sacred fire; the consciousness "without me, life cannot survive"; the mother being milked by her children instead of teaching them the discipline whereby they can tie in to their energy source. This is a very subtle perversion because it's always trying to feed you.

On the seven o'clock line of Leo, the line of God-gratitude, there is the lion of ingratitude. We think of the lion as the king of the beasts, but there is also a perversion here of the lion consciousness that is ingratitude—it is the beast that is ready to pounce.

The eight o'clock line is the line of Virgo—the Earth Mother. Her sons are in a constant state of struggle because of a sense of injustice. The injustice is the warring in our members:[38] our emotions versus the mind, the mind versus the emotions, the memory interfering, the sense that someone has wronged us, the sense of struggle that makes the struggle. That sense of injustice comes out when you have a division in the members on the Gemini line, the Gemini members warring—always the sense that we've been wronged, life has cheated us.

All of these struggles are really internal, but we imagine that we are acting them out with other individuals, other people who are really other aspects of God in various stages of evolution. Each time we engage in that struggle over the sense of injustice, we leave a record in the subconscious. To overcome this sense of injustice, we have to rise to the statement of Portia, "There is no injustice anywhere in the universe." If something unjust happens to us, we transmute it with the violet flame, challenge it, get to the bottom of it, find out what our karma is and move on. Let go of it. As Jesus said, "What is that to thee? follow thou me."[39]

Now we come to the miscreations of the physical quadrant typified on the nine o'clock line as an octopus, the record of the misuse of the ego. It's the other side of the pirate of the three o'clock line. The ego in its own defense must use treachery and intrigue—the undercover, underwater consciousness, the sliminess of getting away with as much as it can get away with by subterfuge.

The ten o'clock line is the scorpion, a manifestation of selfishness, grasping, an imperfect vision of God—the scorpion sting instead of the eagle's All-Seeing Eye of God. The sign of Scorpio is one or the other, the eagle or the scorpion.

On the eleven o'clock line we see the dinosaur form, which is the dragon that we read about in the Book of Revelation. In order to gain our absolute God-victory by the Cosmic Christ Lord Maitreya, we have to gain the victory on all the preceding lines. We come to the eleven o'clock line for the slaying of the dragon itself. It is the logical conclusion of the serpent that began in Genesis.[40] That little serpent in Genesis allegorically becomes the dragon in Revelation, the dinosaur consciousness of revenge.

Resentment, revenge and retaliation is the energy that opposes your God-victory in Sagittarius on the eleven o'clock line. In Revelation, Satan is depicted as this dragon that goes forth to make war with the Woman to prevent her from giving birth to the Divine Manchild.[41] The dragon of our own carnal mind is pitted against our own soul, or feminine potential. But we find that we ourselves have created this dragon. It is the revenge against the light of Christ within.

The Dweller-on-the-Threshold

In the very center of the clock is the dweller-on-the-threshold. It is a combination of all other perversions of God combined into an identity that is your unreal personality. Just as we show you the Chart of the I AM Presence and the Holy Christ Self, the Chart of Your Real Self, this electronic belt is an archetypal chart of your unreal self.

The dweller is much bigger than the individual. The serpent or serpentine mind is a clever mind, a deceiving mind. The origin of the dweller, which is inordinate desire, must be slain before we can attain the Christ consciousness.

The reason we need a guru who is an ascended master, an archangel, an Elohim, a cosmic being, the reason we need the entire Spirit of the Great White Brotherhood is that this dweller-on-the-threshold and all of the beasts of prey that sit on those four quadrants have become more powerful than we have. We have literally surrendered our God energy and endowed these creations with this power. So now we cannot slay them of ourselves.

At the Core of the Subconscious the Lie, "Thou Shalt Not Surely Die."

We see at the very core of the subconscious, at the very base of this spiral, the belief in the lie that the serpent gave to Eve, the archetype of the soul of humanity. Eve said, "God has said, 'You should not eat of this fruit of the tree of the knowledge of good and evil because in the day that you eat thereof, you will die.'" But the serpent said to Eve, "Ye shall not surely die."[42]

What does that mean?

You may die, and you may not?

It is the attempt to convince the soul, as the feminine potential of both man and woman, that the wages of sin is not death. But the prophet said, "The soul that sinneth it *shall* die."[43] No ifs, ands or buts. And in the Last Judgment it is clearly recorded that they are judged "every man according to their works."[44] This is a judgment of deeds, or as the ascended masters would say, of karma. It is not a judgment of doctrine or dogma or philosophies or belief systems. All the believing in the world won't get you anywhere unless your belief has become the action of glorifying God in your soul and in your heart, in your body temple and in your good works.

"Ye shall not *surely* die." It is the confusion of the Law. It is the logic of the serpentine mind. It is the introduction into the subconscious of humanity of what we call "sweet death." If we're going to sin and die, we might as well die sweetly. "Eat, drink and be merry, for tomorrow we die." As long as we're going to rebel against God, as long as we're going to die anyway, let's have fun doing it.

The sweet sense of death is the whiling away of the energies in time and space until the end finally comes. Don't you see a lot of people doing that today? No awareness that life is finite; it is as though they were going to live forever—the grasshopper consciousness. The core, the inception of the energy veil is the belief in the lie, "Thou shalt not surely die."

The programming of death, the programming of the death cult, permeates at least nine-tenths of our civilization today. We have become habituated to it, indoctrinated by it. We go along with it; we go along on the downward spiral that is the downward course of civilization.

What can we do about it?

We return to the point of invocation. We call upon the Holy Spirit.

The Holy Spirit—Destroyer of Human Miscreation and the Human Miscreant

The Hindus have their names for the Trinity of Father, Son and Holy Spirit: Brahma, Vishnu and Shiva. They think of

Brahma, or Father, as the Creator; Vishnu, the Christ, as the Preserver; but the Holy Spirit they call the Destroyer. When we understand that the Holy Spirit is the Destroyer and what this destruction is, we are grateful that God has manifested this aspect of the Trinity.

The Destroyer is the cloven tongues of fire,[45] the sacred fire that consumes on contact every creation of man and woman that is not worthy to be perpetuated in God or in our own higher consciousness. Therefore, we have recourse. We can call upon the law of forgiveness, we can call for the aid of the Holy Spirit, and we can ask that that fire descend upon us that descended on the day of Pentecost[46] to consume our sin, our awareness of sin, our struggle against the Person of the living Christ who comes to initiate us on our own road to Damascus. ("It is hard for thee to kick against the pricks."[47])

Violet Flame—Gift of Christ, Action of Holy Spirit

The invocation of the violet flame is the most fantastic gift that Christ has given to us. It is the action of the Holy Spirit. Jesus promised that he would send the Comforter;[48] he would not leave us alone. The Comforter is another word for the Holy Spirit.

When Jesus ascended, the Comforter came. It gave the apostles understanding and teaching, the nine gifts of the Holy Spirit that we long for and that we pray for.[49] One of these gifts is this action of the cleansing of the subconscious by the fires of the Holy Spirit.

What do we do to get the violet flame? What do we do to get this fire flowing within us, once we understand the purging and the purifying that is needed in our subconscious?

After we see the mess *we* have made from our own misuse of free will, we realize that whatever else happens, we must be free from our self-imposed bondage. We *want* to be free. We *want* to claim our heirship as joint-heirs with Christ,[50] of his consciousness of the mind of God. We determine in God that *we will be free* because he ordained our cosmic freedom from the beginning. Therefore, we invoke the sacred fire in the name of Jesus Christ and in the name of God I AM THAT I AM.

"Whatsoever ye shall ask the Father in my name, he will give it you."

Jesus taught us how to pray. Just before he took his leave of this plane he said, "Whatsoever ye shall ask the Father in my name, he will give it you."[51] To me that is one of the most important statements of cosmic law. I absolutely believe without any question or fear or doubt that when I say, "In the name of Jesus the Christ, I call to God for the action, the manifestation and the sacred fire of the Holy Spirit within me," that instantaneously it is manifest, because he promised that God would give us whatever we called for in his name. And we are not asking amiss, but we are asking according to the will of God and the promise that our sins would be transmuted. "Though your sins be as scarlet, they shall be as white as snow; though they be red like crimson, they shall be as wool."[52]

To me the Laws of God are absolutely unfailing. I could more conceive of the laws of mathematics or the laws that govern the earth's rotation failing than I could conceive of this promise failing. And so when I make my invocation to the Holy Spirit, I say just that:

In the name of Jesus the Christ, in the name of the Christ-potential within me, I call to God for the release of the violet flame.

And then I make the affirmation that where I am, God is the action of the violet flame. I say:

I AM a being of violet fire,
I AM the purity God desires!

The word *I AM* was given to Moses. It is the confirmation of God's Being where I am. If he is not where I am, then I could not be alive, I could not live. I could not exist; for I only exist by the presence of God's grace.

So when I say the name I AM, I understand that it means "God in me is." Right where I am, God is. Right where I am, that flaming flame is burning. If it was where Moses was, then it can be where I am, because there isn't any time and space. And so, we give the simple mantra to affirm that where I AM, there God is as the action of the violet transmuting flame.

A mantra is the flow of the energy of God, the Science of the Spoken Word accompanied by prayer and meditation. There are Eastern and Western mantras. This is a very special mantra for the Aquarian age. It is for the transmutation of mankind's misuses of God's energy of the Piscean age and in every preceding age.

I AM a being of violet fire,
I AM the purity God desires!

As you say this mantra, stand and visualize yourself in the center of the violet flame holding your arms and hands in the receptive mode like the lower figure in the Chart of Your Divine Self. Realize that God is above you, the Divine Monad is focused above you, its light emanations all around you. Christ is also right there above you and pulsating in the threefold flame upon the altar of your heart. This is your own Christ-potential quickened by Jesus the Christ and all ascended masters whose souls have reunited with the God flame. We have but to make the call, and the call, by cosmic law, compels the answer.

"I AM the Resurrection and the Life"

There is another mantra we can give for the affirmation of this sacred fire. It was given to us by Jesus when he said, "I AM the resurrection and the life."[53] God in me is the resurrection and the life.

In the name of Jesus the Christ, I call to the Father for
the light of the resurrection flame, the blessed flame of the

Holy Spirit, the blessed flame of life to enter now the worlds of all who by free will, will use the power of the spoken Word to confirm congruency with God in Christ.

In the name of Jesus the Christ, we call to the Father for the filling of our four lower bodies—the mind, the feelings, the physical form and the memory—with the action of the resurrection.

I AM the Resurrection and the Life!

Figure 30 The Resurrected Subconscious

In figure 30, we see the resurrected subconscious. It comes through the flow of the sacred fire of the Spirit through the subconscious mind for the cleansing of that mind. The whirling action of the fire of Christ has removed all of the impressions of the programming within and without—the programming of our own rebellion, the programming of the mass hypnosis of the collective unconscious. We see, then, the original purpose of the subconscious to be the reflection of First Cause, of God, of the Super-conscious Being and of the Divine Monad.

We Need to Use the Holy Spirit

We need to use the Holy Spirit, and the Aquarian age is the age of the Holy Spirit. It is the age of the action of love in freedom, and freedom in the love of God—God's intense love for us, the love of Christ for us. "I will not leave you comfortless, I will not leave you alone. I will send to you the Comforter."[54]

If by our own dullness and density we are living in this plane without the awareness of the Presence of our Lord, then we can have by his promise the revitalizing action of the Holy Spirit. The comfort of God is the law of the Holy Spirit, destroying that which is unworthy.

Destroying is not quite an accurate term, because nothing is destroyed—it is transmuted. The altar is the place where we alter the human, where we exchange the human for the divine. The energies of the Holy Spirit pass through the subconscious and that same energy, which is God in its origin, is freed from the imperfect forcefield, from the bondage of our creation, and then it rises. It is weightless. So erg by erg, our energy ascends back to God, back to the Source.

When all of the energy that is misqualified has ascended back to God, then we ascend also. And this is what is meant by going into heaven, into the kingdom of God, going into the consciousness of God.

Free Will Equals Cosmic Accountability

Figure 30 represents an individual who has balanced 100 percent of his karma, who has surrendered all desire that is less than God, who has totally given his life to Christ. You can become this. You can express and accept the programming of God. You can accept the programming of Christ. It is a daily choice, an hourly choice, a momentary choice.

These choices we were created to make, we were given free will to make. Can we ever accept, then, the fact that we are not cosmically accountable? Accepting cosmic accountability means accepting responsibility for change, for overcoming, for understanding that "I can do all things through Christ which strengtheneth me."[55] God has given to us an opportunity for self-mastery. If we bypass this opportunity in this life, we will be accountable.

"By thy word thou shalt be justified, by thy word thou shalt be condemned."[56] The Word is the flow of God's grace and energy through us. By the science of that Word we confirm our Reality. We return to the state of paradise or the consciousness of bliss that we knew before we ever created that negative spiral. We are found once again in purity and in holy innocence.

The Subconscious Mind—An Energy Field

The subconscious mind is a latticework, an energy field, an opportunity for God to express himself through us, for God to work his works through us. We are free to be free in God. We no longer say, "I can't, I won't, I am limited, I am mortal," but we say, "Here I am, God. You have created me; do what you will with me. Use my mind; use every aspect of my mind to manifest your light, your life, your healing, your service to everyone I meet."

We have a responsibility to give back to God our feelings, our emotions, our mental body, our memory, our physical life. Giving this energy to him, he fills it with light and uses it to bring humanity to their own awareness of the Self in Christ. Would we not all rather have an open door for Christ to enter in than a clogged subconscious filled with every manner of misuse of the sacred fire that is a repellent to the light of Christ?

A Rising Spiral of Energy

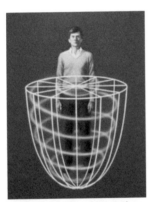

Figure 31 The Ascension Spiral in the Subconscious

Instead of the negative spiral we have created through our self-pity, we are creating a positive, rising spiral of energy. This is the white light that ascends, even from subconscious levels, creating a coil of energy whereby the greatest teachers and saints who have come to us in every age have had the gifts of the Spirit, and they have been anchored right here on earth as a witness unto their devotion to God.

Figure 31 shows the ascension spiral. We reestablish the flow of the figure eight. We reestablish contact with the body of First Cause, and it is instantaneously accessible to us. We get in a right relationship to the flow, to the energy, and we find that with God, with consciousness, with wholeness, all things are possible.[57]

Now we are ready to take cosmic accountability for our nation, for our earth, because the same law that has worked in us to consume the cause and core of evil can work at planetary levels, can work through millions of souls. The same prayer that says, "In the name of Jesus the Christ, I call forth the fire of the Holy Spirit to consume the energy veil within me," is adequate to call forth the fire that will consume the entire subconscious of the race.

God Is the Doer

It is only an equation of cosmic law, and it is only our sense of limitation that makes us think it cannot be done. Why do we think it? Because we think we are the doers.

God is the doer. God is the doer, or the door.[58] God is the door of energy, of flow. When we think we are running the show and doing everything, we block the flow. If God is the doer, he can consume the subconscious of the race as easily as he can consume our own. What is the difference between a grain of sand and a mountain? There is no difference in God, only in relativity.

Take Dominion of Consciousness— Master the Molecules of Matter

In figure 32, we see the balance, as Above, so below. Here on earth we are manifesting the God of our heaven. As Above, so below, we are here to prove that in earth we can take dominion, answering the challenge that God gave when he created male and female and sent them forth to take dominion.[59] Taking dominion over the earth means taking dominion of consciousness and thereby mastering the molecules of Matter.

Now we see the rings of self-conscious awareness expanding by the very action of the flow of the fire. We have a greater and greater awareness of Christ living in us, and therefore we can serve greater and greater numbers of people.

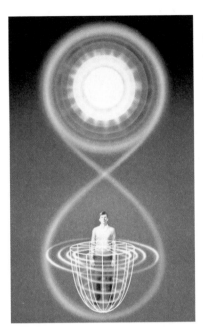

Figure 32 As Above, So Below:
The Macrocosm That Is God
Reflected in the Microcosm
That Is Man

Why do we limit ourselves? Jesus did not. He fed the five thousand as easily as he fed his disciples. It is a question of getting over relativity in time and space, getting over that fruit of the knowledge of good and evil. It is the knowledge of good and evil, of time and space, of relativity that makes us think all of this is impossible. But it *is* possible because God lives in us, and that is the real reason, and we need no other.

We reestablish the flow of that figure eight, that movement of energy, and we have those moments of awareness in meditation when there is no separation between the self and God; and that is because we are experiencing the same energy—above in the Macrocosm that is God and below in the microcosm that is man.

Libra

The Psychology of Wholeness

Melchisedec, king of Salem,
priest of the most high God,…
without father, without mother, without descent,
having neither beginning of days, nor end of life;
but made like unto the Son of God;
abideth a priest continually.

—Hebrews

CHAPTER 10

The Psychology of Wholeness:
The Karmic Clock

In Our Microcosm We Must Reflect the All of the Macrocosm

The point that we must grasp when we contemplate the Chart of Your Divine Self (page 24) is that we must become whole. The Chart of the Presence is a picture of our wholeness—the wholeness of God and God's manifestation in us. And therefore, as we look at the causal body, the I AM Presence, the Christed One and the flame descending as the Holy Spirit, we realize that we must contain all of this. Every part of God must be inside of us: and the definition of our wholeness is when we contain the Allness of God.

Some have said this is not possible. It is possible qualitatively if not quantitatively—but even quantities are nonexistent in infinity.

If we are ever missing any aspects of God's consciousness, we have a distortion or an omission of the Divine, and then we have a problem in our personal psychology—we are not a cosmically integrated being, we are not integrated in the microcosm, and we cannot reflect the integration of the Macrocosm or the superconscious mind. Here below in our microcosm we must reflect the all of the Macrocosm. Therefore, in our state of incompleteness we remain on the quest for wholeness.

Modern psychology since Freud has been examining these issues from many standpoints and many schools of thought. If you see here and there in this explanation what seem to be pieces of various psychologists, it is perhaps incidental because, after all, all mankind have access to the mind of God, and I would like to believe that some have actually interpreted some of this psychology of wholeness.

The Sign of Cosmic Integration

We must realize, then, that wholeness is possible of achievement in Matter. We know it is possible because masters have gone before us and have accomplished it. So that settles the matter—it can be done. We can become the living example, the receptacle, the Christed One.

The Buddhas in meditation are an example. They are the sign of wholly integrated being. They are in meditation upon the flow of the causal body from the Superconscious to the subconscious. This is what every Buddha is doing. Every statue of the Buddha is the focus of that cosmic integration of the flow of the figure-eight pattern, and their chakras are wide-open doors for the release of this energy into the world and the taking in of the world's energy for its transmutation.

A statue of Buddha in your home is a focal point for your own individual cosmic integration. A focus of Mother Mary shows the action of cosmic integration defined through the complete mastery of Matter in the feminine ray, and it is the point for the release of the energies of Spirit in Matter. It symbolizes the attainment—through that mastery—of the white chakra (the base-of-the-spine chakra). Pictures of the Christ healing and teaching show the same action of flow, of cosmic integration and change.

The Essential Theme of Flow, Movement, Oneness, Wholeness

Our misunderstanding of this essential theme of flow, of movement, of oneness and wholeness in God, has led to every form of misuse of the sacred fire. The masters have defined these misuses on the twelve lines of the clock (fig. 19, page 96). In all perversion and misuse of life's energy, it is because wholeness is sought outside of the Self instead of inside of the Self. From war to crime to hatred to arguments to injustice to misuses of sex to the taking of drugs—all of these are done because people continually seek to complete themselves outside of themselves, instead of within.

The Cosmic Clock: A Diagram of Wholeness

The cosmic clock diagrams the wholeness we must manifest. It was given to us by Mother Mary specifically so that we could know how to transmute the substance of our electronic belt, and the knowing how is the knowing of the cycles of its release.

The mind of God and its action within us is a cosmic computer ticking off the manifestation of our energies. That computer, precisely according to our individual cosmic clock, or our cosmic astrology, releases to us hour by hour, day by day, that which represents our challenge on the path of initiation—our own individual karma.

Simultaneously, we receive the challenge of planetary karma, and this comes along a parallel line with our individual karma. There are many cycles within cycles, but they all follow the same diagram of this cosmic clock, Alpha and Omega making the whole into the polarity and the forcefield of consciousness—the Father-Mother God becoming the four quadrants in Matter and in Spirit.

The four cardinal points of Being become the twelve as there is a continuous breakdown of frequency and vibration. These twelve in turn become 144 and so on until point by point around the circle of infinity, there is a new experience in God. If you could count how many dots you could put on the circle, you could count how many states of awareness you could have in higher consciousness.

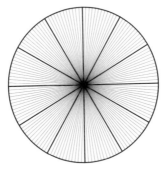

Figure 33 144 Points of God Consciousness

We Create Our Own Astrology—We Create Ourselves

By our uses and misuses of God's energy we create our own astrology. The astrology chart with which you were born—your sun sign, your rising sign, your moon sign and all of your planets—indicates stages of mastery, God-mastery, as well as stages of opportunity for that mastery, and also the opportunity to redo the failures of the past. So truly, right down to the last erg of energy that is in our world, we create ourselves.

The Mandala of Christ and His Apostles

This cosmic clock is the mandala of each esoteric unit, each unit in hierarchy of the guru and of twelve disciples. The twelve disciples of Jesus are figured on these lines. Jesus is the white-fire core in the center, and the positioning of the disciples on the clock was an assignment to each one for the mastery of that line. Each disciple was required to focus one-twelfth of the clock of wholeness, whereas Jesus was required to focus the mastery of all twelve.

Andrew, Philip and Thomas hold the flame in the etheric body. They serve under the hierarchies of Capricorn, Aquarius, Pisces to teach those who are disciples of Christ how to master the energies of God-power, God-love and God-mastery. If you are born under any one of these three sun signs, you can call to the causal body of the disciple on your line to lend you the momentum of his attainment on that line, that you might serve with him in the mandala of the Christ.

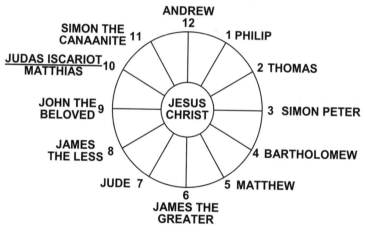

Figure 34 The Apostles on the Lines of the Clock

In the mental quadrant are Simon Peter, Bartholomew and Matthew serving on the lines three, four and five—Aries, Taurus, Gemini. If you are one of these three signs, call in the name of the Christ that the causal body of attainment of that one be transferred to you as a mantle, a momentum of victory.

In the emotional quadrant, serving the hierarchies of Cancer, Leo and Virgo, are the apostles James the Greater, Jude and James the Less. They were intended to master those emotional energies, and so whatever attainment they did manifest is yours for the calling, yours for the asking, by the fiat in the name of the Christ.

In the physical quadrant, serving on the lines of Libra,

Scorpio and Sagittarius, are John the Beloved, Judas Iscariot (who was replaced by Matthias) and Simon the Canaanite. One of those three disciples, then, is your partner if you were born under one of those three signs, and you work with them to hold the mandala of the Christian dispensation, the Piscean dispensation.

As far as we know, John the Beloved is the only one of the twelve who made his ascension at the conclusion of that life—all of the rest reembodied. Whether the apostle on your line has ascended or not, you can still call to the causal body for their attainment. However, if they have not yet ascended, there is a momentum of misqualified energy on that line that is in opposition to the full manifestation of Christianity. While you are serving on that line, you can call for the transmutation of the electronic belt of that apostle. By doing so, you assist that one in keeping the flame and the focus on that line.[1]

We know of two more apostles who have ascended since their Galilean embodiment. One of these is Judas Iscariot on the ten o'clock line. In his next embodiment, so filled with remorse, he gave such devotion and such intense prayer and such intense application to the flame of Jesus Christ that he did make his ascension.

Clara Louise Kieninger

Only a few years ago, the apostle who was embodied as James on the six o'clock line made his ascension from a feminine incarnation as the first Mother of the Flame of the Keepers of the Flame Fraternity, Clara Louise Kieninger. The story of her overcoming and her final victory is recorded in her memoirs, the paperback book *Ich Dien,*[2] which means "I serve." That was her motto, as she was a nurse. So, that makes three that I am aware of who have ascended—three out of twelve. We can call for the ascension and for the fulfillment of the mission of the remaining apostles.

The Karmic Clock: Balancing 100 Percent of Our Karma

The ascended master John the Beloved has given us an understanding of this karmic clock and our psychology of wholeness:

> I remember well when the angel of the Lord came to me on the isle of Patmos and I received the message of Jesus Christ to be sealed and signified by that angel, to remain untouched through these two thousand years.[3] And therefore the authority of the Christ and of the Logos did seal that revelation as two-thirds of the initiatory spiral of the thirty-three. And in the twenty-two chapters of this proclamation of the Word, you will find the key for the transmutation of two-thirds of your own karma and of the balance of energies and of your debts to life.
>
> Listen well and hear well as you read the Holy Book, and see how you can perceive therein the unwinding of the coils of identity and the moving of energy into the flame cycle by cycle; for therein is contained the entire subconscious of the race.
>
> Understand, then, how that collective subconscious must come to the fore, must come there to the moment of the appearing where the subconscious becomes the conscious. And therefore, to slay the dragon and the beast and the beast that riseth up out of the sea and the beast that cometh up out of the earth, the false prophet, the great whore and the fallen ones and all these identities of the carnal mind,[4] you must understand that the moment they appear on the world scene, the moment they appear from subconscious depths of your own psyche, you must stand as the victor, as the Christ, taking the sword of the one who comes with those eyes as pools of fire, one like unto the Son of God, your own Christed Self, and slay the action of the misuse of the sacred fire.
>
> The sword is the sacred sword, the *Sacred Word.*

It must go forth. As the fire proceeds out of the mouth of the two witnesses[5] and the sword comes out of the one who champions the cause of righteousness,[6] so let the sword coming forth from the mouth of the Christ symbolize that which cleaves asunder the Real from the unreal by the fiat of the Lord, by the power of the spoken Word manifest in you....

And for those of you who pass the tests line by line, verse by verse, of that which is recorded in the Book of Revelation, there is prepared for you the revelation of the mysteries whereby you can overcome the remaining third of your karma. The goal of life for total victory is wide open! And you are invited by the LORD of hosts this day to balance 100 percent of your karma, to return to God as victors and champions proving the law of righteousness, proving the balance of harmony as that harmony equals, line by line, the mastery of the feminine ray and of the white-fire core of being. See, then, how God has already marked clearly within you and in *akasha* and in prophecy the path of salvation.[7]

As we consider the assignment to balance 100 percent of our karma, we could logically conclude that 25 percent of this karma falls within each quadrant of the clock. Percentages do not tell us quantities. You may have balanced 10 percent, 30 percent, 40 percent of your karma, but that does not tell you how much karma you have in total as a burden of darkness that must become a burden of light. If you have a thousand tons of karma, your percentages are more; it takes a little bit more time and space to balance your 25 percent than your neighbor might to balance his 25 percent.

Nevertheless, this karma is ours. It's our creation. And unfortunately, we really have to admit that our karma is our sense of wholeness. It's the best we've done with God's energies to manifest the wholeness of his being.

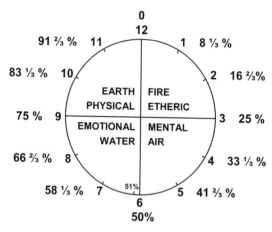

Figure 35 The Karmic Clock

Balancing 51 Percent of Our Karma

Since the inauguration of the new dispensation early in the twentieth century, it is possible to ascend having balanced at least 51 percent of one's karma. Prior to this time, the requirement for the ascension was to have balanced 100 percent of one's karma.

Whether to your outer consciousness or to your soul, the very moment that you balance 51 percent of your karma, you are contacted by Serapis Bey, hierarch of the Ascension Temple, and your Christ Self. You are given notice that you have balanced this quantity of karma, and you are given the opportunity to make your ascension or to remain on earth, staying longer to balance a greater quantity and to be of more service.

You make your decision in consultation with your Christ Self. Most chelas who have no reason particularly to take their ascension, if they are not mature in years, will remain to balance a greater percentage of karma and therefore focus a greater manifestation of attainment as an example to others on the Path.

Those who ascend without all of their karma balanced must remain in the ascended state with earth's evolution. They are not free to go off in service elsewhere in cosmos. Their karma ties them to the system of worlds where they made that karma, and they must work it out from the ascended state by helping chelas on the Path and by working through them.

Balancing the Remaining 49 Percent from the Ascended State

The more karma you balance, you might think, the easier the Path would be. But this is not true. The ascended masters changed the dispensation from 100 percent to 51 percent as the requirement for the ascension in this age—at the conclusion of the Piscean dispensation and the dawn of Aquarius—so that more souls could take advantage of this liberation. This does not mean that the remaining 49 percent is not balanced; it means that the remaining percentage must be balanced from the state of being an ascended master.

I have learned that the reason that 51 percent is the turning point is that the second half of karma is much, much more difficult to balance than the first half and requires much more intense initiations. And it is these initiations that we're going to discuss, because I believe (as the masters believe, and they have an accurate record to look at) that many students of the masters have what it takes to balance more than 51 percent of their karma, and they are on their way to doing this.

They may not have balanced 51 percent yet, but many have youth, energy and tremendous devotion. Given the constancy, the staying power they have shown over a year or two or five or ten years, projecting that on the graph of a lifetime, all other factors being equal, it would be determined that many would have balanced more than 51 percent by the time they had lived out a normal life-span.

The First 25 Percent—Clearing Records

As we work through our percentages of karma, we see, therefore, that with the first 25 percent, we are mainly involved in clearing records—records of past embodiments that are recorded in the etheric body, the fire body, the first quadrant. We don't seem to notice much self-mastery on the surface of being because our giving calls to the violet flame, our clearing action with Astrea is taking place at very deep subconscious levels. And so we go on in faith, we walk in the teachings, we apply the teachings, and we are really going through embodiments that go back several hundred thousand years. This is the etheric memory.

It becomes a more active pursuit of the Law when we have balanced 25 percent and we come into the area of the mental body where, in order to balance this karma, we need to have an active knowledge of the Law, a dedication to the Christ, the hierarch of this quadrant, and a mastery of the mind that is the mind of God. This balancing of karma goes round and round in cycles, in spirals. It doesn't mean that we're just sitting in these quadrants, but it means that they are the base of transmutation.

Most people are not really energetic enough to even enter the Path unless they are approaching 25 percent of their karma balanced: they're not even interested in the Path because they're so weighted down with density it's impossible to perceive even that the Path exists. If you are interested in this subject, you probably should assume that if you're not nearing the completion of the first quadrant, you have completed it and you are in the mental quadrant. This is why you are reading this book. You are so hungry for the Law because your karma demands that you know the Law in order to tackle the next levels of energy.

Animal Magnetism

Magnetism is what binds us to the earth—to the earth plane. Magnetism can be equated with desire. It is the transmutation of every desire that frees us from bondage to the earth and from the round and the wheel of rebirth.

The masters teach us that in addition to being free from desire, we must transmute the cause and core of that desire in the four lower bodies. This desire manifests as the magnetism that is animal-like, in that it is carnal. The masters call it *animal magnetism.* You could just as easily call it carnal magnetism. It's a magnetism that creates the allure and the illusion of *maya* in each of the four lower bodies.

In the etheric body, it is a malicious magnetism, including black magic and witchcraft. It is the willful malice of hatred, of condemnation. It takes a conscious foreknowledge for it to manifest. When we consciously think evil and project evil, we are engaged in this and we are perverting that quadrant.

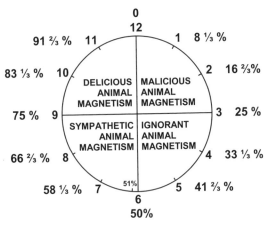

Figure 36 Four Types of Animal Magnetism

Then there is the ignorant form of magnetism that is a total perversion of the mind of Christ that comes with the abuses of the three hierarchies in the mental body.

In the third quadrant, it is a sympathetic magnetism—very sympathetic and very much putting on, swimming in the sea of human emotion and being totally dominated by others' emotions and by our own emotions. It's a very heavy magnetism that includes the magnetism of the family when the family is not based on Christ relationships.

In the physical quadrant, this substance is named as delicious magnetism. It is the magnetism of the senses, of sensuality and of experiencing in the physical body the aspects of the flesh, indulgences in the flesh that keep us from our spiritual reunion.

For the purposes of charting the cycles of our karma, let us assume that each 25 percent of our karma is going to deal directly with one of these four types of magnetism. Again, you can assume that you are moving from the malicious to the ignorant, the first side of the clock, which is the Alpha thrust, and from the sympathetic to the delicious on the second, which is the Omega return.

The Thirty-Six-Turn Spiral: Initiations for the Mastery of the Seven Rays

One of the ways in which we can chart the path of life is as a thirty-six-turn spiral (fig. 37). Evolution starts in the very center, the point of origin—the white-fire core of Alpha and Omega. We come out from the core and begin at the twelve o'clock line in the hierarchy of Capricorn.

Each turn of this spiral can be interpreted as greater or lesser periods in time and space. We can think of each turn as a year, and when we do so, we can see the first seven years of our life (marked at the first dot), the second seven years, the third seven years and the fourth seven years brings us to the age of twenty-eight.

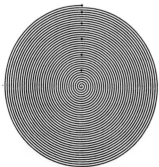

Figure 37 The Thirty-Six-Turn Spiral

The first seven years we are mastering the etheric—the blueprint is being brought forth in the physical plane. The maximum growth and potential of the individual comes forth from the point of conception to the seventh birthday. At that point the blueprint is anchored and the maximum realization of the etheric memory is manifest.

The second seven years sees the development of the mind. From seven to fourteen, the mind is absorbing the maximum potential of the mental quadrant.

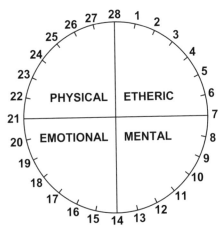

Figure 38 The Mastery of the Four Lower Bodies through the Seven-Year Cycles

From fourteen to twenty-one—the emotional quadrant—there is the mastering of desires, the feelings, the water energies. This period of adolescence to maturity is often a rocky period, as we all know, and the reason is the mastery of the astral plane of the self and of the planet and also the beginning of the descent of individual karma.

The fourth set of seven years, from age twenty-one to twenty-eight, is the mastery of the physical—completing the education, settling down, having a family, having a home, having a profession. This is the culmination of the mastery of the first round of the cycles of seven through the cosmic clock.

Initiations for the Mastery of the Five Secret Rays, the Christ and the Buddha

At the point of age twenty-eight, when things are somewhat now at a level of being settled, there comes a period of going within. It's time for inner mastery in the five secret rays, and that brings us five turns of this wheel to age thirty-three. These years are for the initiations of Christhood that Jesus demonstrated.

From age thirty-three to thirty-six are the initiations of the Buddha. Gautama attained enlightenment at age thirty-six—his consciousness, then, the three times twelve in the Buddhic light, three cycles through the cosmic clock. At that point of thirty-six we start all over again, and if we're lucky, we have another set of opportunity that would bring us to age seventy-two.

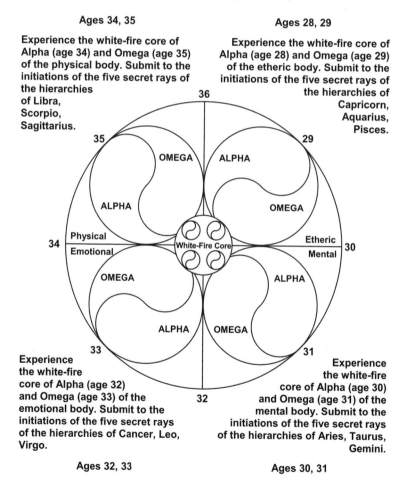

Ages 34, 35

Experience the white-fire core of Alpha (age 34) and Omega (age 35) of the physical body. Submit to the initiations of the five secret rays of the hierarchies of Libra, Scorpio, Sagittarius.

Ages 28, 29

Experience the white-fire core of Alpha (age 28) and Omega (age 29) of the etheric body. Submit to the initiations of the five secret rays of the hierarchies of Capricorn, Aquarius, Pisces.

Experience the white-fire core of Alpha (age 32) and Omega (age 33) of the emotional body. Submit to the initiations of the five secret rays of the hierarchies of Cancer, Leo, Virgo.

Ages 32, 33

Experience the white-fire core of Alpha (age 30) and Omega (age 31) of the mental body. Submit to the initiations of the five secret rays of the hierarchies of Aries, Taurus, Gemini.

Ages 30, 31

Figure 39 Initiations for Reaching the Attainment of the Buddha by Age 36

Many people do not reach that age; and therefore, at whatever point their karma demands on these cycles, at whatever point their karma becomes heavier than their ability to sustain the threefold flame, they may be removed from the screen of life—either quite suddenly or through a prolonged or contracted illness.

The Challenges of the Quadrants

As these spirals unwind, we are going through all of the four lower bodies, and the balancing of karma is really in all of these bodies simultaneously. But when we draw the karmic clock and show four quadrants, we show this so you can see how it adds up; and as it is added, it goes through the four quadrants.

What impressed me, when I began studying the karmic clock and the demands I made on the cosmos, were God's answers to the question, What are the challenges of each quadrant?

If I'm going to balance my karma and if the chelas of the ascended masters are going to balance their karma, they must know the challenges of each of the quarters of the clock. If we know the challenges, we can summon our forces to meet those challenges.

The Etheric Quadrant: 0–25 Percent

So we look at the etheric quadrant. What are the challenges of balancing the first 25 percent of karma? If we have already balanced this karma, then we are in a position to teach others how to balance it; and even if we've balanced it ignorant of this knowledge, this knowledge will help others.

The challenge is first to balance 25 percent of your karma, which means that 25 percent of all energy given to you in all of your embodiments has either been constructively qualified or transmuted through the sacred fire. Much of your energy is in your causal body. That doesn't count; it's already there. We're talking about the energy that is left in Matter in the subconscious and the conscious levels of being.

To balance it means that it must be passed through the sacred fire, through the violet flame, by our invocation to the Trinity or the representatives thereof in the cosmic hierarchy, or we must balance it in service. Day by day in service to life, that karma, that energy, is being balanced. One of the two must be manifest. The best manifestation is the two in combination—using the violet flame and serving the Brotherhood wholeheartedly and simply serving people anywhere and everywhere that there is a need.

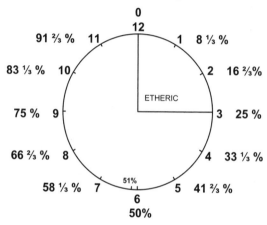

Figure 40 Challenges of the First Quarter
of the Karmic Clock and of the Etheric Plane
Balance 25% Karma—Master Etheric Plane

The second requirement, the second challenge: master the etheric plane, master the memory body, master the fire element, master the lessons taught by the hierarchies of Capricorn, Aquarius and Pisces. You can pretty well determine whether or not you have that mastery by seeing how you feel and how you act when either the sun or the moon are in those signs. If you are steady in maintaining a flow of joy as power, love and mastery, you may have a good mastery of those three. If you do not, you know what you have to work on: criticism, condemnation and judgment, hatred and mild dislike, fear, doubt, human questioning and records of death. Those are the tests of the first quadrant.

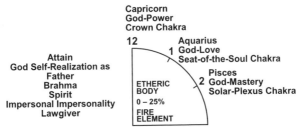

Figure 41 The Mastery of the Etheric Quadrant

The next challenge is to anchor the flames of God-power, God-love, God-mastery in the quadrant that is governed by God the Father—in the fire element, the etheric body and in three chakras: the crown chakra for the twelve o'clock line, the seat-of-the-soul chakra for the one o'clock line and the solar plexus at the two o'clock line.

Next challenge: attain God Self-realization as Father. Have an identity within yourself—the identity of wholeness as Father, as Brahma, as Spirit, as the Impersonal Impersonality and as the Lawgiver. Transmute the misqualified energies on these three lines of the clock: criticism, condemnation and judgment, all black magic; hatred and mild dislike, witchcraft; doubt, fear, human questioning and records of death. Stand, face and conquer the personification of evil, or the energy veil, as that which is anti-God that manifests as the dragon or the beast or as malicious animal magnetism. Overcome the misuses of the crown chakra, the seat-of-the-soul chakra and the solar-plexus chakra in the Father quadrant.

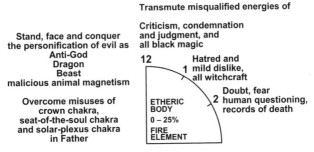

Figure 42 Negative Momentums to Be Overcome in the Etheric Quadrant

Now, you will not do this 100 percent until you have balanced 100 percent of your karma, because all balancing is really going through all of the quadrants. But you must have at least 25 percent mastery to go on; and you will be going on and you will be coming back, because in every cycle you will touch on all of these points.

The final challenge of this quadrant is to master the fire element (because it is a fire quadrant) and the etheric plane through the balance of the Trinity—the blue, the pink, the yellow in the trines that touch this quadrant.

The Trines of the Etheric-Quadrant Signs

When you are dealing with the initiations of each sign of this quadrant, you also have corresponding initiations on the trines. The first trine that touches this quadrant is the earth trine, because the first sign, Capricorn, is an earth sign. You can't master Capricorn without mastering Taurus and Virgo. They are the three earth signs, they are integrated, they function together. So to get to the core of every etheric record under Capricorn, you have to be mastering Taurus and Virgo too. Capricorn is the blue earth sign, Taurus is the pink earth sign, and Virgo is the yellow earth sign (fig. 15, page 52).

These challenges and what is required may make you think that you are going to become a cosmic juggler. And it is true, because each one of the challenges is another sphere of energy that you are balancing, and pretty soon you have nine or ten of these spheres that you are balancing all simultaneously as you are watching, day by day, your cycles unfold.

The second trine that you are concerned with is the one that includes the hierarchy of Aquarius on the one o'clock line, which is Aquarius, Gemini and Libra—the air signs. So this trine relates to the mental quadrant.

Pisces on the two o'clock line is a water sign, so it will connect you with the hierarchies of Cancer and Scorpio, which must be manifested simultaneously. This is the pink trine, and it relates to the feeling body.

That concludes the first quadrant with its challenges. They are not really that complicated once you become familiar with them and once you are familiar with the clock.

The Mental Quadrant: 25–50 Percent

The second quarter of the karmic clock is the mental plane. What challenges do we face when we encounter the karma that represents the misuse of the mind of Christ? First of all, we are building on the previous quadrant, so that of itself is a prerequisite.

The challenge of this quadrant is to balance 50 percent of our karma and to master the mental plane. That's quite a big order when you think of all of the misuses of the mind that we have on earth and all the philosophies and the theories and the education that we go through, only to find out that it is not the true teaching of the Christ or the Great White Brotherhood.

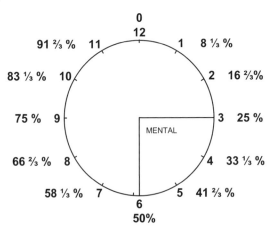

Figure 43 Challenges of the Second Quarter
of the Karmic Clock and of the Mental Plane
Balance 50% of Karma—Master Mental Plane

The three o'clock line is the line on which Lucifer fell.[8] He fell on the line of pride, but pride has many forms. People don't quite understand what is pride, and they don't feel that they have pride.

But people have a need and a desire for recognition by their peers, human recognition, the desire to be recognized for what and who they think they are and for what they are accomplishing.

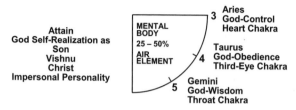

Figure 44 The Mastery of the Mental Quadrant

On this line we are required to overcome these perversions of Lucifer. And we do so by anchoring the flames of God-control under Aries, God-obedience under Taurus and God-wisdom under Gemini. We anchor these flames in the Christ, or the Son, in the air element, in the mental body and in the chakras. The heart chakra is on the three o'clock line, the third eye on the four, and the throat chakra on the five. Heart, throat, third eye—these key chakras associated with the mental body must be mastered.

We must attain God Self-realization as the Son; we must become sons and daughters of God; we must become Christed Ones. By the time you've balanced 51 percent of your karma, you are showing forth a great radiance of the Christ, which is recognizable by others. This is the manifestation of Vishnu, the Impersonal Personality.

On the four o'clock line, you have balanced approximately 33 percent of your karma; on the five o'clock line, approximately 42 percent. Now if you are aware that you are dealing excessively with a certain type of human creation, it enables you by the process of induction to see where you are on the karmic clock. If you are constantly bumping into a problem of ego and the transmutation of the ego, your karma may be moving from 25 percent to 33 percent. If you're in a heavy area of coming to grips with individual and planetary rebellion, you may be working on the four o'clock line at the 33 percent. It may not always hold true, but it is a good index.

When Jesus said, "Verily, verily, I say unto you, Except ye eat the flesh of the Son of man, and drink his blood, ye have no life in you,"[9] he was referring to the need in his followers for wholeness—wholeness as a focus of the Father-Mother God, as the basis for this transmutation. To be a disciple, to conquer in this plane, you need a firm understanding of yourself as Christ. And to have and be the Christ, you need to know who Father and Mother are, because Father and Mother give birth to the Christ. Many of Jesus' followers who heard his words left him because they did not have this understanding.[10]

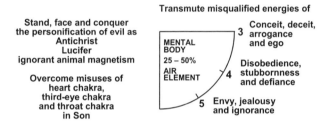

Figure 45 Negative Momentums to Be Overcome in the Mental Quadrant

In this quadrant, you must stand, face and conquer the personification of evil as Antichrist, as Lucifer, as ignorant animal magnetism. You must transmute misqualified energies of conceit, deceit, arrogance and ego; disobedience, stubbornness and defiance of the Law; envy, jealousy and ignorance of the Law. You have to overcome the perversions of the Son: the carnal mind, intellectual pride, ambition and competition, and the failure to surrender the ego. Then you overcome the misuses of the heart chakra, the third-eye chakra and the throat chakra in the quadrant of the Son.

This quadrant demands that you master on the three o'clock line the fire trine under the fire signs of Aries, Leo and Sagittarius; on the four o'clock line the earth signs again of Taurus, Virgo and Capricorn; and on the five o'clock line the air signs of Gemini, Libra and Aquarius. You can see that whatever mastery you attain, it holds you in good stead for the next point of initiation. What you have already won in the etheric plane will assist you in the mental plane. Attainment is cumulative.

The Emotional Quadrant: 50–75 Percent

Now we come to the challenges of the third quarter of the karmic clock and of the astral plane. This is where we begin the very steep upward climb; this is where all of the mastery that has gone before on the seven rays is brought to bear on the extreme testing of the soul in the astral plane and on the five secret rays.

This quadrant is the pink energy of love. It is water. It presents the greatest challenge of all. If you master this, it's downhill in the physical quadrant from 75 to 100.

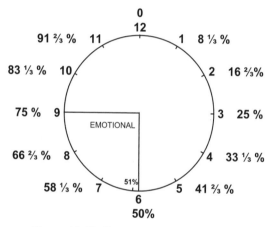

Figure 46 Challenges of the Third Quarter
of the Karmic Clock and of the Astral Plane
Balance 75% Karma—Master Astral Plane

This is the crux and the most difficult test, and the masters have found that sometimes when people don't take their ascension at 51 percent, in the following years they make more karma and they lose the 51 percent of balanced karma that they had already achieved. There is great danger in this, and it is always a possibility. Having balanced the first half does not mean that you can't retrograde and go back and then fall beneath the requirement for the ascension. So holding one's own and maintaining one's attainment is as big a challenge as getting there in the first place.

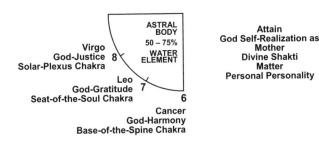

Figure 47 The Mastery of the Emotional Quadrant

In this quadrant you must balance 75 percent of your karma and master the astral plane. This is the time when you attain God Self-realization as Mother. Here you become the Mother.

Every experience under these three hierarchies—six, seven and eight: Cancer, Leo and Virgo—is an experience in becoming Mother. You become the Divine Shakti, the point for the release of the energy of the masculine principle of the Godhead. You are in polarity to Father; you are opposite the twelve o'clock line. You are going to have to master the base-of-the-spine chakra of the Mother and all of the energies of purity in that chakra. You're going to anchor the flames of God-harmony, God-gratitude and God-justice.

In this quadrant you move from the tests of the seven rays, which go from the twelve to the six o'clock line, and you begin the test of the five secret rays, which are on the seven, eight, nine, ten and eleven o'clock lines. The secret rays are the Buddhic initiations. Here you must prove in the white-fire core of the secret rays of Alpha and Omega what you have demonstrated on the circumference of life on the seven rays.

The chakras of this quadrant are the base-of-the-spine chakra on the six under the hierarchy of Cancer; the seat of the soul that you first were working on in Aquarius, you are now mastering in Leo; and the solar plexus that you began in Pisces, you are now mastering in Virgo.

On the six o'clock line, you are required to transmute the misqualified energies of indecision, self-pity and self-justification. You may be a very decisive person ordinarily, but when you bump into this quadrant and the tests of the hierarchy of Cancer, you suddenly find that you can't make up your mind about a thing. It doesn't matter which way you go; it could be equally possible either way. You can see all sides of the question, and a decision is almost the last thing you want to be involved with! This brings on extreme self-pity for your plight and then self-justification because you didn't make the decision.

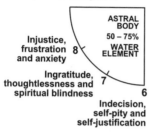

Transmute misqualified energies of

Injustice, frustration and anxiety 8

ASTRAL BODY
50 – 75%
WATER ELEMENT

Ingratitude, thoughtlessness and spiritual blindness 7

6

Indecision, self-pity and self-justification

Stand, face and conquer
the personification of evil as
Anti-Mother
Anti-Matter
Great Whore
sympathetic animal magnetism

Overcome misuses of
base-of-the-spine chakra,
seat-of-the-soul chakra
and solar-plexus chakra
in Mother

Figure 48 Negative Momentums to Be Overcome
in the Emotional Quadrant

On the seven o'clock line, there is ingratitude that comes through the failure to appreciate God in the seat-of-the-soul chakra, that comes on as thoughtlessness and spiritual blindness and carelessness. It's a very dense kind of consciousness, like the bull in the china shop. On the eight o'clock line of Virgo, we transmute injustice, frustration and anxiety.

In this quadrant we stand, face, and conquer the personification of evil as anti-Mother, or anti-Matter—all of the misuses of the plane of Matter, the ecology of the four quadrants, the Great Whore and the sympathetic animal magnetism. We have to overcome the perversion of Mother as the cow consciousness—possessive, sympathetic, overbearing. We need to overcome the misuses of the base-of-the-spine, the seat-of-the-soul and the solar-plexus chakras.

If that is not enough, we have the challenge of dealing with the entire collective unconscious of the race of mankind and what they have polluted the astral plane with. And the astral plane is in various stages—it moves from purgatory to what is known as hell. We're not going to consume that entire plane, but we're going to be able to live in the midst of it without being moved by it.

The first trine we deal with in this quadrant is on the six o'clock line, again the water signs of Cancer, Scorpio, Pisces; on the seven o'clock line will be the fire signs of Leo, Sagittarius, Aries; on the eight o'clock line will be the earth signs of Virgo, Capricorn, Taurus.

The Physical Quadrant: 75–100 Percent

The fourth quarter of the karmic clock is the physical plane. The challenge is to balance 100 percent of your karma and master the physical plane.

In this quadrant you should be manifesting several if not all of the nine gifts of the Holy Spirit: the word of wisdom, the word of knowledge, faith, the gifts of healing, the working of miracles, prophecy, discerning of spirits, divers kinds of tongues and the interpretation of tongues.[11] You should be well on your way as a chela of the Master Alchemist—alchemy as precipitation, doing the works of Jesus, the works of Gautama.

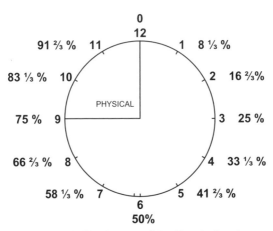

Figure 49 Challenges of the Fourth Quarter
of the Karmic Clock and the Physical Plane
Balance 100% Karma—Master Physical Plane

In the physical quadrant all of the mastery of the preceding three comes home. You have earned it, you have the right to manifest it. Your cycles move from the etheric, to the mental, to the emotional, and you stand in the physical with Jesus, master of time and space, receiving the all-power of heaven and earth,[12] because you are approximating wholeness.

Here you attain God Self-realization in and as the Holy Spirit—Shiva, the Destroyer, the Personal Impersonality. Here you anchor the flames of God-reality in Libra, God-vision in Scorpio, God-victory in Sagittarius—in the Holy Spirit, in the earth element, the physical body.

The heart chakra is on the nine o'clock line opposite the three, where you began its mastery; the third eye on the ten opposite the four, where you began its mastery; and the throat chakra on the eleven opposite the five, where you began its mastery.

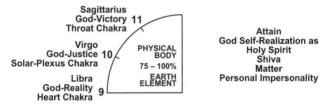

Figure 50 The Mastery of the Physical Quadrant

In this quadrant you must stand, face and conquer the personification of evil as what we call *anti-Spirit*—that which is *anti* (against) the Holy Spirit. The Holy Spirit occupies space; and therefore, all that is not hallowed in your space is anti-Spirit. It comes forth through the False Prophet, the false teachers, the false hierarchy. There is a very real false hierarchy abiding in the astral plane. To be the master of the astral and the physical, you need to be aware of its teachings and how to overcome them, how to resist them.[13]

The physical quadrant is where you stand, face and conquer delicious animal magnetism—you are no longer a slave to your physical body, to its demands, its preoccupations. You overcome the misuses of the heart, the third eye and the throat in the third, fourth and fifth secret rays. And you transmute the misqualified energies of dishonesty, intrigue and treachery; lust, greed, selfishness, self-love and idolatry; and resentment, revenge and retaliation.

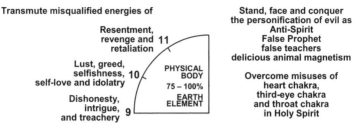

Figure 51 Negative Momentums to Be Overcome
in the Physical Quadrant

The trines that are affected in this quadrant are the air signs on the nine o'clock line—Libra, Aquarius, Gemini; the water signs on the ten o'clock—Scorpio, Pisces, Cancer; and the fire signs on the eleven o'clock—Sagittarius, Aries, Leo. And thus you manifest the balance of the Trinity in this quadrant.

51 Percent—The Turning Point

As I mentioned, the great difficulties presented in the astral plane necessitate that 51 percent be the turning point. This takes us just past the six o'clock line, just into the Mother, just turning the balance from Alpha to Omega. It is quite a tremendous changing of gears when you move from 50 to 51 percent. It can be a time of great upheaval in your life. The ascended lady master Portia has said:

> As you come to the place where you are balancing greater quantities of karma, personal and planetary, you come to the supreme testing of the avatars where your assignment, after having balanced 51 percent of your karma, is to then begin to work away at the transmutation of the entire astral plane as well as your own astral body.

This reminds us of the story from India of the mother squirrel who takes on the ocean because the ocean has swallowed up her young. And she goes to the ocean and beats the ocean with her tail, and drop by drop she takes the ocean and puts it on the land.

That is the determination of the Mother to overcome the astral plane. Portia continues:

> The reason that the Lords of Karma gave the dispen-
> sation for the ascension of souls after the balance of 51
> percent is because the next 24 percent is entirely the
> descent into the astral plane.... So many among mankind
> who were pursuing the Path, when they came to that level
> of transmutation, fell back and lost even the 51 percent
> that they had gained, so treacherous is the walk in the
> labyrinth of the astral plane.[14]

The Dark Night of the Soul
and the Dark Night of the Spirit

Once you start penetrating the astral body, you really get into the darkness of the dark night. Saint John of the Cross wrote of the dark night of the soul and the dark night of the Spirit, and this quadrant of the clock is where these tests occur.

Sometimes I receive letters from chelas on the Path who are going through great difficulty, and they describe it as the dark night of the soul. I do not question their analysis of their own experience, but I might say that while there may be little portions of these dark nights that come to prepare you for the intensity of the experience, the fullness of these two dark nights is not upon you until you have balanced 51 percent of your karma.

The test of the dark night of the soul is to be cut off from the light of God and the masters and the ministering angels. The "darkness that covers the land" is the weight of each individual's own returning karma as he is also learning to come to grips with world karma. Both types of karma eclipse for certain cycles the light of the soul and therefore its discipleship under the Son of God. Before God can infuse the soul with great power, the individual must also be bereft of pride. The testing of the dark night may endure for several hours, several days, several embodiments—according to the acceleration or the deceleration of cycles. The dark night of the soul is experienced by more chelas than is the dark night of the Spirit.

The dark night of the Spirit occurs concurrently with the crucifixion. This dark night is an inflow of such great light as to make one feel completely unclean and wretched and unworthy of that very light. It seems that God is against you and that God has rejected you. So much impurity is beheld in this great light that the soul feels it will never be worthy of blessings again. Saint John of the Cross wrote: "The soul must first be set in emptiness and poverty of spirit and purged of every natural support, consolation, and apprehension, earthly and heavenly. Thus empty, it is truly poor in spirit and stripped of the old man, and thereby able to live that new and blessed life which is the state of union with God, attained by means of this night."[15]

In the dark night of the Spirit, the light of the I AM Presence is eclipsed by planetary karma as well as Christic initiation. Jesus met this test in the ninth hour when he cried out in a loud voice, "Eloi, Eloi, lama sabachthani?... My God, my God, why hast thou forsaken me?"[16] That experience is to be totally cut off from the God Presence and the Christ Self and to sustain your own momentum solely by the light and attainment you have anchored in the heart chakra and your other chakras through the balance of your karma.

Entering the astral plane is like crawling through the sewer of the planet. The only thing that you have to light your way is the flame in your heart and the karma that you have balanced. This flame represents the Brotherhood, the teaching and everything that you have garnered from the Path. This is enough to get you through this heaviest aspect of your karma, if you rely on it. If you are swallowed up with doubts, you may sink beneath the waves of the emotional body, as Peter did.[17]

As we enter this quadrant, we find that the wholeness of Alpha and Omega within us has been replaced at subconscious levels by false images of Father and Mother. These false images we have inherited through our heredity, through our ancestral lineage, and this residue lies within the subconscious. In this quadrant, because we are entering the initiations of the five secret rays, we come face to face with the perversions of Alpha and Omega, represented in the whirling energy of the T'ai Chi.

Two Mackerels in the Subconscious

The T'ai Chi (page 30) is spoken of as the two fishes following each other—each fish has an eye and a tail. The fish is also the symbol of the Piscean dispensation. This symbol is drawn as two arcs, with the crossing of the arcs forming the tail. And each one of the arcs of energy is half of the caduceus, the intertwining of the energies of the Father and the Mother.

As I have actually examined the subconscious of chelas and of the race of mankind, I have seen in the subconscious the focal

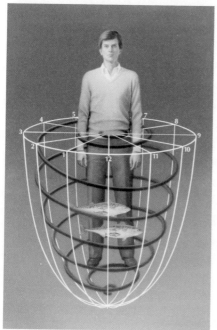

point for the perverted Father and the perverted Mother in the form of two mackerels—believe it or not. You never know what you're going to bring up out of that subconscious!

The mackerels symbolize the misuse of the caduceus, the misuse of Pisces, the misuse of the Christ consciousness. It is accepting our origin in human parents.

And so we seem to have two undigested mackerels within the subconscious. What do we do with them? There they are, sitting in the electronic belt.

Figure 52 Two Mackerels in the Subconscious Symbolize the Perverted Father and Mother

Well, you know that you have to pass the violet flame through them. But it takes more than this. You have to undo the concept; you have to undo the core of what has created this. You can give the violet flame all day, but until you surrender your mackerels, you don't get rid of them! And so you have to know that they are there.

Human Lineage, Human Ancestry, Human Karma

We have to get rid of our sense of a human lineage. Those beings who were truly free are described in the Old Testament, like Melchizedek: "Without father, without mother, without descent, having neither beginning of days, nor end of life."[18] That's a very important key to the mastery of this quadrant. What it means is that Melchizedek had overcome the concept of a human lineage and a human ancestry. By transmuting it, he could no longer be the inheritor of the human karma of his parents, his grandparents, and so forth.

Now you find what's worse is that there are mackerels within mackerels! You have grandparents on either side. One mackerel represents your mother, one represents your father. Then you have your mother's parents and your father's parents, and you are the inheritor of their human creation and their human patterns that you are outpicturing through your genes and chromosomes. And so there are other tiny little mackerels within those mackerels, because each of those grandparents had parents.

What we need to do is to assimilate our awareness of the Self as God the Father and God the Mother. As we assimilate the qualities and the virtues of Alpha and Omega—and that includes the whole clock, the two halves of the whole, the T'ai Chi, Spirit and Matter—we become our own Father and Mother. When we become our own Father and Mother—because we are Father, we are Mother, Father-Mother God in manifestation—we are able to then pass through the digestive tract of the subconscious, the unwanted elements of the unreal aspects of father and mother that we have inherited.

Our parents may have also had a good realization of the Self as Father-Mother God, and this they also passed on to us as virtue. This awareness is locked in the causal body, and all we ever see in the electronic belt is the negative programming. So you could assume that you have inherited a tremendous good from your parents as they set the example of love and obedience and wisdom and good training and proper morals and an understanding of religion and obedience and honor, and so forth.

But when we start to examine our relationship with our parents, we also find that there is a push-pull action of karmic substance such as rebellion, resentment, even hatred, dislike, irritation, a sense of injustice, egos vying with one another. All of this that is not so nice in our relationship with parents (and as our parents had not-so-nice relationships with their parents) is what coalesces as these mackerels within mackerels—as the human lineage, the human hereditary patterns.

So we stand in the violet flame. It looks like we are completely surrounded by our sense of human family. And in real life, is this not so? We are sometimes so dominated by the family that we cannot cut ourselves free to balance our karma. Invoking the violet flame, we find that we can eat away, little by little, the substance of this generation.

The Ancestral Tree

We find that the mackerels produce by their manifestation what is called the *ancestral tree*. As we invoke the violet flame, the violet flame tackles simultaneously this ancestral tree and the mackerels—the consciousness of lineage from which it came forth.

This tree is very complex. It has layers and layers, and its roots go through and around the planet. These are karmic ties; all of those roots are our ties to every other lifestream. The Hindus say that we have been everybody's mother, everybody's father, sister and brother, and so on—we've had so many incarnations that we're all related. Buddha said in the very numerous and varied life-spans of each man, every other being has at one time or another been dear to him.

Figure 53 Violet Flame and Blue Lightning Can Dissolve
the Human Lineage of the Ancestral Tree

We need to invoke the violet flame and the action of blue lightning, tackling the human lineage and the tree. As long as there is an ancestral tree, there will be the mackerels. As long as there are mackerels, there will be the tree. The violet flame—our salvation, our hope, our life, the action of the Holy Spirit. Lo and behold, we're getting rid of the sense of lineage! As we're taking bites out of the human concept of parents, that energy is transmuted. It ascends to the causal body, and we're coming into a greater and greater awareness of the Self as Father and Mother.

What we discover when we have invoked the light of God to take down the ancestral tree and to transmute the mackerels within mackerels within mackerels is that all of this substance in our astral body, in our subconscious, has buried our true identity as the Father-Mother God. And down underneath, the roots of the tree have surrounded—and in their tightly gnarled manifestation not only surrounded but completely buried—a blue egg.

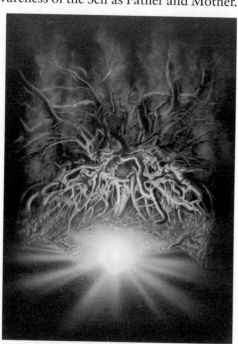

Figure 54 A Blue Cosmic Egg Is Revealed as the Ancestral Tree Is Transmuted

The Blue Cosmic Egg

It is a blue cosmic egg. That egg is our T'ai Chi in Matter; it is our Father-Mother God. Our real Father-Mother has been buried by our sense of the human lineage and by the karma of the ancestral tree. All the genes and chromosomes have prevented it from manifesting, and not until we have purified ourselves do we have this influence in life.

Once we have taken down the tree and slain the perversions, we then find a final action of the violet flame, removing the obstacle, liberates this egg, and the egg can rise. In the process of transmutation—the action of the violet flame—all of the atoms and molecules of energy have been going over the spiral for repolarization to our own Great Central Sun, the individual I AM Presence, the center of that Presence, the white-fire core (fig. 56).

So each time you invoke the violet flame and the blue lightning, the energy is broken down and cycles back to the Great Central Sun. These particles rise over the fiery coil, moving in a clockwise direction, going to the center of Being, and you are attaining greater light in your causal body. And as you know, this doesn't happen all at once, but it happens each time you use the violet-flame mantras and decrees.

Now that the egg is uncovered, the Angel of the Presence takes the egg and carries it—carries it now not to the ancestral tree, but to the Tree of Life.[19] The angel places the egg carefully in the Tree of Life, and it becomes the very center of your Tree of Life. And your Tree of Life and its branches represent your causal body, the Father-Mother God firmly placed in the center. Now you can bring this causal body into manifestation (fig. 55).

You see the "twelve manner of fruits"[20] of the Tree of Life manifesting as the jewels and the gems, the fruits of good works in the twelve spheres of the causal body.

We see, then, that beautiful blue egg focused above in the plane of the I AM Presence. We move to the center of our own higher consciousness forged and won in Matter because we've had the awareness to perceive the challenges of the quadrants, because we have known what needed to be transmuted.

Our Real Family Tree

What a great gift it is from Mother Mary and the Holy Spirit that we would know how to tackle the mackerels, how to tackle

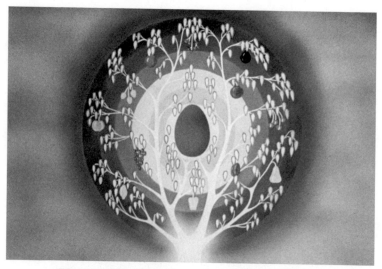

Figure 55 The Blue Cosmic Egg in the Causal Body
and the Twelve Manner of Fruits

the ancestral tree to get to this place of this glorious higher
consciousness!

Higher consciousness is not just a mist; it is a very specific
outlining of God. This tree is the real family tree. It is the family
of ascended masters, chelas on the Path and devotees. It is our
real family of the mystical body of God on earth and in heaven.

You Become the Tree of Life

The egg in the center of the Tree of Life is the white-fire core.
When you have that causal body, the birds of the air come to nest
in it.* These are the aspirations of mankind, pilgrims of the Path.
Millions of people can live out of the attainment in your causal
body, which you bring forth like the Buddha. You become a Tree
of Life to all mankind with this mastery.

Coming down the trunk of the Tree of Life, we are passing
over what we would call the "crystal cord" of the I AM Presence.

---

* "The kingdom of heaven is like to a grain of mustard seed, which a man
took, and sowed in his field: which indeed is the least of all seeds: but when
it is grown, it is the greatest among herbs, and becometh a tree, so that the
birds of the air come and lodge in the branches thereof." [Matt. 13:31–32]

Figure 56 Atoms and Molecules of Energy Return
to the White-Fire Core for Repolarization

And at the plane of the Christ, there is the same awareness of the Father-Mother God in the individual Christ Self, depicted as another cosmic blue egg (fig. 57).

As we come to the roots of the Tree of Life, they are like the *antahkarana,* or the pattern, the cosmic blueprint that is intended to manifest in the electronic belt. The manifestation of these roots of the Tree of Life rather than of the ancestral tree shows that you are totally nonattached to the human sense of ancestors, to the human sense of heredity.

You are free, yet profoundly grateful to the lineage of sons and daughters of God who have gone before you as father, as mother, to bear the seed and the egg, the genes and chromosomes of Alpha and Omega through which the genius of the Christ has been transmitted to you according to the descent of the Holy Spirit through your family from generation to generation.

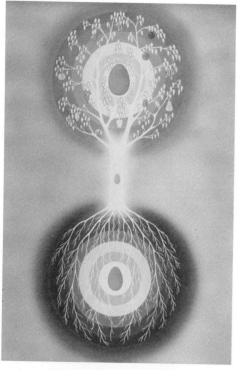

Figure 57 The Tree of Life
"In the midst of the street of it, and on either side of the river, was there the Tree of Life, which bare twelve manner of fruits, and yielded her fruit every month: and the leaves of the Tree were for the healing of the nations." (Rev. 22:2)

All of the veins of consciousness, going to the fiery core of the planet itself, draw forth the virtues, the entire momentum of God-mastery of the causal bodies of all who have ever overcome and attained Christ-mastery on earth. You are cut free from your origins in Matter, your origins in human creation, and you are taking your stand to be totally a son of God. You are totally separated out of the mass consciousness so that now within your subconscious, within your electronic belt where we saw the mackerels, now you have the focus of this cosmic blue egg of Father-Mother God.

Going through the process of identifying this substance and removing it is quite a surgery. It is quite a weaning process, especially when it is conscious. It might not always be conscious, because the violet flame may transmute it for you, but it is difficult to detach oneself from family because of the sympathetic ties.

It is the fine line between honor, compassion and the ties of the heart that can never be broken, and the sympathy, the domination and the possessiveness that must be broken if the soul is to one day take flight of its earthly moorings. Now you are in the class with Melchizedek—"without father, without mother, without descent, having neither beginning of days, nor end of life; but made like unto the Son of God; abideth a priest continually." You can see that with this point of attainment, with this balancing of your astral plane, what a servant of God you can be—a clear latticework of the Tree of Life on earth.

John saw the vision of our tree. He said: "And he shewed me a pure river of water of life, clear as crystal, proceeding out of the throne of God and of the Lamb."[21] This is what you have become, standing in the violet flame. This is the lower portion of self now become spheres of light. "In the midst of the street of it, and on either side of the river, was there the Tree of Life, which bare twelve manner of fruits, and yielded her fruit every month: and the leaves of the Tree were for the healing of the nations."[22]

Another Chart of Your Divine Self

This is another way, then, of depicting the Chart of Your Divine Self. The Trinity again—Father, Son and Holy Spirit—

perfect alignment. Now inside of you are the four quadrants of Matter: the Father-Mother God, the Christ, the Holy Spirit. You can see why I said the physical quadrant is downhill when you get this mastered, because you have all of that attainment.

This entire ritual of clearing the ancestral tree must be completed before you can balance 75 percent of your karma. You then take your full mastery into the physical plane, performing the altogether scientific experiments of Jesus, going through the initiations of the transfiguration, the crucifixion, the resurrection and the ascension.

Jesus went through this ritual of balancing nearly 100 percent of his karma even before his final incarnation, in which he revealed, by the transparency of his soul, the image of the Son of God. Yet he had to prove it again. He had to reconfirm his victory.

"Who is my mother? and who are my brethren? And he stretched forth his hand toward his disciples, and said, Behold my mother and my brethren! For whosoever shall do the will of my Father which is in heaven, the same is my brother, and sister, and mother."[23]

The Tree of Life

CHAPTER 11

Scorpio

The
Dividing
of the Way

The ascended lady master Leto works with seekers of all ages and especially with children and youth who desire to walk the spiritual path and engage in the service of mankind. As a scientist on Atlantis and later as a mystic in China, she devoted her energies to the precipitation of the flame of truth. She is a true scientist of the Spirit and teaches students how to consciously leave the body and reenter at will and also how to draw upon their experiences in the masters' retreats during the sleep of the physical body.

In this discourse, Leto gives a key that can help us make right choices at each point of our initiations on the cosmic clock.

CHAPTER 11

The Dividing of the Way
by the Ascended Lady Master Leto

Out of the depths of love, I, Leto, am called by Saint Germain to be here with you today, adorned by the light of the Cosmic Mother entering now your heart. I would abide there with Lord Gautama to instruct you in the principles of divine law, to impart to you out of the cosmic field of Omega that which comes from Lord Maitreya.

The teaching our Lord has already brought to you, beloved, has come as a sword, not only to set asunder light and darkness but even to separate brother from brother, as only the sword of Maitreya can show the seed of the wicked sitting side by side with the seed of Christ. Therefore, the teaching must be progressive. For in answer to the call of the judgment, so it is the cosmic teacher and the teaching that is the dividing of the way. Thus, my discourse to you today is entitled "The Dividing of the Way."

With each new dissertation from the Mystery School, you discover, beloved, that one is taken and another is left, one is summoned into the heart of the mountain, where disciples meet with the Lord, and the other is left to his own devices, still sowing and reaping in the field of world karma. Therefore, come to know, beloved, that the return of the Mystery School can only mean that the angel with the flaming sword keeping the way of the Tree of Life must stand and say unto those who are not worthy of the teacher or the teaching: "You shall not pass here! Who goes there? Let the thief and the robber be bound! And let the one whose own tree is full of fruits of righteousness, laden with ripe fruit, let *him* enter in."

I tell you, then, of the dividing of the way in consciousness. For when truth does appear as teacher and teaching of the Divine Mother, of Sanat Kumara, it does create a presence in one's life whereby one must continually choose between this thought and that, this course of action and another, this ideology and another that may be offered or may have been espoused for many centuries by the soul. The gait of a man, the posture, the swing of the arm and the tilt of the head all reveal the penchant of a lifestream for this or that form of error or truth, self-righteousness or the LORD's.

A Formula to Chart the Way

I would give to you, then, this day that which you might call a formula, even though we have said the path to the ascension may not be reduced to a formula. This formula, then, is not absolute but will provide a guide when you know not the way to go.

Beloved ones, when you come to the crossroads of life, to know the way to go, right or left or straight ahead, you must first determine where you are—who am I? Positioning, then, according to the directions of the compass makes more accurate than guesswork the choice at hand.

Without the stars to chart the way or the compass, man is adrift at sea, often subject to the very forces that he would eschew. Let it be realized, then, that if the choices may be made plain each step of the way and if each step of the way you know where you are in the grid of life, then, beloved, you may be true to your Highest Self and pass those initiations that do indeed require sometimes a greater sacrifice than anticipated. Indeed, one can make sacrifices that one anticipates, but often on the path of discipleship it is the unexpected that becomes the failed test.

I say, then, proceed with the science that I bear. Add to the knowledge of your personal cosmic clock a new way of realizing when you stand at the Y and why the Y is so important.

A Mystery of the Divine Mother Unveiled

Beloved ones, mysteries are mysteries until they are unveiled. I unveil one mystery of the Divine Mother from the heart of Maitreya today in order that you yourself might unveil the next. The mystery beyond my own must remain yours to unveil. It is the mystery of self, your self, and whither thou goest. For, beloved, though you may ask the way of teacher or mother or father, if the will be not harnessed to the Higher Self, then even if the way be known, it will be the way not taken.

Now let us see, when the choices are at hand, which is the best way to take and which ought to be the way not taken, though many of you have often taken the latter and rejected the former, not because of disposition or want of heart but surely only due to base ignorance.

I am your friend of light and your teacher serving on the second ray of illumination, the powerful light of the sixth ray. Thus, we two together and many may pursue this course. You may remember me as the instructor of your twin flames. This teaching, then, I promise you is given at inner levels to your beloved twin flame simultaneously as I speak to you....

Beloved, life may be for you an unending circle, but we hope not. For the circle must be a spiral that rises; otherwise, the circle can be nothing more than a treadmill and even a life of confusion. I am certain that you do not desire to see this lifetime be recorded as a perpetual merry-go-round. For many it is so and they pass from the screen of life with no regret whatsoever, even when they see that they have pursued merriment round and round and round. And so they have been almost as gamblers who say, "And where she stops nobody knows." What a pity to be an accident of fate. What a pity to derive from merriment the light that ought to be conserved for the thrust of the upward spiral.

Each day you build a spiral that mounts the spinal altar, beloved. And therefore, spiral upon spiral and tier upon tier, you are building a powerful magnet of identity. With consistency and constancy, then, you are building a pillar of selfhood. Now then, with this technique, watch how the spirals can be unerring.

Tests of the Water Trine

Look, then, now to the triangle in question. It is the trine of the signs of water converging in Cancer (see page 52). Isolate, then, this trine and contemplate it. Each point of the triangle is a V. As you stand facing each point, you can see that the tree of self addressing the V forms the Y. At each gate of these three solar hierarchies, man, woman and child may ask the question: "Why am I here? From whence have I come? And where am I going?"

The positioning at the point of the trine is always the Y. Standing, then, as you are this day of the entrance of the sun under the hierarchy of Cancer,* you are positioned at the point of the six o'clock line. The choice is yours to take the left-handed path or the right. This, then, is the formula—to choose the right-handed path of God-mastery under the hierarchy of Pisces or to choose the left-handed path under the hierarchy of Scorpio of the fallen self, of selfishness and self-love.

To go to the left, then, in Cancer will always be the initiation of Scorpio and the Scorpio line to indulge oneself in over-self-concern and in the squandering of light. The right-handed path, when you stand in the hierarchy of Cancer, will always be the choice for God-mastery over this selfish self.

Now, when you move to the position of Scorpio in this trine (whether it is in the solar year of your planet or of your birth chart), when you are passing through this sign, now you are

---

* This dictation was delivered June 22. The sun entered Cancer June 21.

positioned in Scorpio. The Y that will be the choice throughout that cycle of Scorpio, whether for a day, a month or a year, will be whether to take the left-handed path of fear and doubt and human questioning in Pisces or to take the right-handed path of God-harmony in Cancer.

The formula we unveil, then, is that on each line of the clock, the temptation that would thwart your victory on the right will be the misqualified energy of the trine that is formed from that sign on the left. For example, you are now standing on the two o'clock line of Pisces, perhaps in your birth year or in your month. You see the goal of Pisces. It is a fulcrum for attainment— attainment, then, to your right hand, of God-vision. It is your assignment from the base of God-mastery to attain God-vision. You look to the left. That which will deprive you of your victory, which may become a subtle choice for the left-handed path, will be the perversions of God-harmony on the six o'clock line, therefore the indulgence in self-pity, self-justification, indecision, chaos and confusion as the perversion of this line. Thus the left-handed perversion prevents the right-handed victory.

When you go the way of the downward spiral that leads and culminates in the misuse of the base chakra, you cannot also go the way of the right-handed path of God-vision of the raising of that sacred fire in the All-Seeing Eye of God. This is most graphic when you understand the turn in the road of life. When you make the choice on the road of life, it is not easy, and next to impossible, to regain one's position and reaffirm the other choice.

Lifetimes are linear. Mistakes made may be transmuted and transcended by new action, but few mistakes can be redone at the point where the mistake was made. For the cosmic cycles move on and the mighty circle of life is turning. While you are walking through the hierarchies of the sun and the stations of the cross, the cosmic clock is not static. It, too, is turning. And many clocks within your being and system and causal body are also turning. Thus, there is a vast astrology of the configuration and the conjoining of circles of light and forces.

Tests of the Earth Trine

Take, then, for instance, the great God-mastery that is required of you in this hour of the earth trine. Take the power of Gautama Buddha. Take the hierarchies of the Great Divine Director, of Godfre. Take the full power of the line of justice under Lord Lanto and many masters of light. This mastery in the earth, beloved, is being challenged in the face of the Dark Cycle of planetary karma. Mastery in the earth is wanting, hence the pollutions of the body, the mind, the elements and the soul.

When you arrive at the cycle of initiation under the hierarchy of Capricorn, as you initiate your birth year and the year of the planetary home, you have heretofore considered that your challenge is a challenge of God-power, and indeed it is. But in terms of the choice at the Y—the choice that is made by the advanced initiate to choose to become the Christ or to choose to embody the dweller-on-the-threshold—it is power already realized in many previous cycles that enables one to choose, then, the right-handed path of God-justice as opposed to the left-handed path of disobedience, stubbornness and defiance of the Law.

Thus, you see, many rings on the trunk of the Tree of Life, many rings of the causal body, then demand that each point of the clock now become the springboard of victory. With this God-power you must say to yourself: "Shall I become the fullness of Christ as the selfless servant of the light in all? And by that God-power, shall I go forth to champion the cause of divine and human justice? Or shall I choose, then, to take that power and exalt myself in the fallen sign of Taurus as a rebel against that Christhood?"

Thus we see that the choice of the Y can only come when one has attainment in the position where one is standing. For the attainment is the accumulation of light on each point of the clock. That attainment, then, becomes the choice, how to use the ripened fruit from the Tree of Life—whether to eat it up unto the glory of the ego, whether to break the bread of life or to share that fruit that others might partake of that Christhood.

Correspondingly, then, standing at the Y of Taurus, one may choose the right-handed path of God-power, exercising, then, obedience to cosmic law to align power as the will of God to the glory of God in every endeavor. That which will prevent this victory will be the downward spiral of the left-handed path, choosing the perversion under the hierarchy of Virgo. This, then, would mean indulgence in a sense of injustice.

Beloved ones, there are individuals on this planet, both on the Path and not, whom you might compare to a wound-up toy. All the day they never cease to speak of injustices to themselves and to others, to condemn their leaders for injustice. They are bound by a coil, even a snarl, of the misuse of this line of Virgo. Therefore they espouse every cause; and many times when they come to the heart of the cause, they reject both it and the leader as unjust.

Thus, the left-handed path may be the squandering of the light of divinity, even as it may be the launching of an aggressive attack against the light of the lightbearers who are God-victorious on the corresponding right-handed path, which in this case is the path of God-power under the Great Divine Director.

Tests of the Air Trine

This formula, then, is easy to understand. Whenever you come to a new line of the clock, draw the trine. Analyze the techniques and knowledge required for the mastery of the signs and chakras corresponding to those points.

Thus, in Aquarius, Libra and Gemini, you have the challenge of the air sign, the diamond-shining mind of God. Wherever you stand on this trine, you will always be in the challenge to master the air element—at one point, of course, in the fire body; at another, in the air body; at another, in the earth body.

Thus, the Y of Libra presents its choice to take the right-handed path under the hierarchy of Gemini of God-wisdom, defeating, then, not only the left-handed path of the fallen Aquarian of anti-love, mild dislike, criticism, all forms of antagonism toward the person embodying the Aquarian-age man or woman but also, beloved, the base forces of envy, jealousy and ignorance that would prevent the use of your momentum of God-wisdom for the victory of the right-handed path. Since you have made many choices in past ages, the victory of the right-handed path, then, in Gemini becomes a fulcrum of victory and over-turning of past wrong choices electing the left-handed path in either of the points of the trine.

The Trine Is a Trinity of Victory

The trine, as you know, is a trinity. It is a tremendous force—the equilateral triangle. The greatest power you have of God-victory in the trines is the balancing of the threefold flame under each of those signs. As you study the meaning of the chakras—in this case you find the seat of the soul, the heart chakra and the throat chakra—when you understand the combination of those chakras and how they must be harmonized and brought to the apex of the victory of the power of the three-times-three (three on each side of the threefold flame), you will then realize that out of each trine, there may be drawn lines of force that meet in the very center of your cosmic clock. As you come to the center, then, you are bringing the offering of your victory.

Thus you understand that the mystery teachings have por-trayed that at a certain point in life, the individual will come to the place of the Y. And he must choose in that place whether to glorify God or to glorify the lesser ego.

Now you will understand that this choice is indeed a succession of choices. There are rounds that you make around this cosmic clock year upon year and lifetime upon lifetime wherein, beloved, you are making smaller choices. These choices build spirals and momentums. The lesser choice to indulge in fear and doubt on the point of Pisces instead of the victory of light in Cancer, the hate and hate creation on the line of Aquarius instead of the God-wisdom of Gemini—those choices may be indulgences where you accumulate karma. Karma, then, accumulated becomes a dweller-on-the-threshold within the cosmic clock of the electronic belt. That dweller-on-the-threshold, then, will be a momentum to be overcome at the ultimate choice, when one is making the choice for Christhood, for God—or for the lesser self.

Anticipate Your Victory Each Month

Thus, it is wise to use the decree for the cosmic clock.* It is wise, beloved, to clear the lines of the clock when the cycles are open. You know that the cycle of the sun is opened each month as the sun sign changes. In this hour, all of the experiences under the hierarchy of Cancer on a planetary and personal scale are open to you for transmutation of the negative, for exaltation or multiplication of the positive. Therefore, you must make haste and understand that the work that is at hand and the opportunity to perform it is according to these cycles.

When you build monuments to your mighty I AM Presence of achievement, you will find them waiting for you in the hour when here below you need maximum reinforcement and cosmic strength for that victory. For as soon as you make the choice—for instance, facing the Y in Sagittarius—for the right-handed path under Leo, all of the forces of the electronic belt misused on the three o'clock line of Aries will come to the fore. And as these run rampant, so will be unleashed the misuses of light on the seven and the eleven.

In this diagram, you come to an understanding that there is a prize waiting for you at the end of each month's cycle. It is a prize of light and a point of attainment. As you begin a new sign of your year or month or of the solar sign of the earth, anticipate with joy your victory. Go forth with armour to descend into the bottomless pit of your own electronic belt, to slay the forces on that line, to pour pots of violet flame into those holes, to direct

---

* "Round the Clock Protection" decree (see page 143).

blue-lightning rays, also, for the dislodging of that substance, being not satisfied until you have implored Cyclopea intensely to expose that which can be released into the sacred fire.

Understand the Cycles of Your Day

Let us, then, fight this good fight of the victory in each twenty-four-hour cycle. Not to burden you, beloved, but to acquaint you with the intricacies of the mathematics of free will, I must tell you that in every hour, every minute, every twenty-four-hour cycle, you are making these choices on each line of the clock.

You can understand, then, the cycles of your day—when you have the greatest strength, when your energies are lowest, when you have mastery, and when you find it difficult to concentrate or you are not at your best. Then summon your knowledge. Bring all things to bear—the knowledge of health, re-creation of the four lower bodies, centering in the light. Allow yourself to have maximum reinforcement by the application of the science of being. The alchemy of the physical body is most necessary on this path of attainment. It is difficult to make right choices when you are undernourished, or malnourished, or without sufficient prana.

Therefore, observe yourself and give to yourself all that is necessary to greet the day as a victor and to greet every hour of the day, not to put the demands upon yourself or your family members or children when you know that that individual is at the weakest or lowest level of energy, but to support that hour or time, whether with devotion or prayer, rest or a change of activity. To press yourself and then to find that the energies are explosive and uncontrolled and to repeat this process daily is only to fall into the trap of making an unwanted and undesired decision for the left-handed path, one day to find, beloved, that the repetition of the cycle has created a monster of neglect that waits to deprive you of your victory in these choices.

See, then, how the power of the victory of one trine begets another. Sometimes the combined astrological charts of family members or guru and chela or husband and wife can produce a grand trine showing reinforcement, one with another, to meet the crucial tests of life. This is the sign that the cooperative venture— whether of a business or a community such as is yours to create —can be victorious, supported, then, by the combined strengths of the members.

In your causal bodies of light, the members of this community are intended to reinforce not alone four trines of light or five or ten, but 360 degrees of trines now formed and many in between unto infinity. A mandala is complete when the sufficiency of the presence of many lifestreams can combine a victory on these trines, therefore safeguarding and protecting right choice of the individual disciple each step of the way.

The Love of Christhood

I would speak to you, then, of the love of Christhood at each gate of the Holy City, at each door of initiation where Christ does knock and bid you allow him enter your heart. And having so allowed him, you may knock at the gate of that city and receive the Great Initiator.

Rejoicing, then, in the newness of God's consciousness in each of these signs and solar hierarchies, you value the attainment of Christhood far more than you would allow the giving in to the lesser self and lesser momentums. It is no longer desirable to slide down the chute of the old spirals of negativity, which does take place as easily as a child slides down his slide. But rather, the external things, the pulls and the pressures, the old arguments, the old habits of discord—these things are cast aside as outworn and useless. For the fire of the heart, the love of the heart who has found the living guru, who has found the Divine Mother in this sign of Cancer, forsakes all for the sake of mastery. This, then, is the choice in the hierarchy of Cancer.

Realize that if you lose your God-harmony at the Y, you have no energy to travel the right-handed path to God-mastery. The availability of the choice depends upon the solidity of the individual in the God-quality of the point of the Y that he is facing.

The Love for the Mother and Her Children

I say to you, then, that in this month, under the hierarchy of the Divine Mother Omega, place yourself firmly, securely in the seat of authority of the hierarchy of Cancer and the quality of God-harmony. Out of God-harmony choose the right-handed path of God-mastery and defeat the selfish self. This is the challenge of the month, beloved.

I bid you try, using all of the alchemical formulas of Saint Germain. I bid you tarry, then, in the sign and the house of the Divine Mother and to love and to be—being that Divine Mother or being her child or being her son or daughter. So love the Divine Mother in this month, beloved, that you do not stray into the discords that are generated by self-pity, the need to justify oneself, and every form of indecision that comes from the idling of the energies of the base chakra when that sacred fire is not raised. Indecision, then, begets chaos and confusion.

I pray that this community ... shall have in this hour a great victory of the fountain of light of the Mother. As each of you does keep that flame and thereby attain your God-mastery, you will see the defeat, not only in yourself and in the community but worldwide, of the nefarious forces who misuse, on the left-handed path, the line of Scorpio with the sting of death....

Thus, consider how great is your love for the Mother and her children. And greater love than this hath no disciple that he should lay down his life for the cause of the Woman and her seed. Those, then, who proclaim to be deliverers of the freedom fighters spiritually and physically, let them show that they may stand in the light of the Divine Mother, raising up that sacred fire to defeat the horrendous hordes of world selfishness that descend upon nations....

Therefore, you will see no path of victory in the trines of life without tremendous love for those who will be the benefactors of your God-mastery. Only love begets the desire for victory that results in the action of victory.

Beloved ones, those on the left-handed path gain adeptship not by love but by the love to control others, an all-consuming base anti-force of love whereby they make any and all sacrifices for the sake of controlling others with their adeptship on the left-handed path. There are many black magicians in the world today, beloved, especially those arrayed in the camps of World Communism and those who support them. Therefore, if they will make the sacrifice necessary to destroy America and the Divine Mother for which she stands and which is her reason for being, can you not, more so by love, make the sacrifice necessary to attain this victory?

This is my question to you today. It has perhaps been brought to you in various forms through messages of the ascended masters. I bring it again as a reminder that the love is not only flowing from your heart as the cup of desire to serve, but it flows from God's heart as the most powerful force in the universe, which you will attract by your love. And it is God's love, beloved, that is your victory. It is God's love that makes it true that with God all things are possible. With God's love and yours, multiplied thereby, you can have the victory of the trines every day and every hour of your life. Thus, may you love unto the fulfillment of Christ-victory.

I Am Your Teacher of Love

I am with Maitreya in the Retreat of the Divine Mother. I am your teacher of love in the science of being. I place your hand now in the hand of your twin flame. And I bid you walk, walk now in this hour, beloved, a concerted victory within and without in the Alpha, in the Omega of thyself—not self-concern but concern for the Great God Self appearing in these little ones. Let us move to create for all of these the Place Prepared.

I am joyous as a builder, and you will see me side by side with you, moving with the construction crews, for I love to build in the physical octave. Now build your temple, beloved, that more than Christ might enter there, truly that the Beloved might knock and enter and love's union be here and now below as is Above.

In the fullness of love, I am come, your teacher of light. I seal you now in the foreverness of the sphere of light.

Leto

Sagittarius

CHAPTER 12

Timing Is Everything

There is a tide in the affairs of men
Which, taken at the flood, leads on to fortune;
Omitted, all the voyage of their life
Is bound in shallows and in miseries.

—Shakespeare

CHAPTER 12

Timing Is Everything

As you walk the path of life, you are carrying a flame.

You are carrying that flame from the point of origin, which is Capricorn, to each of the twelve houses of the hierarchies.

You carry the torch of Capricorn, and you deposit it in the house of Aquarius; you lay it upon the altar. You take up the torch of Aquarius, and you carry it to the house of Pisces, and so on. You are carrying the flame of each hierarchy as an emissary of that hierarchy during that particular month of your year. You are a Christed one—one anointed with the flame of Christ— accepting the challenge of going forth to consume the cause and core, not only of personal karma and personal misuses of that hierarchy, but also of planetary karma.

The influence of your I AM Presence moves from the microcosm to the Macrocosm when you begin to manifest the God-mastery established through a daily ritual of decrees and invocations. Thereby you invoke enough fire so that when you give forth your calls in the morning, your energies are sufficient not only to transmute your own karma for that day under a house and sign, but also to make a considerable dent in planetary karma on that day.

Balancing Both Personal and Planetary Karma

The path of Christhood and Buddhahood should be considered as the parallel lines of personal and planetary initiation, a movement to the right and to the left—the right signifying the balancing of personal karma through service, self-sacrifice and surrender, and the left signifying the taking-in of planetary karma and the balancing of this karma in the sacred fires of the heart. So, right and left, right and left, we must walk these parallel lines of self-mastery.

We cannot ascend back to the heart of God unless we contribute to the balancing of planetary karma. Everyone who has shown us the path of mastery has demonstrated that it is necessary, at a particular point, to go from the personal to the planetary. The significance of Jesus dying for our sins on the cross was that he was transmuting planetary karma. And everyone who attains that mastery must go through the initiation of the crucifixion—not necessarily surrendering the physical body, but being willing to take into that body spirals of planetary karma to balance them in the threefold flame within the heart.

Anticipate Your Karma and Your Dharma

The science of the cosmic clock enables us to anticipate our daily karma, our dharma of the day, our duties of the day; it enables us to anticipate our initiations in the way of the Christ and the Buddha—karma, dharma, initiation.

Sometimes God uses our own karma to initiate us. Sometimes he uses the karma of another to test our patience and our tolerance and our compassion. Sometimes he uses the karma of the world or of the nation or of the group we are involved with.

So there is no need to be in a state of blame, of pointing the finger, of trying to say who did this and who did that and where is that vibration coming from. It doesn't matter where that vibration is coming from. It's polluting Matter. It's polluting the four lower bodies of a planet. It's polluting your four lower bodies. Put it into the flame. Let go of it. Let go of the personality cult.

Do you know what the personality cult is? It's attachment to personalities, preferences for personalities, getting involved in cliques of personalities, and imagining that certain personalities are great and others aren't so great. It is an idolatry cult, a mutual admiration society.

Get rid of the personality cult. Depersonalize. Get centered in the sacred fire and be ready at any moment of the day or night to release the flame to consume the misqualified energies.

You can examine the clock, analyze the qualities of God, analyze their perversions, see how they come up for transmutation. Be a guard, be a watchman on the wall of your consciousness. Don't let the negative energies in. Don't entertain them. Know them for what they are, and know that every day of your life until the hour of your ascension you are required by the law of your being to put something into the flame.

Timing Is Everything

Line by line, you can replace misqualified energy with God's pure energy. But because of the nature of cycles, you have to be at the "right place" at the "right time"—you have to know what cycles are manifesting in your world. In mastering the cosmic clock, the cycles of energy that govern all life, timing is everything.

You know how precise you have to be in playing a game of baseball. You have to swing the bat when the ball gets to the right place—when you swing your bat, it's going to hit, and by practice you get an innate sense of exactly when this is going to happen. In your subconscious mind you have a computer that tells you how long it takes the ball to travel from the pitcher to home plate, how long it takes you to swing the bat, and when the two will meet. It takes precision.

The same is true of the law of cycles. If the sun comes into position, are you going to bat it a week later or the day before?

Cycles are very accurate. It's when the wave of God's energy is at its peak that you have your supreme opportunity to counteract the misqualified energy that is opposing it. You have to find a crest of light from the sun, by the sun sign, by the hour in which you're working. You have to take full advantage of that cycle.

The science of the cosmic clock, when you understand it, enables you to make very specific, precise, scientific calls. There is no point making a call for something that is not prominent, or, as we say, "up for transmutation." There are certain cycles of energy that are there, energy that needs to be transmuted at a particular time in your personal cycles and also because of the configurations not only of the sun and the moon, but of the planetary bodies—all of which have their influences of misqualified energy, not only because of the forcefield they occupy in time and space, but also because their lifewaves (those which have evolutions in either the etheric, the mental, the astral or the physical plane) have polluted the sacred fire. We feel that flow of energy from bodies within our solar system and from bodies beyond.

The understanding of these cycles and of astrology lets you know specifically—it pinpoints in the cosmos—where the testing is, so that you can put your attention upon it, so that you can prepare for it, so that you can invoke the violet flame to consume the cause and core even before the test comes.

In the days just before the turn of the cycle of the month, you begin to prepare for that testing. You anticipate it. Call for the violet flame to transmute the cause and core of all misuses of that line of the clock. Call to the hierarchies on that line, the masters on that line and all powers known or unknown who are serving the light at that moment. And then you have to demand that your human creation and that of the world be counteracted. You clear the ground, and this makes the testing that much simpler because you are there ready to seize that energy, ready to welcome the Lords of Karma and your Christ Self, who deposit that energy on your heart's altar for its transmutation.

It would be pointless after a baseball game was over to go out on the field and start swinging your bat and then to wonder why you didn't get any results. It's so obvious on the physical plane. Yet we tend to think that just by accident we're going to conquer cycles at the etheric and spiritual planes. It's really a much more involved science.

The Science of Astrology

If you really go more deeply into astrology, you can check where each of the planets is each day. The planets move through these signs, and according to their specific vibration in combination with that sign, you will get the returning karma of misqualified energy. But remember, you always get the good karma of light simultaneously.

So when you are in a Taurus cycle, you can expect to receive out of your causal body great momentums of your own obedience to the Law. Where you have obeyed God and loved him and kept his commandments, where your twin flame has done the same, that is your momentum of attainment for that cycle. It's the crest of the wave of your cosmic light.

Take the strength of good momentums to challenge the darkness, transmute any misuses, and increase the light. Taurus is an earth sign, and any earth sign means that you can do something that's physical. It's a sign of building and completion and organizing in the physical plane. When you are in a Taurus cycle, you take your momentum of love of God through obedience and you ride the crest of that good momentum. You take the strength of your good momentum, your good Alpha thrust, to challenge and transmute in the Omega return any misuses on that line and to increase the light.

You always should know at least where the sun and the moon are, or you're not going to be on top of the astral plane for the day. These are your tools. This is the New Age science. But always remember that where our knowledge of science leaves off, the masters will supply it. So at the end of every call, you can always say, "Let this call be adjusted according to the will of God." And in the end, after you've figured out and charted all of these various cycles of energy, you realize that God already is the master of all cycles that could ever be, going out to all points of the cosmos—every star, every sun, every moon, every particle of dust in the entire universe.

Retreating to the inner plane of the Christ consciousness, you can recognize the Presence of God in you as your Great Central Sun, in its full-orbed mastery right now.

Your Divine Destiny

Predicting your future with the cosmic clock is predicting what karma will befall you month after month and year after year.

Is this clock accurate? It is so accurate, it is awesome! It would be frightening if we did not understand and love the Law that governs a cosmos. It is so exact that if you know the hour of your birth, every month at this hour you will actually be able to observe the shifting of the cycle. The exactness of the flow of energy-spirals in the cosmos is a wonder. It's like the wonder of the human body and of cells and of the flow of life and the vastness of the design of the body temple we live in. But the wonder of wonders is to perceive how this cosmic clock works.

As we are dealing with ourselves, as we find ourselves at this time in space, as we come to grips with our karma and our karmic cycles, we can make the most of the clock whatever age we are, because the sacred fire, the transmuting flame, can consume the cause and core of all past misuses of the qualities of God on all lines of the clock.

If all goes according to clockwork and we earn the flame of our God-mastery, then we walk the earth as teachers, as unascended members of the Great White Brotherhood. If we fail our tests year by year, making more karma than we balance, accumulating not only the increment of the past that we vowed before the Lords of Karma to balance in this life but also the increment of karma from present infractions of the Law—which pile up into another mountain of karma in this embodiment—then when we finally surrender our life to the path that is set before us, the path of initiation, we will have to intensify our invocation to the flame of life. We will have to intensify our momentum of service to the cause of the Great White Brotherhood in order to fulfill our divine plan in this life.

It is still a supreme opportunity! It is still a supreme moment of victory! And Saint Germain has promised us that if we apply this teaching and the law of the violet flame and all that the masters have given through their teachings, the soul can ascend either in this life or in the next life—the requirement being the balancing of 51 percent of all misuses of these twelve flames and the fulfillment of the divine plan.

Divine destiny leads us to the heart of God. The Path is a spiral of love, and the road map is the cosmic clock, which ticks off the cycles of that ultimate destiny.

Eternity is a clock—
a cosmic clock, if you will.
Its face is that of
your mighty I AM Presence
(superimposed upon the rainbow rings
of your causal body)
measuring out segments of life.
Even your heartbeat is a reminder
that time is finite
and that the tick-tock of
"Forever—never! Never—forever!"
will come to an end.

What matters is neither the endings
or the beginnings
nor the separations
that time and space bring,
but that you have filled
those cosmic intervals
with éternité.

For if you do,
when the mold is broken,
your soul,
once the prisoner of time-space,
spreads its wings to fly—
already a part of eternity.

And in this alchemy
wherein time is tolled
in the chiming of the spheres
of universal awareness,
and finite space
becomes infinite grace,
the soul takes all of her eternities with her;
for now that she is perfected
in eternity's hours,
she can contain them all.

CONCLUSION

Predicting Your Future

Is it *really* possible to predict your future?

We are not talking about your daily horoscope, fortune-tellers, crystal balls or the psychic hotline. We are not talking about meeting "a tall, handsome stranger."

Rather we are talking about patterns. This is the science of a cosmos, the rhythm of life.

Cycles are apparent in everything—from the hum of the whirling of the electron, to the rising and setting of the sun, to the changing of the seasons, to the turning of the galaxy in millions of years. It is the regularity of cycles that makes life possible.

We can predict that the sun will rise at a certain time tomorrow morning. Spring surely brings new life after the dormancy of winter. Meteorologists can predict the weather with some degree of accuracy based on their understanding of cycles of the atmosphere and the oceans. It is all a part of natural law. The more we know about this law, the more we can know of the world around us and thereby know what is likely to happen.

The same holds true for spiritual law. The great precept of Hermes Trismegistus tells us that what we see in this world is a reflection of the worlds of higher realms; the cycles we see around us are a reflection of cycles in spiritual dimensions. This is the key to understanding the realms of Spirit.

We have a physical body with its own internal cycles. This body also interacts with the cycles in the world around us. Beyond the physical body, we have other bodies that interact with influences on their own planes. As scientists are learning to understand the cycles of the physical body, so the workings of the finer bodies can be understood by the scientists of the Spirit.

Challenges and Opportunities

Most basic of the influences we deal with each day is the law of karma—as you sow, so shall you reap. But how long after the seed is planted does the harvest come? It comes according to cycles. There are longer cycles of returning karma and shorter ones. But each day, we find returning to us a portion of energy we have sent out in the past—both good and bad.

We also meet each day the increments of light that come from the spiritual hierarchies—what El Morya has called "the light of far-off worlds"—as well as increments of planetary karma coming due.

The complex interaction of all these cycles, our personal ones and the cycles of the planet, determines the circumstances we will face each day. The more we understand the cycles of our own cosmic clock and the cycles written in the heavens, the more clearly we will know what to expect.

Charting these cycles will not tell us every detail of what the day will bring—but it can help us be aware of strong possibilities. For one thing, many of the causes we have set in motion are from past lives and we no longer remember the details of those events; thus we do not know in exactly what fashion the energy must appear in order to be balanced. What we can know is the basic outline—the matrix, the pattern—and the type of energy we will be dealing with as it is outplayed in the details of life.

This science is accurate, and by being aware of your position on the cosmic clock, you can have a foreknowing of the energies each day will bring. However, knowing what the future will bring is only the beginning. In fact, if you leave it there, will you really be any better off after having read this book?

The real question is: Now that you know how to predict the future, what are you going to *do* about it?

Taking Action

This is what much of this book has really been about—not just how to know what the future will bring, but the tools and techniques that can help you make the most of every opportunity. These cycles of returning energy do not need to catch you off guard. You are meant to have mastery over them—to embrace the positive and dissolve the negative.

If you are in a Capricorn cycle, for example, you know that you will be dealing with the return of negative energies of the light of that hierarchy. You can therefore maintain a greater equanimity when you find a weight of condemnation or criticism coming your way. You don't let yourself internalize it by condemning yourself, and you watch out for the tendency to criticize others. You can depersonalize the energy and see it as an opportunity for negative energy to simply pass into the flame and be transmuted into the buoyancy of God-power.

You also know that Capricorn is the twelve o'clock line. It is the first line of the clock and represents the start of a new cycle. It is a time of new beginnings, a time when you can use the increment of God-power that descends to initiate projects and positive momentums in your life. (For example, the Capricorn cycle of the planet is when people make their New Year's resolutions.) So you try to make the most of these cycles as opportunities.

It is like riding a surfboard—if you start paddling at the right time, you can catch the momentum and ride the wave. If you start a little bit late, you may have to paddle much harder, or you may miss that particular wave altogether. Catch the wave of Capricorn and use it to lay a foundation for a whole cycle of the cosmic clock. Then you get ready for each succeeding line as it appears.

Will your new beginning (or your New Year's resolution) make it through the testings of love in Aquarius? Will you let fear and doubt on the line of Pisces get you off track, or will you use that energy to gain greater God-mastery? Each line, in turn, has its opportunities and its tests.

If you know what is coming on each line, you can be prepared. You can make the most of the opportunities of light and positive energy that come your way, and you are less likely to be caught off-guard by the challenges. Call to the master and the hierarchy of each line to lend you their momentum of mastery. You don't have to do this alone, and the masters are here to help. They will fill in the gaps of your attainment until you are ready to handle it on your own.

Perhaps the greatest opportunity the cosmic clock gives us is to use the violet flame and the Science of the Spoken Word to help balance the karma that will be coming due. Each morning at dawn, the karma of the day is released. It's like a little paper sack delivered to your doorstep by the angels. If you give your calls and decrees for "Round the Clock Protection" and the violet flame early in the day, a large percentage of that bundle of returning karma can be transmuted—it doesn't all have to manifest as illness, accidents, conflicts, burdens and all the many ways that karma outplays. In fact, it is a lot easier to deal with this energy before it becomes physical.

You will find several violet-flame mantras in the last section of this book. You will also find decrees to Archangel Michael (for protection of your life and plans each day) and to Astrea (a very powerful action for the clearing of negative energy and forcefields of darkness). If you would like to find out more about this science and what it can do in your life, a good place to start is *The Science of the Spoken Word,* by Mark L. Prophet and Elizabeth Clare Prophet.

Free Will

The fact that you can predict your future does not mean that there is predestination. We live in a universe of free will. Each day you are presented with challenges and opportunities related to how you have by free will used and misused energies in the past. And each day you must choose what you will do with these new situations.

Your present is the result of choices you have already made—in this and in many past lives.

Your future is as yet unwritten.

The converging of cycles of light and darkness can be predicted with accuracy. But the final outcome depends on the choices you make—today and every day for the rest of your life.

The present is the cusp of opportunity.

It is the place of decision.

It is where you write your future—a future that will be, ultimately, what *you* make it.

This is the meaning of free will.

The science of the cosmic clock is the great gift and opportunity that life gives us.

Please take this teaching, so lovingly given to each one by Mother Mary and Elizabeth Clare Prophet, and use it daily to win your ascension in this life.

Sincerely,

Annice Booth

Meditations
and
Mantras

Thus saith the Lord,
the Holy One of Israel, and his Maker,
Ask me of things to come concerning my sons,
and concerning the work of my hands
command ye me.

—Isaiah

I AM THE VIOLET FLAME

In the name of the beloved mighty victorious Presence of God, I AM in me, and my very own beloved Holy Christ Self, I call to beloved Alpha and Omega in the heart of God in our Great Central Sun, beloved Saint Germain, beloved Portia, beloved Lanello, the entire Spirit of the Great White Brotherhood and the World Mother, elemental life—fire, air, water and earth!

To expand the violet flame within my heart, purify my four lower bodies, transmute all misqualified energy I have ever imposed upon life, and blaze mercy's healing ray throughout the earth, the elementals, and all mankind and answer this my call infinitely, presently, and forever:

> I AM the violet flame
> In action in me now
> I AM the violet flame
> To light alone I bow
> I AM the violet flame
> In mighty cosmic power
> I AM the light of God
> Shining every hour
> I AM the violet flame
> Blazing like a sun
> I AM God's sacred power
> Freeing every one

And in full faith I consciously accept this manifest, manifest, manifest! (3x) right here and now with full power, eternally sustained, all-powerfully active, ever expanding and world enfolding until all are wholly ascended in the light and free!

Beloved I AM! Beloved I AM! Beloved I AM!

VIOLET FLAME FROM THE HEART OF GOD

In the name of the beloved mighty victorious Presence of God, I AM in me, my very own beloved Holy Christ Self, beloved Lanello, the entire Spirit of the Great White Brotherhood and the World Mother, elemental life—fire, air, water and earth! I decree:

Violet flame from the heart of God, (3x*)
    Expand thy mercy through me today! (3x)
Violet flame from the heart of God, (3x)
    Transmute all wrong by forgiveness ray! (3x)
Violet flame from the heart of God, (3x)
    Blaze into action through all to stay! (3x)
Violet flame from the heart of God, (3x)
    O mercy's flame, fore'er hold sway! (3x)
Violet flame from the heart of God, (3x)
    Sweep all the earth by Christ-command! (3x)
Violet flame from the heart of God, (3x)
    Thy freeing power I now demand! (3x)

    Take dominion now,
    To thy light I bow;
    I AM thy radiant light,
    Violet flame so bright.
    Grateful for thy ray
    Sent to me today,
    Fill me through and through
    Until there's only you!

And in full faith I consciously accept this manifest, manifest, manifest! (3x) right here and now with full power, eternally sustained, all-powerfully active, ever expanding and world enfolding until all are wholly ascended in the light and free!

Beloved I AM! Beloved I AM! Beloved I AM!

---

* "3x" means to give each line three times.

LORD MICHAEL, CUT ME FREE!

In the name of the beloved mighty victorious Presence of God, I AM in me, my very own beloved Holy Christ Self, Holy Christ Selves of all mankind, beloved Archangel Michael, beloved Lanello, the entire Spirit of the Great White Brotherhood and the World Mother, elemental life—fire, air, water and earth! I decree:

1. Lord Michael, Lord Michael,
   I call unto thee
   Wield thy sword of blue flame
   And now cut me free!

Refrain: Blaze God power, protection
   Now into my world,
   Thy banner of faith
   Above me unfurl!
   Transcendent blue lightning
   Now flash through my soul,
   I AM by God's mercy
   Made radiant and whole!

2. Lord Michael, Lord Michael,
   I love thee, I do
   With all thy great faith
   My being imbue!

3. Lord Michael, Lord Michael
   And legions of blue
   Come seal me, now keep me
   Faithful and true!

Coda: I AM with thy blue flame
   Now full charged and blest,
   I AM now in Michael's
   Blue flame armor dressed! (3x)

And in full faith...

DECREE TO BELOVED MIGHTY ASTREA
The Starry Mother

In the name of the beloved mighty victorious Presence of God, I AM in me, mighty I AM Presence and Holy Christ Selves of all mankind, by and through the magnetic power of the sacred fire vested in the threefold flame burning within my heart, I call to beloved Mighty Astrea and Purity, Archangel Gabriel and Hope, beloved Serapis Bey and the seraphim and cherubim of God, beloved Lanello, the entire Spirit of the Great White Brotherhood and the World Mother, elemental life—fire, air, water and earth! to lock your cosmic circles and swords of blue flame in, through, and around: my four lower bodies, my electronic belt, my heart chakra and all of my chakras, my entire consciousness, being and world. [____ name other conditions or qualities of negativity on specific lines of the clock____.]

Cut me loose and set me free (3x) from all that is less than God's perfection and my own divine plan fulfilled.

1. O beloved Astrea, may God Purity
   Manifest here for all to see,
   God's divine will shining through
   Circle and sword of brightest blue.

First chorus: Come now answer this my call
   Lock thy circle round us all.
   Circle and sword of brightest blue,
   Blaze now, raise now, shine right through!

2. Cutting life free from patterns unwise,
   Burdens fall off while souls arise
   Into thine arms of infinite love,
   Merciful shining from heaven above.

3. Circle and sword of Astrea now shine,
   Blazing blue white my being refine,
   Stripping away all doubt and fear,
   Faith and goodwill patterns appear.

Second chorus: Come now answer this my call,
Lock thy circle round us all.
Circle and sword of brightest blue,
Raise our youth now, blaze right through!

Third chorus: Come now answer this my call,
Lock thy circle round us all.
Circle and sword of brightest blue,
Raise mankind now, shine right through!

And in full faith...

I AM THE LIGHT OF THE HEART
by Saint Germain

I AM the light of the heart
Shining in the darkness of being
And changing all into the golden treasury
Of the mind of Christ.

I AM projecting my love
Out into the world
To erase all errors
And to break down all barriers.

I AM the power of infinite love,
Amplifying itself
Until it is victorious,
World without end!

SAINT GERMAIN'S MANTRA
FOR THE AQUARIAN AGE

I AM a being of violet fire,
I AM the purity God desires!

DJWAL KUL, COME!
A Meditation of the Heart on the Twelve Solar Hierarchies by the Tibetan Master

In the name of the beloved mighty victorious Presence of God, I AM in me, my very own beloved Holy Christ Self, Holy Christ Selves of all mankind, beloved Djwal Kul, beloved Lanello, the entire Spirit of the Great White Brotherhood and the World Mother, elemental life—fire, air, water and earth! I decree:

> Djwal Kul, come!
> In the center of the One,
> Anchor now thy radiant sun,
> Magnet of the threefold flame,
> Expand God's aura in God's name!
>
> Djwal Kul, come!
> Threefold fountain, fill my heart;
> Let thy angel now impart
> The name of God—I AM THAT I AM,
> I AM THAT I AM, I AM THAT I AM,
> I AM THAT I AM!
>
> Djwal Kul, come!
> Flame of gold, pink, blue and white,
> Seal thy victory star of light;
> Renew my vows to God's own name;
> Come, O Christ, in me now reign!
>
> Djwal Kul, come!
> Expand the fire of the Sun;
> Alpha 'n Omega, make us one,
> Seal my energies in Christ,
> Raise my energies in light!
>
> Djwal Kul, come!
> Align my consciousness with thee,
> Make us one, O make me free!
> Seal my heart and hand in thine,
> In God's mind I AM divine!

Djwal Kul, come!
Blaze the action of the Whole,
With light of victory fill my soul;
Return me to the Flaming One,
I AM begotten of the Son!

Coda: I AM God-power, I AM God-love,
I AM THAT I AM, I AM THAT I AM,
    I AM THAT I AM!

I AM God-mastery and God-control,
I AM THAT I AM
AUM (chant)
I AM THAT I AM
AUM (chant)

I AM God-obedience now,
To thy Law I vow,
I AM THAT I AM, I AM THAT I AM,
    I AM THAT I AM!

God-wisdom flame I AM,
God-wisdom flame I AM,
God-wisdom flame I AM!
AUM—God-har-mo-ny (chant)
AUM—God-har-mo-ny (chant)
AUM—God-har-mo-ny! (chant)

God-gratitude, God-gratitude, God-gratitude!
I AM God-justice in full view,
I AM God-justice in full view,
I AM God-justice in full view!

God-re-al-i-ty! (chant)
I AM God-vision, God-victory won,
I AM God-vision, God-victory won,
I AM God-vision, God-victory won!

And in full faith...

NOTES

INTRODUCTION
1. Shakespeare, *Julius Cæsar,* Act iv, Sc. 3.
2. Job 7:17–18.

CHAPTER 1
The Law of Cycles

Opening quote: Gen. 8:22.
1. John 1:1, 3.

CHAPTER 2
The Psychology of Being

Opening quote: Inscription on the Oracle of Apollo at Delphi, Greece, 6th century B.C.
1. John 14:18, 26.
2. *Meister Eckhart: Sermons and Treatises,* trans. and ed. M. O'C. Walshe (Logmead, Shaftesbury, Dorset: Element Books, 1987), 3:107.
3. Matt. 6:6.

CHAPTER 3
Your Personal Cosmic Clock

Opening quote: Eccl. 3:1, 2.
1. According to esoteric tradition, there are seven primary groups of souls who have been assigned to planet Earth for their soul evolution. The first three root races lived in purity and innocence upon earth in three golden ages before the Fall of Adam and Eve. Through obedience to cosmic law and total identification with the Real Self, these three root races won their immortal freedom and ascended from earth. It was during the time of the fourth root race, on the continent of Lemuria,

that the allegorical Fall took place under the influence of the fallen angels known as Serpents. The fourth, fifth and sixth root races remain in embodiment on earth today. See Mark L. Prophet and Elizabeth Clare Prophet, *The Path of the Higher Self,* ch. 3.

2. Heb. 12:29.
3. Mark L. Prophet and Elizabeth Clare Prophet, *Saint Germain on Alchemy* (1993), pp. 74–75.
4. John 4:24.
5. John 1:14.

CHAPTER 4
Hierarchy

1. Exod. 33:20.
2. Rev. 1:8; 21:6; 22:13.
3. Gen. 1:3.
4. Job 38:7.
5. John 1:14.
6. John 5:30; 14:10; 5:17.
7. Matt. 13:24–30, 36–43.
8. Henry Wadsworth Longfellow, "The Builders," stanza 5.
9. El Morya, *The Chela and the Path* (1978), p. 60.
10. J.R.R. Tolkein, *The Two Towers* (Boston: Houghton Mifflin, 1999), ch. 4.
11. Voltaire, *Oeuvres.* Lettre cxviii., ed. Beuchot, lviii., p. 360, quoted in Isabel Cooper-Oakley, *The Count of Saint Germain* (Blauvelt, N.Y.: Rudolf Steiner Publications, 1970), p. 96.
12. Further information about Saint Germain's embodiments and background on the masters of all twelve lines may be found in Mark L. Prophet and Elizabeth Clare Prophet, *The Masters and Their Retreats* (2003).
13. Oliver St. John Fogarty, *I Follow Saint Patrick* (London: Rich & Cowan, 1938), p. 298.
14. Rev. 1:4.
15. James 1:8.
16. Matt. 6:22.
17. John 3:30.
18. Matt. 11:11–14; 17:12–13.
19. Matt. 25:40.
20. Matt. 10:41.
21. *Pearls of Wisdom* are weekly letters of instruction dictated by the ascended masters to their messengers Mark L. Prophet and Elizabeth Clare Prophet for students of the sacred mysteries throughout the world. *Pearls of Wisdom* have been published by The Summit Lighthouse continuously since 1958. They contain both fundamental and advanced teachings on cosmic law with a practical application of spiritual truths to personal and planetary problems.

　　In addition to publishing the *Pearls of Wisdom*, The Summit

Lighthouse is the sponsoring organization for the Keepers of the Flame Lessons, which are provided to members of the Keepers of the Flame Fraternity. This fraternity is sponsored by the ascended master Saint Germain, and the lessons he provides are intended to give individuals who have had a basic orthodox background in religion, or no background at all, the first steps on the path of self-mastery. The Keepers of the Flame Lessons are sent monthly to members of the fraternity.

22. 1 John 2:18.
23. James. 3:11.
24. Matt. 7:15, 20.
25. 1 John 4:1.
26. Gen. 28:12.
27. Matt. 11:12.

CHAPTER 5
Charting the Cycles of You and Your Family

Opening quote: Kahlil Gibran, *The Prophet*, "The Farewell."

1. The Montessori system of education was inspired upon the Italian educator Maria Montessori (1870–1952) by Mother Mary. It provides a unique classroom environment whereby the child follows the direction of the inner teacher in choosing the lessons to study. The combined freedom and order in the Montessori classroom is the true Aquarian-age education.

2. A key understanding for teenagers is the path of Jesus during the "lost years" of his life that are not recorded in the Bible. Manuscripts found in the East reveal that he journeyed to India and the Himalayas during this time, studying with the great lights of the East and teaching the sacred doctrines.

   "The lost years of Jesus have hurt the younger generation more than all others, because they have had no one to equate with from the years twelve to twenty-nine. In those very important years from twelve to eighteen, when all of the burdens and temptations of life come upon them, they have not seen the figure of the one who became the master and who now is ready to show them the way." [El Morya, "A Mighty Release of Heart," *Pearls of Wisdom*, vol. 25, no. 70.] For more about these years in Jesus' life, see Elizabeth Clare Prophet, *The Lost Years of Jesus* (1987).

3. For further teaching on the problem of suicide, along with spiritual tools to help deal with this issue, see *Wanting to Live: Overcoming the Seduction of Suicide*, by Dr. Neroli Duffy and Marilyn Barrick, Ph.D., based on the teachings of Elizabeth Clare Prophet.

4. Luke 2:49.

5. See chapter 5, note 2.

6. Summit University was founded by Mark and Elizabeth Prophet in 1971 to offer disciples of East and West the ongoing revelations of the Christ and the Buddha and techniques for self-mastery and self-

realization through the I AM Presence.

CHAPTER 6
The Alpha Thrust and the Omega Return

Opening quote: Rev. 1:8.
  1. 2 Peter 3:8.
  2. Ps. 121:8.
  3. Ezek. 1:16.

THE RITUAL OF THE ATOM

  1. Isa. 65:24.

CHAPTER 7
The Decades of Life

Opening quote: Oliver Wendell Holmes, Sr., "The Chambered Nautilus"
  1. Prov. 22:6.

CHAPTER 8
Karmic Dust

Opening quote: Matt. 24:22.
  1. Eccles. 3:2.
  2. Matt. 6:34.
  3. Matt. 24:22.
  4. John 7:24.
  5. 1 Cor. 15:55.
  6. Jesus Christ, "The Final Judgment of Satan," *Pearls of Wisdom*, vol. 25, no. 16, April 18, 1982.
  7. See chapter 4, note 21.
  8. Isa. 28:10, 13.
  9. 2 Tim. 2:15.

CHAPTER 9
Cosmic Accountability

  1. *The Dhammapada*, trans. P. Lal (New York: Farrar, Straus & Giroux, 1967), p. 39.
  2. Gal. 6:7.
  3. 2 Cor. 6:17.
  4. Gal. 5:7.
  5. 1 Cor. 15:41.
  6. Leto, "Becoming the Christos: The Path of Science," April 15, 1976: "I am counting on you chelas of the masters to become more

scientific in your application of the Law and far less superstitious. The teachings of the masters have no superstition, and yet you make of them a superstition as though you lived in primitive times and places. Let us then with equanimity, with a certainty of the Word that we have been given, without fear, without division apply each law we have been given. Let us apply it with scientific certitude that the law always works when it is correctly applied, that the call always compels the answer when the call reaches the level of the God flame.

"Let us not superstitiously give our decrees as rote, but let us give them as scientists with total concentration, total oneness, using the faculties, God-given, to expand the greater faculties within waiting to be tapped. Let us use the cycles of the cosmic clock with diligence, with discipline. There is so much more of the science of Christhood that each and every one of you could be manifesting with just the law that you know. And if you would give that manifestation of application, you would find that we would run to deliver to you, at your very doorstep, the next step of advanced teachings in the initiation of science."

7. James 1:17.
8. 1 Cor. 15:52–54.
9. John 2:1–11.
10. Matt. 5:48.
11. Wilson Bryan Key, *Subliminal Seduction: Ad Media's Manipulation of a Not So Innocent America* (New York: Times Mirror, New American Library, 1974), p. 16.
12. Rom. 7:19.
13. *Educational Psychology.*
14. Phil. 2:5.
15. Rev. 21:6; 22:13.
16. Rev. 1:8, 11.
17. Exod. 3:2.
18. Exod. 3:13–15.
19. Matt. 6:19–20.
20. Matt. 6:21.
21. 1 Cor. 15:40.
22. 1 Cor. 15:41.
23. Luke 24:50–51.
24. Hab. 1:13.
25. John 14:12.
26. John 20:17.
27. Ezek. 20:47.
28. John 8:58.
29. Lao Tzu, *Tao Te Ching,* trans. Gia-Fu Feng and Jane English (New York: Random House, Vintage Books, 1972), stanza 25.
30. Luke 24:32.
31. Gen. 3:4.
32. 1 Sam. 15:23, 26.
33. Ibid.
34. Acts 10:42.
35. Gen. 2:9, 17.

36. Key, *Subliminal Seduction*, p. 1.
37. Matt. 7:1
38. Rom. 7:23; James 4:1.
39. John 21:22.
40. Rev. 12:3; Gen. 3:1.
41. Rev. 12.
42. Gen. 3:3, 4.
43. Ezek. 18:4, 20.
44. Rev. 20:12, 13.
45. Acts 2:3.
46. Acts 2:1, 2.
47. Acts 9:5; 26:14.
48. John 14:16.
49. The nine gifts of the Holy Spirit are 1) the word of wisdom, 2) the word of knowledge, 3) faith, 4) healing, 5) the working of miracles, 6) prophecy, 7) the discerning of spirits, 8) divers kinds of tongues, 9) the interpretation of tongues (1 Cor. 12:1, 4–11).
50. Rom. 8:17.
51. John 16:23.
52. Isa. 1:18.
53. John 14:18.
54. John 11:25.
55. Phil. 4:13.
56. Matt. 12:37.
57. Matt. 19:26.
58. John 10:9.
59. Gen. 1:27, 28.

CHAPTER 10
The Psychology of Wholeness

Opening quote: Heb. 7:1, 3.
1. For more information on the twelve apostles and their offices under the twelve solar hierarchies, see Mark L. Prophet and Elizabeth Clare Prophet, *The Path of Brotherhood*, pages 151–74.
2. Clara Louise Kieninger, *Ich Dien*, ed. and comp. Elizabeth Clare Prophet (The Summit Lighthouse, 1975).
3. Rev. 1:1; 22:18–19.
4. See Rev. 11–20.
5. Rev. 11:3, 5.
6. Rev. 1:16.
7. Rev. 12:11; John the Beloved, "The Foundation of the New Jerusalem," *Pearls of Wisdom*, vol. 19, no. 37, September 12, 1976.
8. Isa. 14:12.
9. John 6:53.
10. John 6:66.
11. 1 Cor. 12:8–10.
12. Matt. 28:18.

13. Key teachings on dealing with the false hierarchy and their false teachings may be found in "An Exposé of False Teachings," *Pearls of Wisdom,* vol. 19, nos. 1–15, January 4–April 11, 1976, by Kuthumi and the Brothers of the Golden Robe, and in *Mark L. Prophet and Elizabeth Clare Prophet on Strategies of Light and Darkness,* by the Staff of Summit University.
14. Portia, April 17, 1976.
15. St. John of the Cross, *The Collected Works of St. John of the Cross,* trans. Kieran Kavanaugh and Otilio Rodriguez (Washington, D.C.: ICS Publications, 1973), p. 347.
16. Mark 15:34.
17. Matt. 14:25–31.
18. Heb. 7:3.
19. Gen. 2:9, 3:22, 24; Prov. 3:18, 11:30, 13:12, 15:4; Rev. 22:2, 14.
20. Rev. 22:2.
21. Rev. 22:1.
22. Rev. 22:2.
23. Matt. 12:48–50.

CHAPTER 11
The Dividing of the Way

This dictation by Leto was delivered June 22, 1986, at Camelot, Los Angeles County, California.

CHAPTER 12
Timing Is Everything

Opening quote: Shakespeare, *Julius Caesar,* Act iv, Scene 3.

GLOSSARY

Terms set in italics are defined elsewhere in the glossary.

Adept. An initiate of the *Great White Brotherhood* of a high degree of attainment, especially in the control of *Matter,* physical forces, nature spirits and bodily functions; fully the alchemist undergoing advanced initiations of the *sacred fire* on the path of the *ascension.*

Akashic records. The impressions of all that has ever transpired in the physical universe, recorded in the etheric substance and dimension known by the Sanskrit term *akasha.* These records can be read by those with developed *soul* faculties.

Alchemical marriage. The soul's permanent bonding to the *Holy Christ Self,* in preparation for the permanent fusing to the *I AM Presence* in the ritual of the *ascension.* See also *Soul; Secret chamber of the heart.*

All-Seeing Eye of God. See *Cyclopea.*

Alpha and Omega. The divine wholeness of the Father-Mother God affirmed as "the beginning and the ending" by the Lord *Christ* in Revelation (Rev. 1:8, 11; 21:6; 22:13). Ascended *twin flames* of the *Cosmic Christ* consciousness who hold the balance of the masculine-feminine polarity of the Godhead in the *Great Central Sun* of cosmos. Thus through the *Universal Christ* (the *Word* incarnate), the Father is the origin and the Mother is the fulfillment of the cycles of God's consciousness expressed throughout the *Spirit-Matter* creation. See also

Mother.

Ancient of Days. See *Sanat Kumara.*

Angel. A divine spirit, a herald or messenger sent by God to deliver his *Word* to his children. A ministering spirit sent forth to tend the heirs of *Christ*—to comfort, protect, guide, strengthen, teach, counsel and warn. The fallen angels, also called the dark ones, are those angels who followed Lucifer in the Great Rebellion, whose consciousness therefore "fell" to lower levels of vibration. They were "cast out into the earth" by Archangel Michael (Rev. 12:7–12)—constrained by the karma of their disobedience to God and his Christ to take on and evolve through dense physical bodies. Here they walk about, sowing seeds of unrest and rebellion among men and nations.

Antahkarana. The web of life. The net of *light* spanning *Spirit* and *Matter,* connecting and sensitizing the whole of creation within itself and to the heart of God.

Archangel. The highest rank in the orders of *angels.* Each of the *seven rays* has a presiding archangel who, with his divine complement, or archeia, embodies the God consciousness of the ray and directs the bands of angels serving in their command on that ray. The archangels and archeiai of the rays and the locations of their *retreats* are as follows:

First ray, blue, Archangel Michael and Faith, Banff, near Lake Louise, Alberta, Canada.

Second ray, yellow, Archangel Jophiel and Christine, south of the Great Wall near Lanchow, north central China.

Third ray, petal pink, deep rose and ruby, Archangel Chamuel and Charity, St. Louis, Missouri, U.S.A.

Fourth ray, white and mother-of-pearl, Archangel Gabriel and Hope, between Sacramento and Mount Shasta, California, U.S.A.

Fifth ray, green, Archangel Raphael and Mary, Fátima, Portugal.

Sixth ray, purple and gold with ruby flecks, Archangel Uriel and Aurora, Tatra Mountains, south of Cracow, Poland. Seventh ray, violet and purple, Archangel Zadkiel and Holy Amethyst, Cuba.

Archeia (pl. **archeiai**). Divine complement and *twin flame* of an *archangel*.

Ascended master. One who, through *Christ* and the putting on of that mind which was in Christ Jesus (Phil. 2:5), has mastered time and space and in the process gained the mastery of the self in the *four lower bodies* and the four quadrants of *Matter,* in the *chakras* and the balanced *threefold flame.* An ascended master has also transmuted at least 51 percent of his karma, fulfilled his divine plan, and taken the initiations of the ruby ray unto the ritual of the *ascension*—acceleration by the *sacred fire* into the Presence of the I AM THAT I AM (the *I AM Presence*). Ascended masters inhabit the planes of *Spirit*—the kingdom of God (God's consciousness)—and they may teach unascended souls in an *etheric temple* or in the cities on the *etheric plane* (the kingdom of heaven).

Ascension. The ritual whereby the *soul* reunites with the *Spirit* of the living God, the *I AM Presence*. The ascension is the culmination of the soul's God-victorious sojourn in time and space. It is the process whereby the soul, having balanced her karma and fulfilled her divine plan, merges first with the Christ consciousness and then with the living Presence of the I AM THAT I AM. Once the ascension has taken place, the soul—the corruptible aspect of being—becomes the incorruptible one, a permanent atom in the Body of God. See also *Alchemical marriage.*

Aspirant. One who aspires; specifically, one who aspires to reunion with God through the ritual of the *ascension*. One who aspires to overcome the conditions and limitations of time and space to fulfill the cycles of karma and one's reason for being through the sacred labor.

Astral plane. A frequency of time and space beyond the physical, yet below the mental, corresponding to the *emotional body* of man and the collective unconscious of the race; the repository of mankind's thoughts and feelings, conscious and unconscious. Because the astral plane has been muddied by impure human thought and feeling, the term "astral" is often used in a negative context to refer to that which is impure or psychic.

Astrea. Feminine Elohim of the fourth ray, the ray of purity, who works to cut *souls* free from the *astral plane* and the projections of the dark forces. See also *Elohim; Seven rays.*

Atman. The spark of the Divine within, identical with *Brahman;* the ultimate essence of the universe as well as the essence of the individual.

AUM. See *OM.*

Avatar. The incarnation of the *Word.* The avatar of an age is the *Christ,* the incarnation of the Son of God. The *manus* may designate numerous Christed ones—those endued with an extraordinary *light*—to go forth as world teachers and way-showers. The Christed ones demonstrate in a given epoch the law of the *Logos,* stepped down through the manu(s) and the avatar(s) until it is made flesh through their own word and work—to be ultimately victorious in its fulfillment in all souls of light sent forth to conquer time and space in that era.

Bodhisattva. (Sanskrit, 'a being of *bodhi* or enlightenment.') A being destined for enlightenment, or one whose energy and power is directed toward enlightenment. A bodhisattva is destined to become a *Buddha* but has forgone the bliss of *nirvana* with a vow to save all children of God on earth. An ascended master or an unascended master may be a bodhisattva.

Brahman. Ultimate Reality; the Absolute.

Buddha. (From Sanskrit *budh* 'awake, know, perceive.') "The enlightened one." Buddha denotes an office in the spiritual *hierarchy* of worlds that is attained by passing certain initiations of the *sacred fire,* including those of the *seven rays* of the Holy Spirit and of the five secret *rays,* the raising of the feminine ray (sacred fire of the Kundalini) and the "mastery of the seven in the seven multiplied by the power of the ten."

Gautama attained the enlightenment of the Buddha twenty-five centuries ago, a path he had pursued through many previous embodiments culminating in his forty-nine-day meditation under the Bo tree. Hence he is called Gautama, the Buddha. He holds the office of *Lord of the World*, sustaining, by his *causal body* and *threefold flame*, the divine spark and consciousness in the evolutions of earth approaching the path of personal Christhood. His aura of love-wisdom ensouling the planet issues from his incomparable devotion to the Divine *Mother*. He is the hierarch of Shamballa, the original *retreat* of *Sanat Kumara* now on the *etheric plane* over the Gobi Desert.

Lord Maitreya, the *Cosmic Christ*, has also passed the initiations of the Buddha. He is the long-awaited Coming Buddha who has come to the fore to teach all who have departed from the way of the Great *Guru*, Sanat Kumara, from whose lineage both he and Gautama descended. In the history of the planet, there have been numerous Buddhas who have served the evolutions of mankind through the steps and stages of the path of the *bodhisattva*. In the East Jesus is referred to as the Buddha Issa. He is the World Saviour by the love-wisdom of the Godhead.

Caduceus. The Kundalini. See *Sacred fire*.

Causal Body. Seven concentric spheres of *light* surrounding the *I AM Presence*. The spheres of the causal body contain the records of the virtuous acts we have performed to the glory of God and the blessing of man through our many incarnations on earth. See also *Chart of Your Divine Self*.

Central Sun. A vortex of energy, physical or spiritual, central to systems of worlds that it thrusts from, or gathers unto, itself by the Central Sun Magnet. Whether in the *microcosm* or the *Macrocosm*, the Central Sun is the principal energy source, vortex, or nexus of energy interchange in atoms, cells, man (the heart center), amidst plant life and the core of the earth. The Great Central Sun is the center of cosmos; the point of integration of the *Spirit-Matter* cosmos; the point of origin of all physical-spiritual creation; the nucleus, or white fire core, of the *Cosmic Egg.* (The God Star, Sirius, is the focus of the Great Central Sun in our sector of the galaxy.) The Sun behind the sun is the spiritual Cause behind the physical effect we see as our own physical sun and all other stars and star systems, seen or unseen, including the Great Central Sun.

Chakra. (Sanskrit, 'wheel, disc, circle.') Center of *light* anchored in the *etheric body* and governing the flow of energy to the *four lower bodies* of man. There are seven major chakras corresponding to the *seven rays,* five minor chakras corresponding to the five secret rays, and a total of 144 light centers in the body of man.

Chart of Your Divine Self. There are three figures represented in the Chart. The upper figure is the *I AM Presence,* the I AM THAT I AM, the individualization of God's Presence for every son and daughter of the Most High. The Divine Monad consists of the I AM Presence surrounded by the spheres (color rings) of *light* that make up the body of First Cause, or *Causal Body.*

The middle figure in the Chart is the Mediator between God and man, called the *Holy Christ Self,* the *Real Self* or the *Christ* consciousness. It has also been referred to as the Higher Mental Body or one's Higher Consciousness. This Inner Teacher overshadows the lower self, which consists of the *soul* evolving through the four planes of *Matter* using the vehicles of the *four lower bodies*—the *etheric* (memory) *body,* the *mental body,* the *emotional* (desire) *body,* and the *physical body*—to balance karma and fulfill the divine plan.

The three figures of the Chart correspond to the Trinity of Father, who always includes the *Mother* (the upper figure), Son (the middle figure) and Holy Spirit (the lower figure). The latter is the intended temple of the Holy Spirit, whose *sacred fire* is indicated in the enfolding *violet flame*. The lower figure corresponds to you as a disciple on the *Path*.

The lower figure is surrounded by a *tube of light*, which is projected from the heart of the I AM Presence in answer to your call. It is a cylinder of white light that sustains a forcefield of protection twenty-four hours a day, so long as you guard it in harmony. The *threefold flame* of life is the divine spark sent from the I AM Presence as the gift of life, consciousness and free will. It is sealed in the *secret chamber of the heart* that through the love, wisdom and power of the Godhead anchored therein the *soul* may fulfill her reason for being in the physical plane. Also called the Christ flame and the liberty flame, or fleur-de-lis, it is the spark of a man's divinity, his potential for Christhood.

The silver cord (or *crystal cord*) is the stream of life, or *lifestream,* that descends from the heart of the I AM Presence to the Holy Christ Self to nourish and sustain (through the *chakras*) the soul and its vehicles of expression in time and space. It is over this 'umbilical cord' that the energy of the Presence flows, entering the being of man at the crown and giving impetus for the pulsation of the threefold flame as well as the physical heartbeat.

When a round of the soul's incarnation in Matter-form is finished, the I AM Presence withdraws the silver cord (Eccles. 12:6), whereupon the threefold flame returns to the level of the Christ, and the soul clothed in the etheric garment gravitates to the highest level of her attainment, where she is schooled between embodiments until her final incarnation when the Great Law decrees she shall go out no more.

The dove of the Holy Spirit descending from the heart of the Father is shown just above the head of the Christ. When the son of man puts on and becomes the Christ consciousness as Jesus did, he merges with the Holy Christ Self. The Holy Spirit is upon him, and the words of the Father, the beloved I AM Presence, are spoken: "This is my beloved Son, in whom I AM well pleased" (Matt. 3:17).

Chela. (Hindi *cela* from Sanskrit *ceta* 'slave,' i.e., 'servant.') In India, a disciple of a religious teacher or *guru*. A term used generally to refer to a student of the *ascended masters* and their teachings. Specifically, a student of more than ordinary self-discipline and devotion initiated by an ascended master and serving the cause of the *Great White Brotherhood*.

Chohan. (Tibetan, 'lord' or 'master'; a chief.) Each of the seven *rays* has a chohan who focuses the *Christ* consciousness of the ray. Having ensouled and demonstrated the law of the ray throughout numerous incarnations, and having taken initiations both before and after the *ascension*, the candidate is appointed to the office of chohan by the Maha Chohan (the "Great Lord"), who is himself the representative of the Holy Spirit on all the rays. The names of the chohans of the rays (each one an *ascended master* representing one of the seven rays to earth's evolutions) and the locations of their physical/etheric focuses are as follows:

First ray, El Morya, Retreat of God's Will, Darjeeling, India
Second ray, Lanto, Royal Teton Retreat, Grand Teton, Jackson Hole, Wyoming, U.S.A.
Third ray, Paul the Venetian, Château de Liberté, southern France, with a focus of the *threefold flame* at the Washington Monument, Washington, D.C., U.S.A.
Fourth ray, Serapis Bey, the Ascension Temple and Retreat at Luxor, Egypt
Fifth ray, Hilarion (the apostle Paul), Temple of Truth, Crete
Sixth ray, Nada, Arabian Retreat, Saudi Arabia
Seventh ray, Saint Germain, Royal Teton Retreat, Grand Teton, Wyoming, U.S.A.; Cave of Symbols, Table Mountain, Wyoming, U.S.A. Saint Germain also works out of the Great Divine Director's focuses—the Cave of Light in India and the Rakoczy Mansion in Transylvania, where Saint Germain presides as hierarch.

Christ. (From the Greek *Christos* 'anointed.') Messiah (Hebrew,

Aramaic 'anointed'); 'Christed one,' one fully endued and infilled—anointed—by the *light* (the Son) of God. The *Word*, the *Logos*, the Second Person of the Trinity. In the Hindu Trinity of Brahma, Vishnu and Shiva, the term "Christ" corresponds to or is the incarnation of Vishnu, the Preserver; Avatara, God-man, Dispeller of Darkness, *Guru*.

The term "Christ" or "Christed one" also denotes an office in *hierarchy* held by those who have attained self-mastery on the *seven rays* and the seven *chakras* of the Holy Spirit. Christ-mastery includes the balancing of the *threefold flame*—the divine attributes of power, wisdom and love—for the harmonization of consciousness and the implementation of the mastery of the seven rays in the chakras and in the *four lower bodies* through the Mother flame (the raised Kundalini).

At the hour designated for the *ascension*, the *soul* thus anointed raises the spiral of the threefold flame from beneath the feet through the entire form for the transmutation of every atom and cell of her being, consciousness and world. The saturation and acceleration of the *four lower bodies* and the soul by this transfiguring light of the Christ flame take place in part during the initiation of the *transfiguration*, increasing through the resurrection and gaining full intensity in the ritual of the ascension.

Christ Self. The individualized focus of "the only begotten of the Father, full of grace and truth." The *Universal Christ* individualized as the true identity of the *soul*; the *Real Self* of every man, woman and child, to which the soul must rise. The Christ Self is the Mediator between a man and his God. He is a man's own personal teacher, master and prophet.

Color rays. See *Seven rays*.

Cosmic Being. (1) An *ascended master* who has attained cosmic consciousness and ensouls the *light*/energy/consciousness of many worlds and systems of worlds across the galaxies to the Sun behind the *Great Central Sun*; or, (2) A being of God who has never descended below the level of the *Christ,* has never taken physical embodiment, and has never made human karma or engaged in sin but has remained a part of the Cosmic Virgin and holds a cosmic balance for the return of souls from the vale (veil) of sorrows to the Immaculate Heart of the Blessed Mother.

Cosmic Christ. An office in *hierarchy* currently held by Lord Maitreya under Gautama *Buddha,* the *Lord of the World.* Also used as a synonym for *Universal Christ.*

Cosmic Egg. The spiritual-material universe, including a seemingly endless chain of galaxies, star systems, worlds known and unknown, whose center, or white-fire core, is called the *Great Central Sun.* The Cosmic Egg has both a spiritual and a material center. Although we may discover and observe the Cosmic Egg from the standpoint of our physical senses and perspective, all of the dimensions of *Spirit* can also be known and experienced within the Cosmic Egg. For the God who created the Cosmic Egg and holds it in the hollow of his hand is also the God flame expanding hour by hour within his very own sons and daughters. The Cosmic Egg represents the bounds of man's habitation in this cosmic cycle. Yet, as God is everywhere throughout and beyond the Cosmic Egg, so by his Spirit within us we daily awaken to new dimensions of being, soul-satisfied in conformity with his likeness.

Cosmic law. The Law that governs mathematically, yet with the spontaneity of Mercy's flame, all manifestation throughout the cosmos in the planes of *Spirit* and *Matter.*

Crystal cord. The stream of God's *light,* life and consciousness that nourishes and sustains the *soul* and her *four lower bodies.* Also called the silver cord (Eccles. 12:6). See also *Chart of Your Divine Self.*

Cyclopea. Masculine Elohim of the fifth ray, also known as the All-Seeing Eye of God or as the Great Silent Watcher. See also *Elohim; Seven rays.*

Deathless solar body. See *Seamless garment.*

Decree. A dynamic form of spoken prayer used by students of the *ascended masters* to direct God's *light* into individual and world conditions. The decree may be short or long and is usually marked by a formal preamble and a closing or acceptance. It is the authoritative *Word* of God spoken in man in the name of the *I AM Presence* and the living *Christ* to bring about constructive change on earth through the will of God. The decree is the birthright of the sons and daughters of God, the "Command ye me" of Isaiah 45:11, the original fiat of the Creator: "Let there be light: and there was light" (Gen. 1:3). It is written in the Book of Job, "Thou shalt decree a thing, and it shall be established unto thee: and the light shall shine upon thy ways" (Job 22:28).

Dictation. A message from an *ascended master,* an *archangel* or another advanced spiritual being delivered through the agency of the Holy Spirit by a *messenger* of the *Great White Brotherhood.*

Divine Monad. See Chart of Your Divine Self; I AM Presence.

Electronic Presence. A duplicate of the *I AM Presence* of an ascended master.

Elohim. (Hebrew; plural of *Eloah,* 'God.') The name of God used in the first verse of the Bible: "In the beginning God created the heaven and the earth." The Seven Mighty Elohim and their feminine counterparts are the builders of form. They are the "seven spirits of God" named in Revelation 4:5 and the "morning stars" that sang together in the beginning, as the Lord revealed them to Job (Job 38:7). In the order of *hierarchy,* the Elohim and *cosmic beings* carry the greatest concentration, the highest vibration of *light* that we can comprehend in our present state of evolution. Serving directly under the Elohim are the four hierarchs of the elements, who have dominion over the elementals—the gnomes, salamanders, sylphs and undines.

Following are the names of the Seven Elohim and their

divine complements, the ray on which they serve and the location of their etheric *retreat:*

First ray, Hercules and Amazonia, Half Dome, Sierra Nevada, Yosemite National Park, California, U.S.A.

Second ray, Apollo and Lumina, western Lower Saxony, Germany

Third ray, Heros and Amora, Lake Winnipeg, Manitoba, Canada

Fourth ray, Purity and Astrea, near Gulf of Archangel, southeast arm of White Sea, Russia

Fifth ray, Cyclopea and Virginia, Altai Range where China, Siberia and Mongolia meet, near Tabun Bogdo

Sixth ray, Peace and Aloha, Hawaiian Islands

Seventh ray, Arcturus and Victoria, near Luanda, Angola, Africa

Emotional body. One of the *four lower bodies* of man, corresponding to the water element and the third quadrant of *Matter;* the vehicle of the desires and feelings of God made manifest in the being of man. Also called the astral body, the desire body or the feeling body.

Entity. A conglomerate of misqualified energy or disembodied individuals who have chosen to embody evil. Entities that are focuses of sinister forces may attack disembodied as well as embodied individuals.

Etheric body. One of the *four lower bodies* of man, corresponding to the fire element and the first quadrant of *Matter;* called the envelope of the *soul,* holding the blueprint of the divine plan and the image of *Christ*-perfection to be outpictured in the world of form. Also called the memory body.

Etheric octave or etheric plane. The highest plane in the dimension of *Matter;* a plane that is as concrete and real as the physical plane (and even more so) but is experienced through the senses of the *soul* in a dimension and a consciousness beyond physical awareness. This is the plane on which the *akashic records* of mankind's entire evolution register individually and collectively. It is the world of *ascended masters* and their *retreats,* etheric cities of *light* where *souls* of a higher order of evolution abide between embodiments. It is the plane of Reality.

The lower *etheric plane,* which overlaps the astral/mental/physical belts, is contaminated by these lower worlds occupied by the false hierarchy and the mass consciousness it controls.

Etheric temple. See *Retreat.*

Fallen angels. See *Angels.*

Father-Mother God. See *Alpha and Omega.*

Four Cosmic Forces. The four beasts seen by Saint John and other seers as the lion, the calf (or ox), the man and the flying eagle (Rev. 4:6–8). They serve directly under the Elohim and govern all of the Matter cosmos. They are transformers of the infinite light unto souls evolving in the finite. See also *Elohim.*

Four lower bodies. Four sheaths of four distinct frequencies that surround the *soul* (the physical, emotional, mental and etheric bodies), providing vehicles for the soul in her journey through time and space. The etheric sheath, highest in vibration, is the gateway to the three higher bodies: the *Christ Self,* the *I AM Presence* and the *Causal Body.* See also *Physical body; Emotional body; Mental body; Etheric body.*

Great Central Sun. See *Central Sun.*

Great Hub. See *Central Sun.*

Great White Brotherhood. A spiritual order of Western saints and Eastern adepts who have reunited with the *Spirit* of the living God; the heavenly hosts. They have transcended the cycles of karma and rebirth and ascended (accelerated) into that higher reality that is the eternal abode of the soul. The *ascended masters* of the Great White Brotherhood, united for the highest purposes of the brotherhood of man under the Fatherhood of God, have risen in every age from every culture and religion to inspire creative achievement in education, the arts and sciences, God-government and the abundant life through the economies of the nations. The word "white" refers not to race but to the aura (halo) of white *light* surrounding their forms. The Brotherhood also includes in its ranks certain unascended *chelas* of the ascended masters.

Guru. (Sanskrit.) A personal religious teacher and spiritual guide; one of high attainment. A guru may be unascended or ascended.

Hierarchy. The universal chain of individualized God-free beings fulfilling the attributes and aspects of God's infinite Selfhood. Included in the cosmic hierarchical scheme are *Solar Logoi, Elohim,* Sons and Daughters of God, ascended and unascended masters with their circles of *chelas, cosmic beings,* the *Twelve Hierarchies of the Sun, archangels* and *angels* of the *sacred fire,* children of the *light,* nature spirits (called elementals) and *twin flames* of the *Alpha/Omega* polarity sponsoring planetary and galactic systems.

This universal order of the Father's own Self-expression is the means whereby God in the *Great Central Sun* steps down the Presence and power of his universal being/consciousness in order that succeeding evolutions in time and space, from the least unto the greatest, might come to know the wonder of his love. The level of one's spiritual/physical attainment— measured by one's balanced self-awareness "hid with *Christ* in God" and demonstrating his Law, by his love, in the *Spirit-Matter* cosmos—is the criterion establishing one's placement on this ladder of life called hierarchy.

Higher Mental Body. See *Chart of Your Divine Self.*

Higher Self. The *I AM Presence;* the *Christ Self;* the exalted aspect of selfhood. Used in contrast to the term "lower self," or "little self," which indicates the *soul* that went forth from and may elect by free will to return to the Divine Whole through the realization of the oneness of the self in God.

Higher consciousness.

Holy Christ Self. See *Christ Self.*

Human monad. The entire forcefield of self; the interconnecting spheres of influences—hereditary, environmental, karmic—which make up that self-awareness that identifies itself as human. The reference point of lesser awareness or non-awareness out of which all mankind must evolve to the realization of the *Real Self* as the *Christ Self.*

I AM Presence. The I AM THAT I AM (Exod. 3:13–15); the individualized Presence of God focused for each individual *soul.* The God-identity of the individual; the Divine Monad; the individual Source. The origin of the soul focused in the planes of *Spirit* just above the physical form; the personification of the God Flame for the individual. See also *Chart of Your Divine Self.*

I AM THAT I AM. See *I AM Presence.*

Kali Yuga. (Sanskrit.) Term in Hindu mystic philosophy for the last and worst of the four yugas (world ages), characterized by strife, discord and moral deterioration.

Karmic Board. See *Lords of Karma.*

Keepers of the Flame Fraternity. Founded in 1961 by Saint Germain, an organization of *ascended masters* and their *chelas* who vow to keep the flame of life on earth and to support the activities of the *Great White Brotherhood* in the establishment of their community and mystery school and in the dissemination of their teachings. Keepers of the Flame receive graded lessons in *cosmic law* dictated by the *ascended masters* to their *messengers* Mark and Elizabeth Prophet.

Kundalini. See *Sacred fire.*

Lifestream. The stream of life that comes forth from the one Source, from the *I AM Presence* in the planes of *Spirit,* and descends to the planes of *Matter* where it manifests as the *threefold flame* anchored in the heart *chakra* for the sustainment of the *soul* in Matter and the nourishment of the *four lower bodies.* Used to denote souls evolving as individual "lifestreams" and hence synonymous with the term "individual." Denotes the ongoing nature of the individual through cycles of individualization.

Light. The energy of God; the potential of the *Christ.* As the personification of *Spirit,* the term "Light" can be used synonymously with the terms "God" and "Christ." As the essence of Spirit, it is synonymous with *"sacred fire."* It is the emanation of the *Great Central Sun* and the individualized *I AM Presence*—and the Source of all life.

Logos. (Greek, 'word, speech, reason.') The divine wisdom manifest in the creation. According to ancient Greek philosophy, the Logos is the controlling principle in the universe. The Book of John identifies the *Word,* or Logos, with Jesus Christ: "And the Word was made flesh, and dwelt among us" (John 1:14). Hence, Jesus Christ is seen as the embodiment of divine reason, the Word Incarnate.

Lord of the World. *Sanat Kumara* held the office of Lord of the World (referred to as "God of the earth" in Rev. 11:4) for tens of thousands of years. Gautama Buddha recently succeeded Sanat Kumara and now holds this office. His is the highest governing office of the spiritual *hierarchy* for the planet—and yet Lord Gautama is truly the most humble among the *ascended masters.* At inner levels, he sustains the *threefold flame,* the divine spark, for those *lifestreams* who have lost the direct contact with their *I AM Presence* and who have made so much negative karma as to be unable to magnetize sufficient *light* from the Godhead to sustain their *soul's* physical incarnation on earth. Through a filigree thread of light connecting his heart with the hearts of all God's children, Lord Gautama nourishes the flickering flame of life that ought to burn upon the altar of each heart with a greater magnitude of love, wisdom and power, fed by each one's own *Christ* consciousness.

Lords of Karma. The ascended beings who comprise the Karmic Board. Their names and the *rays* they represent on the Board are as follows: first ray, the Great Divine Director; second ray, the Goddess of Liberty; third ray, the ascended lady master Nada; fourth ray, the *Elohim Cyclopea;* fifth ray, Pallas Athena, Goddess of Truth; sixth ray, Portia, Goddess of Justice; seventh ray, Kuan Yin, Goddess of Mercy. The Buddha Vairochana also sits on the Karmic Board.

The Lords of Karma dispense justice to this system of worlds, adjudicating karma, mercy and judgment on behalf of every *lifestream.* All *souls* must pass before the Karmic Board before and after each incarnation on earth, receiving their assignment and karmic allotment for each lifetime beforehand and the review of their performance at its conclusion. Through the Keeper of the Scrolls and the recording *angels,* the Lords of Karma have access to the complete records of every lifestream's incarnations on earth. They determine who shall embody, as well as when and where. They assign souls to families and communities, measuring out the weights of karma that must be balanced as the "jot and tittle" of the Law. The Karmic Board, acting in consonance with the individual *I AM Presence* and *Christ Self,* determines when the soul has earned the right to be free from the wheel of karma and the round of rebirth.

The Lords of Karma meet at the Royal Teton Retreat twice yearly, at winter and summer solstice, to review petitions from unascended mankind and to grant dispensations for their assistance.

Macrocosm. (Greek, 'great world.') The larger cosmos; the entire warp and woof of creation, which we call the *Cosmic Egg.* Also used to contrast man as the microcosm ('little world') against the backdrop of the larger world in which he lives. See also *Microcosm.*

Mantra. A mystical formula or invocation; a word or formula, often in Sanskrit, to be recited or sung for the purpose of intensifying the action of the *Spirit* of God in man. A form of prayer consisting of a word or a group of words that is chanted over and over again to magnetize a particular aspect of the Deity or of a being who has actualized that aspect of the Deity. See also *Decree.*

Manu. (Sanskrit.) The progenitor and lawgiver of the evolutions of God on earth. The manu and his divine complement are *twin flames* assigned by the *Father-Mother God* to sponsor and ensoul the Christic image for a certain evolution or lifewave known as a root race—*souls* who embody as a group and have a unique archetypal pattern, divine plan and mission to fulfill on earth.

According to esoteric tradition, there are seven primary aggregations of souls—that is, the first to the seventh root races. The first three root races lived in purity and innocence upon earth in three golden ages before the fall of Adam and Eve. Through obedience to *cosmic law* and total identification with the *Real Self,* these three root races won their immortal freedom and ascended from earth.

It was during the time of the fourth root race, on the continent of Lemuria, that the allegorical Fall took place under the influence of the fallen angels known as Serpents (because they used the serpentine spinal energies to beguile the soul, or female principle in mankind, as a means to their end of lowering the masculine potential, thereby emasculating the Sons of God).

The fourth, fifth and sixth root races (the latter soul group not having entirely descended into physical incarnation) remain in embodiment on earth today. Lord Himalaya and his beloved are the manus for the fourth root race, Vaivasvata Manu and his consort are the manus for the fifth root race, and the God and Goddess Meru are the manus for the sixth root race. The seventh root race is destined to incarnate on the continent of South America in the Aquarian age under their manus, the Great Divine Director and his divine complement.

Manvantara. (Sanskrit, from *manv,* used in compounds for *manu,*

+ *antara,* 'interval, period of time.') In Hinduism, the period or age of a *manu,* consisting of 4,320,000 solar years; one of the fourteen intervals that constitute a *kalpa* (Sanskrit), a period of time covering a cosmic cycle from the origination to the destruction of a world system. In Hindu cosmology, the universe is continually evolving through periodic cycles of creation and dissolution. Creation is said to occur during the outbreath of the God of Creation, Brahma; dissolution occurs during his inbreath.

Matter. The feminine (negative) polarity of the Godhead, of which the masculine (positive) polarity is Spirit. Matter acts as a chalice for the kingdom of God and is the abiding place of evolving *souls* who identify with their Lord, their *Holy Christ Self.* Matter is distinguished from matter (lowercase m)—the substance of the earth earthy, of the realms of maya, which blocks rather than radiates divine *light* and the Spirit of the *I AM THAT I AM.* See also *Mother; Spirit.*

Mental body. One of the *four lower bodies* of man, corresponding to the air element and the second quadrant of *Matter;* the body that is intended to be the vehicle, or vessel, for the mind of God or the *Christ* mind. "Let this [universal] mind be in you, which was also in Christ Jesus" (Phil. 2:5). Until quickened, this body remains the vehicle for the carnal mind, often called the lower mental body in contrast to the Higher Mental Body, a synonym for the *Christ Self* or *Christ* consciousness.

Messenger. Evangelist. One who goes before the *angels* bearing to the people of earth the good news of the gospel of Jesus Christ and, at the appointed time, the Everlasting Gospel. The messengers of the *Great White Brotherhood* are anointed by the *hierarchy* as their apostles ("one sent on a mission"). They deliver through the *dictations* (prophecies) of the *ascended masters* the testimony and lost teachings of Jesus Christ in the power of the Holy Spirit to the seed of *Christ,* the lost sheep of the house of Israel, and to every nation. A messenger is one who is trained by an ascended master to receive by various methods the words, concepts, teachings and messages of the Great White Brotherhood; one who delivers the Law, the prophecies and the dispensations of God for a people and an age.

Microcosm. (Greek, 'small world.') (1) The world of the individual, his *four lower bodies,* his aura and the forcefield of his karma; or (2) The planet. See also *Macrocosm.*

Mother. "Divine Mother," "Universal Mother" and "Cosmic Virgin" are alternate terms for the feminine polarity of the Godhead, the manifestation of God as Mother. *Matter* is the feminine polarity of *Spirit,* and the term is used interchangeably with Mater (Latin, 'mother'). In this context, the entire material cosmos becomes the womb of creation into which Spirit projects the energies of life. Matter, then, is the womb of the Cosmic Virgin, who, as the other half of the Divine Whole, also exists in Spirit as the spiritual polarity of God.

Nirvana. The goal of life according to Hindu and Buddhist philosophy: the state of liberation from the wheel of rebirth through the extinction of desire.

OM (AUM). The Word; the sound symbol for ultimate Reality.

Omega. See *Alpha and Omega.*

Path. The strait gate and narrow way that leadeth unto life (Matt. 7:14). The path of initiation whereby the disciple who pursues the *Christ* consciousness overcomes step by step the limitations of selfhood in time and space and attains reunion with Reality through the ritual of the *ascension.*

Pearls of Wisdom. Weekly letters of instruction dictated by the *ascended masters* to their *messengers* Mark L. Prophet and Elizabeth Clare Prophet for students of the sacred mysteries throughout the world. *Pearls of Wisdom* have been published by *The Summit Lighthouse* continuously since 1958. They contain both fundamental and advanced teachings on *cosmic law* with a practical application of spiritual truths to personal and planetary problems.

Physical body. The most dense of the *four lower bodies* of man, corresponding to the earth element and the fourth quadrant of *Matter.* The physical body is the vehicle for the *soul's* sojourn on earth and the focus for the crystallization in form of the energies of the *etheric, mental* and *emotional bodies.*

Rays. Beams of *light* or other radiant energy. The *light* emanations of the Godhead that, when invoked in the name of God or in the name of the *Christ,* burst forth as a flame in the world of the individual. Rays may be projected by the God consciousness of ascended or unascended beings through the *chakras* and the third eye as a concentration of energy taking on numerous God-qualities, such as love, truth, wisdom, healing, and so on. Through the misuse of God's energy, practitioners of black magic project rays having negative qualities, such as death rays, sleep rays, hypnotic rays, disease rays, psychotronic rays, the evil eye, and so on. See also *Seven rays.*

Real Self. The *Christ Self;* the *I AM Presence;* immortal *Spirit* that is the animating principle of all manifestation. See also *Chart of Your Divine Self.*

Reembodiment. The rebirth of a *soul* in a new human body. The soul continues to return to the physical plane in a new body temple until she balances her karma, attains self-mastery, overcomes the cycles of time and space, and finally reunites with the *I AM Presence* through the ritual of the *ascension.*

Retreat. A focus of the *Great White Brotherhood,* usually on the *etheric plane* where the *ascended masters* preside. Retreats anchor one or more flames of the Godhead as well as the momentum of the masters' service and attainment for the balance of *light* in the *four lower bodies* of a planet and its evolutions. Retreats serve many functions for the councils of the *hierarchy* ministering to the lifewaves of earth. Some retreats are open to unascended mankind, whose *souls* may journey to these focuses in their *etheric body* between their incarnations on earth and in their finer bodies during sleep or *samadhi*.

Root race. See *Manu*.

Sacred fire. The Kundalini fire that lies as the coiled serpent in the base-of-the-spine *chakra* and rises through spiritual purity and self-mastery to the crown chakra, quickening the spiritual centers on the way. God, *light*, life, energy, the *I AM THAT I AM*. "Our God is a consuming fire" (Heb. 12:29). The sacred fire is the precipitation of the Holy Ghost for the baptism of souls, for purification, for alchemy and transmutation, and for the realization of the *ascension,* the sacred ritual whereby the *soul* returns to the One. In the West, the Kundalini has been symbolized in the caduceus, a staff of two intertwined snakes topped by a pair of wings. The Greek god Hermes is shown holding this staff, and physicians have adopted it as their symbol.

Samadhi. (Sanskrit, literally "putting together": "uniting") In Hinduism, a state of profound concentration or absorption resulting in perfect union with God; the highest state of yoga. In Buddhism, samadhis are numerous modes of concentration believed to ultimately result in higher spiritual powers and the attainment of enlightenment, or nirvana.

Sanat Kumara. (From the Sanskrit, 'always a youth.') Great *Guru* of the seed of *Christ* throughout cosmos; hierarch of Venus; the Ancient of Days spoken of in Daniel 7. Long ago he came to earth in her darkest hour when all light had gone out in her evolutions, for there was not a single individual on the planet who gave adoration to the God Presence. Sanat Kumara and the band of 144,000 souls of light who accompanied him volunteered to keep the flame of life on behalf of earth's people. This they vowed to do until the children of God would respond to the love of God and turn once again to serve their mighty *I AM Presence.* Sanat Kumara's retreat, Shamballa, was established on an island in the Gobi Sea, now the Gobi Desert. The first to respond to his flame was Gautama *Buddha,* followed by Lord Maitreya and Jesus. See also *Lord of the World.*

Seamless garment. Body of *light* beginning in the heart of the *I AM Presence* and descending around the *crystal cord* to envelop the individual in the vital currents of the *ascension* as he invokes the holy energies of the Father for the return home to God. Also known as the deathless solar body.

Secret chamber of the heart. The sanctuary of meditation behind the heart *chakra,* the place to which the *souls* of lightbearers withdraw. It is the nucleus of life where the individual stands face to face with the inner *Guru,* the beloved *Holy Christ Self,* and receives the soul testings that precede the alchemical union with that Holy Christ Self—the marriage of the soul to the Lamb.

Seed Atom. The focus of the Divine *Mother* (the feminine ray of the Godhead) that anchors the energies of *Spirit* in *Matter* at the base-of-the-spine *chakra.* See also *Sacred fire.*

Seven rays. The *light* emanations of the Godhead; the seven *rays* of the white light that emerge through the prism of the *Christ* consciousness.

Siddhis. Spiritual powers such as levitation, stopping the heart-beat, clairvoyance, clairaudience, materialization and biloca-tion. The cultivation of siddhis for their own sake is often cautioned against by spiritual teachers.

Solar Logoi. *Cosmic beings* who transmit the *light* emanations of the Godhead flowing from *Alpha and Omega* in the *Great Central Sun* to the planetary systems. Also called Solar Lords.

Soul. God is a *Spirit,* and the soul is the living potential of God. The soul's demand for free will and her separation from God resulted in the descent of this potential into the lowly estate of the flesh. Sown in dishonor, the soul is destined to be raised in honor to the fullness of that God-estate which is the one Spirit of all life. The soul can be lost; Spirit can never die.

The soul remains a fallen potential that must be imbued with the Reality of Spirit, purified through prayer and supplication, and returned to the glory from which she descended and to the unity of the Whole. This rejoining of soul to Spirit is the *alchemical marriage* that determines the destiny of the self and makes it one with immortal Truth. When this ritual is fulfilled, the highest Self is enthroned as the Lord of Life, and the potential of God, realized in man, is found to be the All-in-all.

Spirit. The masculine polarity of the Godhead; the coordinate of *Matter;* God as Father, who of necessity includes within the polarity of himself God as *Mother,* and hence is known as the *Father-Mother God.* The plane of the *I AM Presence,* of perfection; the dwelling place of the *ascended masters* in the kingdom of God. (When lowercased, as in "spirits," the term is synonymous with discarnates, or astral *entities;* "spirit," singular and lowercased, is used interchangeably with soul.)

Spoken Word. The *Word* of the Lord God released in the original fiats of creation. The release of the energies of the Word, or the *Logos,* through the throat *chakra* by the Sons of God in confirmation of that lost Word. It is written, "By thy words thou shalt be justified, and by thy words thou shalt be condemned" (Matt. 12:37). Today disciples use the power of the Word in *decrees,* affirmations, prayers and *mantras* to draw the essence of the *sacred fire* from the *I AM Presence,* the *Christ Self* and *cosmic beings* to channel God's *light* into matrices of transmutation and transformation for constructive change in the planes of *Matter.*

The Summit Lighthouse. An outer organization of the *Great White Brotherhood* founded by Mark L. Prophet in 1958 in Washington, D.C., under the direction of the *ascended master* El Morya, Chief of the Darjeeling Council, for the purpose of publishing and disseminating the teachings of the ascended masters.

Threefold flame. The flame of the *Christ,* the spark of life that burns within the *secret chamber of the heart* (a secondary *chakra* behind the heart). The sacred trinity of power, wisdom and love that is the manifestation of the *sacred fire*. See also *Chart of Your Divine Self.*

Transfiguration. An initiation on the path of the *ascension* that takes place when the initiate has attained a certain balance and expansion of the *threefold flame.* Jesus' transfiguration is described in Matthew 17:1–8.

Tube of light. The white *light* that descends from the heart of the *I AM Presence* in answer to the call of man as a shield of protection for his *four lower bodies* and his *soul* evolution. See also *Chart of Your Divine Self.*

Twelve Hierarchies of the Sun. Twelve mandalas of *cosmic beings* ensouling twelve facets of God's consciousness, who hold the pattern of that frequency for the entire cosmos. They are identified by the names of the signs of the zodiac, as they focus their energies through these constellations. Also called the Twelve Solar Hierarchies.

Twin flame. The *soul's* masculine or feminine counterpart conceived out of the same white fire body, the fiery ovoid of the *I AM Presence.*

Unascended master. One who has overcome all limitations of *Matter* yet chooses to remain in time and space to focus the consciousness of God for lesser evolutions. See also *Bodhisattva.*

Universal Christ. The Mediator between the planes of *Spirit* and the planes of *Matter.* Personified as the *Christ Self,* he is the Mediator between the Spirit of God and the *soul* of man. The Universal Christ sustains the nexus of (the figure-eight flow of) consciousness through which the energies of the Father (Spirit) pass to his children for the crystallization (*Christ-*realization) of the God flame by their soul's strivings in the cosmic womb (matrix) of the *Mother* (Matter).

Violet flame. Seventh-ray aspect of the Holy Spirit. The *sacred fire* that transmutes the cause, effect, record and memory of sin, or negative karma. Also called the flame of trans-mutation, of freedom and of forgiveness. See also *Decree;*

Chart of Your Divine Self.

Word. The Word is the *Logos:* it is the power of God and the realization of that power incarnate in and as the Christ. The energies of the Word are released by devotees of the Logos in the ritual of the Science of the *Spoken Word.* It is through the Word that the *Father-Mother God* communicates with mankind. The Christ is the personification of the Word. See also *Christ; Decree.*

World Teacher. Office in *hierarchy* held by those ascended beings whose attainment qualifies them to represent the universal and personal *Christ* to unascended mankind. The office of World Teacher, formerly held by Maitreya, was passed to Jesus and his disciple Saint Francis (Kuthumi) on January 1, 1956, when the mantle of *Lord of the World* was transferred from *Sanat Kumara* to Gautama *Buddha* and the office of *Cosmic Christ* and Planetary Buddha (formerly held by Gautama) was simultaneously filled by Lord Maitreya. Serving under Lord Maitreya, Jesus and Kuthumi are responsible in this cycle for setting forth the teachings leading to individual self-mastery and the *Christ* consciousness. They sponsor all *souls* seeking union with God, tutoring them in the fundamental laws governing the cause-effect sequences of their own karma and teaching them how to come to grips with the day-to-day challenges of their individual dharma, the duty to fulfill the Christ potential through the sacred labor.

Sources

The material in this volume has been compiled from many lectures by Elizabeth Clare Prophet on the subject of the cosmic clock, as well as published and unpublished writings. Among these sources are the following lectures:

December 31, 1970. "Signs of the Planets."

January 2, 1972. "How the Treasures of Heaven Can Be Obtained."

March 30, 1972. "Cosmic Astrology."

July 1, 1972. "The Psychology of Being."

January 1, 1973. "The Dust Shall Settle: A Karmic Exposé."

January 28, 1973. "Twelve Pillars in the Temple of Our God."

April 21, 1973. "The Prince of This World Cometh and Hath Nothing in Me."

July 1, 1973. "God-Mastery via the Cosmic Clock."

October 3, 1973. "The Ritual of the Atom."

June 15, 1974. "Charting the Cycles of Your Family on the Cosmic Clock."

July 3, 1975. "The Torch Is Passed." Published in *The Great White Brotherhood in the Culture, History and Religion of America.*

July 5, 1975. "The Cosmic Clock: Psychology for the Aquarian Man and Woman." Published in *The Great White Brotherhood in the Culture, History and Religion of America.*

November 23, 1975. "Karma, Dharma, Self-Mastery, Soul

Freedom."

July 1, 1976. "Cosmic Accountability."

July 2, 1976. "The Psychology of Wholeness."

April 22, 1978. "Meditation and Contact with the Beloved through the I AM Presence and the Universal Mind of God."

November 30, 1980. "The Law of Cycles." Published in *The Coming Revolution Magazine,* Fall 1981.

February 25, 1984. Lecture on the Path of the Bodhisattva.

June 7, 1986. "Predict Your Own Future."

June 29, 1988. "Seminar on the Cosmic Clock: Charting the Cycles of Your Karma, Psychology and Spiritual Powers on the Cosmic Clock."

April 8, 1989. Lecture on charting the decades of life on the clock.

December 28, 1990. Lecture on Serapis Bey's 14-month cycles.

January 9, 1991. Lecture on Serapis Bey's 14-month cycles.

FOR MORE INFORMATION

Summit University Press books are available at fine book-stores worldwide and at your favorite on-line bookseller. For a free catalog of our books and products or to learn more about the spiritual techniques featured in this book, please contact:

Summit University Press
PO Box 5000
Corwin Springs, MT 59030-5000 USA
Telephone: 1-800-245-5445 or 406-848-9500
Fax: 1-800-221-8307 or 406-848-9555
www.summituniversitypress.com
info@summituniversitypress.com

Elizabeth Clare Prophet is a world-renowned author. Among her best-sellers are *Fallen Angels and the Origins of Evil, Saint Germain's Prophecy for the New Millennium,* her 10-book series *Pocket Guides to Practical Spirituality* including *How to Work with Angels, Soul Mates and Twin Flames* and *Alchemy of the Heart,* and *The Lost Years of Jesus: Documentary Evidence of Jesus' 17-Year Journey to the East.*

She has pioneered techniques in practical spirituality, including the use of the creative power of sound for personal growth and world transformation. Her books are translated into more than twenty languages.